Communication and Cybernetics   9

Editors: H. Wolter   K. S. Fu   W. D. Keidel

WITHDRAWN

Göran Hammarström

Linguistic Units and Items

Springer-Verlag
Berlin Heidelberg New York 1976

U. Göran E. Hammarström
Monash University, Department of Linguistics
Clayton, Victoria, Australia

ISBN 3-540-07241-1 Springer-Verlag Berlin Heidelberg New York
ISBN 0-387-07241-1 Springer-Verlag New York Heidelberg Berlin

Library of Congress Cataloging in Publication Data. Hammarström, Göran. Linguistic units and items (Communication and cybernetics; 9). Bibliography: p. Includes index. 1. Linguistic analysis (Linguistics). 2. Structural linguistics. 3. Writing. I. Title. P 123. H 26. 410. 75-9679.

This work is subject to copyright. All rights are reserved, whether the whole or part of the material is concerned, specifically those of translation, reprinting, re-use of illustrations, broadcasting, reproduction by photocopying machine or similar means, and storage in data banks. Under § 54 of the German Copyright Law where copies are made for other than private use, a fee is payable to the publisher, the amount of the fee to be determined by agreement with the publisher.

© by Springer-Verlag Berlin Heidelberg 1976.

Printed in Germany.

Typesetting and printing: Carl Ritter & Co., Wiesbaden. Binding: Konrad Triltsch, Graphischer Betrieb, Würzburg.

Preface

This book contains among other things, developments of ideas suggested in my papers "Pseudo-units in phonetics" and "On linguistic terminology" read to the Congresses in Prague and Bucharest (both 1967) and in my book *Linguistische Einheiten im Rahmen der modernen Sprachwissenschaft* (1966), which, in its turn, includes ideas contained in previous papers.

It is my belief that units and relations between units are the basic linguistic facts to be described. Units must be defined in relation to other units, i.e. as elements of systems. Relations or systems contain as elements units having some "positive" definition (and not merely a "negative" one), i.e. units have describable features which can be compared with features of other units. It is not sufficient to establish that different units are functionally different but one must also describe in detail the character of the difference between them. A language has a paradigmatic system, i.e. a network of paradigmatic relations, and a syntagmatic system, i.e. a network of syntagmatic relations.

Following J. Baudouin de Courtenay, F. de Saussure, N. S. Trubetzkoy, L. Hjelmslev and so many others I think that the difference between form and substance, between *units* and their realizations, henceforth called *items*, should be emphasized.

A clear recognition of language facts leads to a drastically increased number of units and items. This will not amaze anybody having at least an intuitive understanding of the immense complexity of a natural language.

The units and items treated in this book are of *general* interest in the sense that they are needed for the description of many different languages. They are not *universal* because the author has not tried to investigate whether any of them exist in all languages. Actually this would be impossible as there are languages which have not as yet been described (and many languages disappeared before they were described at all). (Note that the word universal is here used in the sense of "existing in all languages".)

Our account of units and items can obviously not be exhaustive. The account may well suit the description of major European languages better than other languages.

I believe that the major task of linguistics is classification and definition of units as parts of the overall system of a language. Although many valuable results have been achieved by authors using some variant of the transformational generative approach, I do not think that this approach as such is of any value in the basic, "neutral" description of a language. Generating and (in most cases) transforming intuitively seem to be inadequate procedures. Against the claims which have been made so frequently in recent times, these procedures do not allow the linguist to state anything of value that cannot be stated in another mostly simpler way.

The kind of syntactic-semantic deep structure recently postulated in so many papers and books cannot claim adequately to describe a speaker's "competence". I agree on this point with B. Collinder, *Noam Chomsky und die generative Grammatik. Eine kritische Betrachtung* (Acta Societatis Linguisticae Upsaliensis, Nova series 2:1, 1970). Nor is it possible to maintain that "underlying, abstract" morphological forms are acceptably described in works such as Chomsky-Halle, *The Sound Pattern of English*. See my detailed criticism on p. 103—109 of *The Problem of nonsense linguistics* (Acta Societatis Linguisticae Upsaliensis, Nova Series 2:4, 1971) and in "Generative phonology: A critical appraisal" (Phonetica 27:3, 1973, p. 157—184)[1].

There are many features in transformational generative descriptions which make one believe that they are written to suit the speaker rather than the hearer. Be this true or not, a description taking the speaker (writer) into account rather than the hearer (reader) is not adequate for a basic description, which in my mind should be "neutral" in relation to the speaker and the hearer, i.e. it should not describe processes specifically relatable to the one or the other.

A "neutral", basic description would presumably describe the language that an individual uses both when speaking (or writing) and when understanding spoken text (or reading).

It would be a secondary task (both in regard to importance and in regard to the order in which the study should be undertaken) to study what happens when somebody produces a language message and when somebody interprets it. However, in a more complete description a synthetic grammar, or a grammar from the view point of the speaker, and an analytic grammar, or a grammar from the viewpoint of the hearer, must be added to the "basic" grammar.

In the above I have not implied that what is improper in the "basic" description of a given language could not be used by linguists for other purposes. "Generative" and transformational devices may well be useful, and necessary, in discovery procedures, speaker's grammar, hearer's grammar, comparing different languages, diachrony and machine translation (see below, p. 4).

It should not be denied that one can imagine a "deep structure" that would be universal in relation to all languages. Every language could be transformed into this universal system and each language could be derived from it in a specific way. This would be an economic procedure in machine translation as soon as several languages are involved. This problem is, however, marginal in linguistics. One might even think that it is outside linguistics if linguistics is thought to be the study of normal, natural language.

This book contains few quotations. Influences from other linguists can, however, be traced in corresponding parts of my book *Linguistische Einheiten*. The writings, which have had the most important influence on the way I understand linguistics are those by F. de Saussure, N. S. Trubetzkoy, R. Jakobson, L. Bloomfield, A. Martinet and E. Coseriu. The works of G. Ungeheuer, G. Heike, H. G. Tillmann as well as many personal discussions with these linguists have been particularly valuable for the development of my own thoughts on linguistics.

---

[1] My view points are largely in agreement with those of R. A. Hall, Jr. as expressed in his papers "Some recent developments in American linguistics" (Neuphilologische Mitteilungen **70**, 1969, p. 192—227) and "Underlying representation and observable fact in phonology" (Journal of English Linguistics **7**, 1973, p. 21—42).

J. Platt discussed with me the first version of the manuscript. His criticisms of style and content have been taken into account on almost every page of the book. I am very grateful for his assistance.

A stencilled draft of the book was discussed at meetings of the research seminar of the Linguistics Department, Monash University, mainly in 1971, but also, to some extent, in 1972. Many improvements suggested by the members of the seminar have been included in the final version. In this respect I am particularly indebted to R. Beebe, T. Bell, N. Chadwick, M. Clyne, H. Platt and E. Shaw.

Mr. P. Busby has assisted in proof reading and indexing.

Melbourne 1975   Göran Hammarström

Table of Contents

0. Introduction	1
1. Spoken Language	11
1.1. α-Level	11
1.1.1. Phonemes	11
1.1.2. Prosodemes	30
1.1.3. Syllabemes	39
1.1.4. Morphemes	44
1.1.5. Lexemes	51
1.1.6. Syntagmemes	56
1.1.7. Sememes	85
1.2. β-Level	111
1.3. γ-Level	112
1.4. Phonetics, Morphology, Semantics and Syntax	113
2. Written Language	114
3. Written Language in Relation to Spoken Language	114
4. Spoken Language in Relation to Written Language	115
5. The Tasks of Linguistics	115
Bibliography	117
Author Index	120
Subject Index	121

0. Introduction

1. Linguistics is the science of languages. (The notion of language is defined below, 3.)

2. The title of the book *Linguistic units and items* refers to units and items dealt with in linguistics. In the mind of the author it could be of some advantage to let the adjective *linguistic* refer to linguistics alone and not directly to language itself. To denote that something belongs to language one would say *of language* or *language*, e.g. *sounds of language* or *language development* (not *linguistic sounds* or *linguistic development*).

In our case the distinction is perhaps not very important. The present title using "linguistic" implies that there are *language* units and items to be described. If instead this latter expression had been used, it could perhaps have been said to be self-evident that there is a framework, i.e. linguistics, within which they can be described and which is the real topic of the book.

3. A language is a system of communication such that the expression side is either spoken sounds or written symbols (often letters). The content side is made up by the meanings (this word is taken in a very wide sense and includes "functions", cf. below p. 2—3, 13, 44, 52, 85).

Any language, in the sense of a natural language, is far more complicated than any other system of communication whether or not created by man. By means of a language very complicated content can be conveyed from a speaker (writer) to a hearer (reader) and an extremely high (but not an infinite) number of different utterances can be formed.

4. The units (see below, 7) of a human natural language are basically characterized by the following points:

(a) The expression side of the units is either spoken or written (whereas, for instance, a dog communicates by various means: wagging its tail etc.).

(b) The units are arbitrary in the sense that in one language a particular unit of content is expressed by *ox* whilst in another language a comparable content is expressed by *bœuf*. This shows that there is not a motivated but an arbitrary link between content and expression. If it had been the accepted habit to call an *ox* a *man* and a *bœuf* a *pain* this would also have functioned.

However, once somebody has got used to a particular language, he finds it natural and somehow motivated to employ the words of this particular language and no others.

(c) The units are conventional in the sense that they are habits within particular societies. If one is among speakers of English and if one wants to speak English, *ox* is for instance one of the possible habitual words but not *bœuf*.

(d) Units are segmentable (if they are long enough). An utterance may consist of syntactic constructions. These have words as segments. The words have phonemes (or letters) as segments. Not only the expression side is segmentable. Considering the content side, in the sentence *I like milk* three consecutive (word) meanings add up to contribute to the total meaning of the sentence.

A segment may be so short that it cannot be segmented. In Latin *i* (= go!) can be an utterance, which is a sentence, which is a word, which is a morpheme, which is a syllable, which is a phoneme.

Generally, one can say that units (as well as items) can be used in different combinations as segments of other units (or items).

(e) Units are linear in the sense that segments follow one another in time in spoken languages, and, in space, in (most) written languages. Segments of the same kind are not usually produced simultaneously. In an English word such as *be*, in the spoken form /b/ comes first and /i:/ follows. In the written form *b* comes first and *e* follows. /b/ and /i:/ are not pronounced simultaneously (although there may be some "co-articulation"), nor is *e* written on top of *b*. It should also be noted that the place of the segments is fixed. /i:t/ and *eat* have not the same meaning as /ti:/ and *tea*.

(It goes perhaps without saying that our points (b) to (e) are strongly influenced by F. de Saussure, *Cours de linguistique générale*.)

A language has a "silent" form used in thinking. One would assume that clear and explicit thinking uses silent language in a more complete form but that less elaborate thinking is less bound by the rules of language.

In written language and in spoken recorded language, it is the case that individuals who no longer exist communicate with living individuals.

In the last fifty years or so, linguists have generally emphasized that a language is primarily something spoken. One's most immediate observation would, however, be that most languages of which one has a knowledge have a spoken and a written form. (In some cases, e.g. in most Australian languages, only a spoken form exists. In the case of a "dead" language, such as Latin, there would be some sense in saying that nowadays this language is essentially a written language.) The possibility of describing written language in relation to spoken language and spoken language in relation to written language is largely overlooked.

I intend to treat (I) spoken language, (II) written language, (III) written language in relation to spoken language, (IV) spoken language in relation to written language. However, only (I) spoken language, will be dealt with in detail in this book, and within spoken language only the α-level (see below).

5. In a terminology that I suggested some years ago a language usually has three functions:

α-function. All units of a language which, directly or indirectly, convey the "meanings" have α-function. What has been achieved up to date in linguistics is predominantly related to the α-level. Also the "meanings" may be thought of as α-units.

β-function. Sound properties which inform about the attitude of the producer of an utterance have β-function. Anything can be said in a neutral, an angry, a friendly etc. way. In written language this function is of little importance. However, if "style" in general is considered to be a β-fact, then written language would have even more differences at this level than the spoken language.

γ-function. All facts of language characterizing an individual or a group of individuals have γ-function. "Primarily" these facts do not belong only to phonetics but also to morphology, syntax and semantics (see below p. 13, 28, 38, 43, 48, 51, 55, 82—83, 107, 112—113)[1]. Even β-facts may have an "additional" γ-function.

The γ-function can be subdivided into:

$γ_1$- or *idiolectal function*. Properties which characterize the speaker (writer) as an individual in contra-distinction to other speakers (writers) have this function[2].

$γ_2$- or *sociolectal function*. Properties which characterize groups of speakers (writers) as belonging to particular social groups have this function[3].

$γ_3$- or *dialectal function*. Properties which characterize groups of speakers (writers) relatable to some geographical area have this function[4].

Note that these three functions are called functions of language, which implies that all of them fall within the field of linguistics. Although it seems natural, in the first instance, to let $α$, $β$ and $γ$ refer to expression units, it seems appropriate also to say that their corresponding content, or meanings, belong respectively to the $α$-, $β$- and $γ$-levels.

6. For more than fifty years many linguists have attached much importance to the distinction between the language or the "system of signs" and the speech or the "parole" (often forgetting to mention writing), whereas other linguists have been less interested in this distinction (which is, however, of basic importance).

We suggest that, within an enlarged framework, the difference between the act and the result be also taken into account (although little will be said about the act in this book) and that the following terms be used: The *spoken* and the *written* system. The *speech act* and the *writing act*. The *spoken* and the *written text*. The *spoken* and the *written language* could be general terms each including system, act and text. Thus, the term language would mean more or less what it means in everyday use.

Also the *hearing act* and the *reading act* belong obviously to linguistics.

In each context one would have to state which language one was referring to: the English language, the language of Edinburgh, the language of the lower classes in London, the language of individual A.

In more technical terms, a particular natural language (English, French, German etc.) as a whole could be called *glottolect* with its *glottosystem, glottoacts, glottotexts*. A language of some particular geographical area within a glottolect would be called *dialect* with its *diasystem, diaacts* and *diatexts*. A language of some particular social class would be called a *sociolect* with its *sociosystem, socioacts* and *sociotexts*. The language of an individual would be called an *idiolect* with its *idiosystem, idioacts* and *idiotexts*[5].

---

[1] At this stage an intuitive understanding of the terms phonetics, morphology, syntax and semantics is sufficient. It is hardly necessary that the reader looks up the definitions on p. 113.
[2] See my remarks in *Idiolekt*, p. 312–314 of *Lexikon der Germanistischen Linguistik*.
[3] See Karl-Heinz Bausch, *Soziolekte*, p. 254–262 of *Lexikon der Germanistischen Linguistik*.
[4] The three functions are explained in more detail in *Linguistische Einheiten*, p. 7–14; see also index ("Sachverzeichnis") of this book. For further discussion see my paper "Zur soziolektalen und dialektalen Funktion der Sprache" (Zeitschrift für Mundartforschung 34, 1967, p. 205–216).
[5] My previously expressed ideas on the definitions of language, dialect and sociolect and some points related to the problem of delimitation of dialects and sociolects will not be repeated here. See, however, *Linguistische Einheiten* (Sachverzeichnis) and the paper mentioned in the preceding footnote.

All terms in the foregoing paragraph could be preceded, in a meaningful way, by either "spoken" or "written".

The units (see below, 8) of these different language systems would be *glottounits*, *diaunits*, *sociounits* and *idiounits*. (See below, *glottophoneme*, *glottomorpheme* etc.; *diaphoneme*, *sociophoneme*, *idiophoneme* etc.). The items would be similarly prefixed (see below, 8).

7. "Sounds", letters, words, syntactic constructions etc. can be considered either as *units* (for which "parts of form", "elements of the system", "sets", "invariants", "abstractions", "types" and other terms have been used) or as *items* (for which "parts of substance", "parts of speech acts", "elements of sets", "variants", "concrete examples", "realizations" and other terms have been used).

It appears to be useful, at least in an account aiming at a high degree of detail and exhaustiveness, to consider the units from two viewpoints. Either one stresses that a unit is a set of all its elements (variants, items), which sometimes is required by the purpose of one's investigation of some particular point, or one stresses that a unit is an invariant having, so to speak, no variants, which is required when an account of the exact properties of all the variants is irrelevant or, even, not applicable.

In the first mentioned kind of definition, in principle, all members of the set are included and many minute details may be taken into account. The definition is *narrow*. We suggest that units thus defined be called *n-units* (n-phonemes, n-morphemes etc.).

In the second kind of definition one will use as few and as "abstract" properties as possible to determine the invariant. The definition is *broad*. We suggest that units thus defined be called *b-units* (b-phonemes, b-morphemes etc.).

It seems possible to neglect the difference between n- and b-units in descriptions where great accuracy is not aimed at.

Differences in the definition of phonemes (and other units) found in different authors or in different "schools" can be partly explained as differences between those who have more emphasized the n-aspect and those who have emphasized the b-aspect. (A complete definition should obviously take both into account.)

8. All units (be they n- or b-units) should have names that distinguish them from items[6]. Those units which seem particularly important and frequent in linguistic discussion will have a name ending in *-eme* : *phoneme, morpheme, syntagmeme, sememe* etc. A set of such units will usually have a name ending in *-ememe*, e.g., *phonememe*. There is a possibility of naming certain sets by adding *-eme* to a term prefixed *allo-* (*diallo-*, *triallo-*, etc.) (cf. below, allophoneme, p. 14). Subsets of the unit in *-eme*, going from higher to lower, will be prefixed *allo-, diallo-, triallo-, tetrallo-*, e.g., *allophone, diallophone* etc. (cf. below, p. 14).

A unit may have, in addition to the hierarchy of subsets labelled *allo-, diallo-* etc. (and being perhaps in some way primary), another set of subsets established by some other criterion. It is suggested that this other series of subsets be prefixed *vari-, divari-, trivari-* etc. (cf. below, p. 15).

The set-theoretical approach is taken considerably further than in my previous book *Linguistische Einheiten*. This approach is unrevolutionary as linguistics has always been abundant in implicit, or explicit, set-theoretical statements: a phoneme

---

[6] Cf. my paper "On linguistic terminology" (*Actes du Xe congrès international des linguistes*, Bucharest 1969, p. 321–325).

is a family of sounds; all clauses with certain characteristics are active, in contradistinction to all clauses with other given characteristics which are passive; a language has a number of dialects etc.

I feel that a description using some set-theoretical notions, and formulae, is the most appropriate for basic language facts as it seems to correspond closely to our intuitive knowledge of language.

W. S. Cooper comes to the conclusion, in *Set Theory and Syntactic Description* (The Hague, 1964) that set theory is "rich enough and flexible enough to provide an adequate basis for syntactic description" (p. 16). He discusses several mathematical devices that are more advanced than the elementary set-theoretical notions I have made use of. On the other hand I am concerned with many more units and aspects.

In "*Klasse*" *und Klassifikation in der Sprachwissenschaft* (The Hague 1968) Juilland and Lieb deal, among other things, with set-theoretical notions. The terms "intensional" and "extensional" as explained by these authors (p. 58–65) have meanings which have some similarity to the meanings of my terms "broad" ("b-") and "narrow" ("n-").

9. Units or items that can be combined so that they follow one another in sequence can be considered as *segments*. They are established, so to speak, by making vertical cuts at various points along the "horizontal" dimension (time dimension in speech and line in writing).

A segment may possess simultaneous *components* such as the phoneme components. The phoneme /t/ has in English the components voiceless, alveolar and stop.

10. The two basic kinds of relation between units (or items) are the *paradigmatic* and the *syntagmatic* relation. The structure of a language[7] can be described from the viewpoint of paradigmatics and of syntagmatics. Paradigmatic relations are those between a unit (or item) found in some particular context and another unit (or item) which could have appeared instead of the one under consideration. (This relation can be thought of as being "vertical".) Syntagmatic relations are those between consecutive units (or items). (This relation can naturally be thought of as being "horizontal": various items appear along the line of time, when spoken, and on a line when written.)

When in a paradigmatic way segments (at the level of units or items) are compared with other segments, units with definite paradigmatic characteristics can be established. Relevant similarities, i.e. those appropriate for the broad definition of the unit, warrant membership of some particular unit (set). Relevant partial similarities result in different sub-units (sub-sets). Complete dissimilarity indicates membership of completely different units (sets).

An example from phonetics: All English consonants having the component alveolar form the set of alveolars: /t/, /d/, /s/, /z/, /n/, /l/. Of these /t/ and /s/ are voiceless (dissimilarity in comparison with the others) and form therefore one of the subsets of the set of the alveolars. (It would also be possible to consider voiced and voiceless consonants as higher sets, within which the alveolars were one of the subsets.)

---

[7] Instead of *language* the above-mentioned term *glottolect* could have been used. It should, however, be recognized that some technical terms may be less important than others and can be omitted in certain contexts.

An example from morphology: All words having two syllables form a set: *water, petrol* etc.

An example from syntax: All subjects can be said to form a set (the subjecteme). This set can be subdivided into a number of subsets: subjects such as *the boy, the girl* etc. would form one, and subjects such as *the little boy, the young girl* etc. would form another subset.

Note that in this case a functional criterion groups together the various subsets, but the subsets are constituted by their syntagmatic structure, which is the point in which they differ.

An example from semantics: Some particular component can determine a set. The meanings of the words *boy, girl, dog, cat* etc. have all the component 'animate' and form therefore a set.

In syntagmatics, relations between segments of a sequence, be they units or items, are established.

An example from phonetics: In /wi:/ (*we*), a /w/ is followed by an /i:/.

An example from morphology: In *boys* a stem and a suffix (the plural ending) are combined to form a word.

An example from syntax: In *I came* a subject is followed by a predicate.

An example from semantics: In *this note is very high* the seme (the meaning) of *high* has a particular relation to the seme of *note*, because in this combination the seme of *high* belongs to a particular *alloseme* (*high* on the pitch scale). (Cf., e.g. *this tree is high*, where *high* has a somewhat different meaning.)

One might be induced to think that segmentation is a procedure entirely within syntagmatics. Although the aim of segmentation is to establish segments combinable in different ways, segmentation as such, is however, basically a paradigmatic procedure. Items (being segments) cannot be established until paradigmatically determined sets of items are more or less clearly distinguished. If the linguist possessed only one sentence in a particular language, and if he had otherwise no knowledge of that language, he could not draw definite conclusions about the phonemes of that language, because the necessary comparisons with other sentences would not be possible.

Considering syntagmatics, a unit (or an item) may be determined:

(a) from the viewpoint of its own structure in terms of segments; and

(b) from the viewpoint of its distribution, i.e. its combinability with other segments.

By the very nature of the language studied, a linguist may not only have to attach more importance to either paradigmatics or syntagmatics, but also his general linguistic approach may be influenced. In Latin or German the cases are so obviously important that they require close attention by the linguist. However, a linguist studying English, where cases are less striking, may be more inclined to concentrate on other facts such as word order, which is a syntagmatic problem.

Describing "phonological systems" N. S. Trubetzkoy and R. Jakobson with the early Prague School provided deeper knowledge of paradigmatics. Other linguists, such as L. Bloomfield or Z. S. Harris, have been particularly interested in (syntagmatic) "structures" and "distributional" aspects.

It is obvious that units and items as well as their components should be paradigmatically as well as syntagmatically determined. (There is no doubt that the history of "phonology" shows that many linguists have been inclined to use one of these viewpoints for the definition of the phoneme and neglect or minimize the importance of the other.)

11. The items may receive a detailed description as to their sound properties in spoken language and the shape of the symbols in written (including printed) language.

The spoken sounds can be described from:
(a) an articulatory;
(b) an acoustic; and
(c) an auditory standpoint.

Instead of these three terms another set of terms could be used and given a slightly wider sense:

(a) Although the term articulation is sometimes used in such a wide sense that it includes phonation, it would not be appropriate to let it also include activities in nerves, muscles and brain. If one wants to refer to a more complete account of the production of speech sounds by the speaker, the term *genetic* could, however, be used.

(b) The term *gennemic* could be used in roughly the same meaning as acoustic.

(c) The term *energemic* could include all processes involved when a hearer decodes speech sounds, whereas auditory would refer exclusively to the auditory impressions.

It is important to distinguish among facts from (a), (b) and (c). They are sometimes not in simple one-to-one relation to one another, but often the relations are more complicated. (See *Linguistische Einheiten*, p. 3–6.)

A full description of a language would include (a), (b) and (c) and even all relations between them. In practice one will mostly limit oneself to one of these. A description in (c), i.e. an auditory description, is the most practical and natural choice. As a matter of fact, despite the mainly articulatory terms generally used (dental, palatal, lateral, rolled etc.) descriptions of spoken language carried out to the present date are usually (on the whole) auditory: a linguist listens and writes down what he hears (photos of lips, X-ray movies, palatograms etc. are seldom used, and when they are, the results are sometimes included only in a marginal way). In most cases the predominantly articulatory terms simply describe auditory impressions.

Actually, the auditory description may be thought of as primary in the sense that a linguist studying spoken language cannot do without it but when he has it he can decide not to go on to describing acoustic and articulatory data and still make a coherent description containing all sounds having meaning (including function) and thus including all units of the language.

One can try to establish relevant features directly at the articulatory level. One would accept as relevant articulatory features those that have to be learnt for each language separately, i.e. those belonging to the rules (conventions) of the particular language but not those being necessarily conditioned by physiological facts. It does, however, seem to me that no new distinctive features would be revealed this way. The explanation for this fact would be that articulatory features are almost exclusively learnt when trying to reproduce perceived sounds.

The acoustic description as such is of little interest in linguistics[8] as linguists should be interested in the first instance in the activity of the speaker and the hearer

---
[8] It should not be denied, however, that acoustic investigation often throws interesting light on genetic and energemic facts.

(or put in another way — the speaker-hearer) and in the language known by them. (An ordinary speaker has no sort of knowledge of what is going on in the "medium", i.e. the air)[9].

In most acoustic descriptions, terms are (almost) purely acoustic (as they should be), but in auditory and articulatory descriptions, terms are unfortunately usually a mixture of articulatory, auditory and even acoustic terms. It would be of some advantage if coherent sets of terms were used also in articulatory and auditory studies.

To establish a purely articulatory system of terms does not offer much difficulty. For most distinctions, the terms are already available.

To establish a purely auditory system of terms is more difficult. The /i/ of some language could be called "thin" or "sharp", but how should the rest of the terms necessary for vowels look?

In lectures (at Monash University, 1969) H. Pilch discussed auditory terms and suggested, among other things, that English consonants could be characterized by the auditory features hiss, hush, shrill, hollow etc. (A more definite version of Pilch's auditory features is forthcoming.) For basic sound properties, which, when seen as *courses*, describe facts of what is often called "suprasegmentals", I have suggested[10] the following terms:

(a)	(b)	(c)
frequency of the vocal cords	frequency of the fundamental	pitch
force of articulation	intensity	loudness
form of the vocal tract	spectrum	quality
duration	duration	length

It is seen from the way in which these terms have been divided into three groups that the first column (a) refers to genetic ("articulatory"), the second (b) to gennemic (acoustic), and the third (c) to energemic (auditory) phonetics. (The presentation of the terms might erroneously suggest to an inexperienced reader that there are everywhere simple one-to-one relations between variables for which the terms are to be found on the same line. Even if it is true that the frequency of the vocal cords and the frequency of the fundamental correspond exactly to each other and the duration is the same variable both in genetic and gennemic phonetics, other relations are very complicated.)

Pitch, loudness, quality and length may be called "measured variables" [as the variables under (a) and (b)] on the ground that a listener, particularly if used as a test person in hearing tests, is more comparable to a phonetic instrument than one might think. To measure frequency of the fundamental, for instance, the phonetician reads the appropriate instrument. To measure pitch, he "reads" the test person who responds to stimuli in a way comparable to an instrument.

If a linguist uses the term "pitch" for something observed by a listener, he should not say: "The frequency is one convenient measure of the pitch" or "Cycles per

---

[9] Similar ideas have been expressed in my papers "Inquéritos linguísticos II" (Revista de Portugal **26**, 1961, p. 9–32), p. 10, 24–25; "Dialektologiska undersökningar" (Nordisk tidsskrift for tale og stemme **24**, 1964, p. 27–51), p. 28, 42–43; "L'historique et le programme d'activité de l'Institut de phonétique d'Upsal" (*Communications et rapports du Premier Congrès International de Dialectologie générale*, Louvain 1965, p. 152–156), p. 156.
[10] In "On terminology in genetic, gennemic and energemic phonetics" (Word **23**, 1967, p. 254–256).

second is the measure of pitch preferred by physicists"[11]. It is easy to find other similar mistakes: intensity (defined in acoustics as energy per time per unit area) is used for loudness (a listener's impression), quality is used for spectrum, duration for length or length for duration etc.

An instrument used for measuring the frequency of the fundamental is commonly (and erroneously) called a pitchmeter.

To present only one measurement (or an average of several measurements) the terms suggested for the twelve parameters will be sufficient. To give an account of the variation of the parameters as a function of time, however, it is suggested that the word *course* be used: *course of the frequency of the vocal cords, course of pitch* etc.

The terms *course of duration* and *course of length* require an explanation. When two or more consecutive segments are measured and compared, we get series of varying measurements. If in the verb *impórt* the first vowel is compared to the first vowel in the substantive *ímport*, the vowel of the verb will have less duration or be shorter than the vowel of the substantive. Considering the second vowel of the two words, conditions will be reversed. The course of duration of the vowels, or syllables (which would be analogous in this respect) will then be for the verb: shorter duration + longer duration, and for the substantive: longer duration + shorter duration. The corresponding course of length will be for the verb: shorter length + longer length, and for the substantive: longer length + shorter length[12].

12. In our account, the units of spoken language belonging to phonetics, morphology, syntax and semantics will be treated in this order. If the description of a language is meant only to include few details and describe only what may be thought of as being the basic units, one may well think that syntactic constructions presuppose the knowledge of words and word classes (used to describe syntactic constructions) and that words presuppose the knowledge of phonemes (used to describe words). This would mean that phonemes should come first in the analysis and the description. The words and the syntactic constructions would follow. This was actually thought by many "structuralists". More recently, syntax-semantics is put forward as a kind of starting point. It cannot, however, be convincingly claimed that this procedure is superior. It may certainly be naturally relatable to the way a speaker would be supposed to produce items in the speech act but, if so, it would not at all be relatable to what the hearer does when he interprets items. (He receives sounds to which he attributes words, syntactic constructions and meanings.)

I cannot see any reason for not following the traditional order starting with phonetics. At the same time one would like to stress that in a complete description where all items ("variants", "realizations") are to be accounted for in a detailed way, each of the four main parts of the description presupposes the others. None of the four is an ideal starting point. One would need a circular arrangement (with no beginning or end) impossible in a book (which goes from the first page to the last). Things being as they are, one will have to manage as well as one can using a high number of cross references. (Cf. below, p. 113.)

13. Discovery procedures, sometimes called tests (e.g. "the test of commutation") are often more or less clearly implied in definitions of units. Sometimes they are even

---

[11] Cf. H. A. Gleason, *An Introduction to Descriptive Linguistics* (New York 1961), p. 47, 358.
[12] Cf. *Linguistische Einheiten*, p. 33-37.

explicitly made the base for defining units and items. An item is described as the one which some given discovery procedure provides. It seems preferable, however, to exclude them from basic definitions and state them separately.

It is not possible to believe that discovery procedures would provide a linguist without knowledge of a language with an automatic tool for establishing a definite description of a language[13]. Consequently, if one is to retain the word discovery procedure, one must use it in a weak sense. A linguist having a knowledge of a language may apply discovery procedures to make (some) things clearer to himself and others.

14. Units of content (such as functemes, sememes and expressemes) are established by the linguist who finds and considers their items in some spoken or written text (a "corpus") or in examples constructed by himself. (A linguist aiming at a high degree of exhaustiveness will usually have to use both procedures.) Most units of expression (such as phonemes, lexemes and syntagmemes) are in this book defined in complete dependence of units of content. Syllabemes, which are not connected with meanings, must, however, be discovered by the linguist in a more direct way.

When units (of content and of expression) are established and described in detail, it is particularly important to consider paradigmatic relations. One compares units and items which appear in the same context. These comparisons have different names: oppositions are established, commutation tests are carried out, minimal pairs are found (in phonology) or substitutions are carried out within some frame which is kept constant.

This is a kind of discovery procedure and it should be emphasized again that discovery procedures generally do nothing more than assist the linguist in making his own knowledge of some language clear and explicit. In my paper "Generative Phonology. A critical appraisal", I express the opinion that, to be acceptable, descriptions of languages must be empirically adequate (p. 163): "I suggest that the term *empirical adequacy* be given the following meaning: anything said about a language is empirically adequate, (a) if it is intuitively acceptable to the linguist making the statement and if it seems obvious or is clearly known that other linguists share his intuition; (b) if it is based on the linguist's introspection, whereby it is thought that introspection implies a clearer understanding than just intuition in the sense that the linguist has applied something like a discovery procedure to himself; (c) if it is based on observation of speech whereby the observation may imply not only heard or seen but also measured phenomena; (d) if it is based on tests (discovery procedures) of the knowledge laymen (or linguists) have about their language; (e) if, generally, every part of the description gives account of what has been discovered (see a to d) as directly and naturally as possible.

It should be noted that (a) to (d) are not mutually exclusive.

It may appear that particularly (a) is a weak requirement, but in a case where the object of study is a faculty of human beings intuition must be allowed to play a main role and it is particularly important that statements should not be counter-intuitive."

It should be noted that I have here somewhat reinterpreted the term "empirical" so as to give it the only meaning that I consider to be suitable in linguistics. My use of the term does not imply that I disagree with Esa Itkonen when, in his important

---

[13] Cf. *Linguistische Einheiten*, p. 22–23.

book *Linguistics and Metascience* (1974), he draws the conclusion (p. 7) that linguistics is not "an empirical science in the same sense as physics and other natural sciences", where "empirical" is used in a more traditional sense.

It can be noted that a sketchy and probably somewhat faulty description of a language can certainly be carried out by an observer without previous knowledge of a language but making maximal use of discovery procedures on a "corpus". This is the kind of linguistics discussed by Z. S. Harris in *Methods in structural linguistics*. The non-speaker of the language would obviously have an easier task when describing the expression side than when tackling the content side. The mere observer of language behaviour, with no access to introspection, would, among other difficulties, have no possibility of distinguishing between correct utterances and incorrect ones. It must not be forgotten that the latter do occur in speech acts. [This is a crucial point in Esa Itkonen's paper "Concerning the methodological status of linguistic descriptions" (1972).] The grammar of the mere observer would have to include the same kind of rules for correct and incorrect sentences as all of them would have to be assumed to be correct.

15. I am of the opinion that it is necessary to let the primary, most immediate description of a language be absolutely synchronic[14].

Only facts of which it is reasonable to believe that they co-exist at the same moment of time should be included, because only in this way is it possible to adequately describe a language used by speakers as a means of communication. Everything else must be excluded.

As further steps it is obviously possible to expand towards diachronic or diatopic studies[15]. There will be no diachrony in this book. Some diatopic considerations are, however, included (see, for instance, p. 22–29).

1. Spoken Language

1.1. α-Level

1.1.1. Phonemes

0. In this book the term *phonetics* (and the adjective *phonetic*) is taken in a broad sense. Thus phonetics includes every aspect of the sound used in communication by means of a spoken language.

Segments (phonemes, prosodemes etc.) and components can be studied from the viewpoints of *genetic* (articulatory), *gennemic* (acoustic) and *energemic* (auditory) *phonetics* (see above, p. 7–9). Even when this kind of phonetics is very detailed it is usually the case that it concerns segments and components having functions. One may, however, treat the sound substance in a less detailed way and concentrate instead on

---
[14] Cf. *Linguistische Einheiten*, p. 60–63.
[15] Cf. *Linguistische Einheiten*, p. 64–101.

facts related to function: In a certain position within a syllable, how many different phonemes (functional units which will be defined below) can be found in the language to be described? What is the number of phonemes in the inventory? What is the form of the "phonological system" (definition below)? Etc. Not only function at the α-level but also function at the β- and γ-levels should be taken into account. When phonetics deals with these kinds of problems it could be called functional.

Many linguists, particularly in the U.S., distinguish between segmental and suprasegmental phonemes. In this book we distinguish instead between *phonemes* and *prosodemes* (which terms have the definite advantage of being shorter).

Phonemics can be distinguished from *prosodemics* and these two can be summarized under the label *phonology*.

As phonology is concerned with the α-function only, it occupies not the whole, but only a part of the wider field of functional phonetics.

In the system of terms suggested "phonetic" cannot be opposed to "phonemic", or "phonological", as is done by many other linguists. Instead of the term "phonetic" in the sense "dealing with sounds in a more or less detailed way and without stressing function" we suggest the term *phonic*.

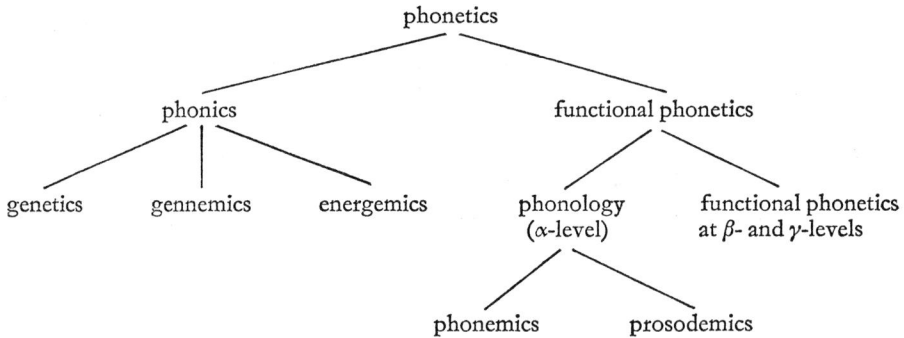

1. *Items : phones*. Uttered sentences or "periods" (see below, p. 58-59) can intuitively be divided into their smallest segments, their "sounds". This operation can be performed even by an intelligent layman. These smallest segments are the phones. They are, among other things, parts of words.

Definition : Phones are the smallest, or shortest, segments which are produced by the speaker, single[16] or in sequences, to contribute to forming spoken words (or lexes), and which the hearer identifies, among other things[17], when he understands a word (a lex).

---

[16] A lex may have only one phone: English *I* (if the diphthong is thought of as being just one phone) or Swedish *i* (= *in*). In this case some other segments ("syllable", lex and its prosode) happen to be as short as the phone but in most cases the phone is indeed the shortest segment.

[17] The other things are syllabs, syllab prosodes, lexes, lex prosodes, syntagms, syntagm prosodes and meaning. It is of interest to note that, although, in a sentence, one or more phones may be so unclear that they provide insufficient clues for their identification, the rest may be sufficient to allow the hearer so to speak to fill in what he has only partly heard clearly, or perhaps not heard at all. Thus it is clear that not only phones but also other factors contribute to the identification of spoken "words".

This function of "building words", the "constructive function", seems to be primary to, and to imply, the function of "distinguishing words". However, it is usually the "distinctive function" that is made the basic one in different varieties of phonology.

A phone as such (an [s], a [t] etc.) has no "meaning" in the narrow, and usual, sense of the word (cf. below, p. 44) but only the "lex-building function", which is a constructive (α-)function. The term "lex building" implies "syllab building" and "morph building" as syllabs[18] and morphs[18] are segments of lexes. It would be a possible alternative to say that a phone has basically "syllab building" (or "morph building") function.

Phones which are not different in their lex building function, may still be heard to be different. I.e. a particular segment in a particular word, e.g. /i:/ in *be*, has many variants. The following circumstances must be taken into account:

(1) There is *free variation*, which means that the speaker does not produce sounds in an absolutely precise way. Even if one tries to pronounce the same phone a couple of times there will be a random variation from time to time. This variation is of no real importance in communication and cannot generally be established by ear. It is, however, easy to establish by articulatory or acoustic measurements.

(2) There is *facultative variation* which is here defined as variation at the β- and γ-levels.

If, for instance, the word *bill* is pronounced in an angry way, one will probably hear, among other things, a particularly long and loud [b]. When segments are varied in this way they have different *phone contours* (β-level).

When a segment is considered as belonging to a particular individual, it will have characteristics different from those of other individuals. Each individual has his *idiophones* (γ-variation).

Different groups within a society may have different pronunciation of segments or different *sociophones* (γ-variation).

Pronunciations in different geographical regions may differ. There may be different *diaphones* (γ-variation) in a language.

(3) There is *positional variation*, which is conditioned by the position of the segment in relation to other segments. The [k] in *key* is not the same as a [k] in *cool* (see below, 2.1).

Phones are notated in square brackets: [...] or in a more explicit way: ph[...].

2.1. *Units: allophones. Definition*: Phones having definite relevant "positions", or, said in another way, a *given distribution*, and differing among themselves only through *free* (point 1 above) and *facultative* (point 2 above) variation form a set called *allophone*.

Two [k] in [ki:] (*key*) pronounced differently on different occasions (by the same speaker or by two different speakers) would belong to the same allophone, as the difference is conditioned by free and facultative variation.

A [k] in [ki:] could be comparable, from the viewpoint of free and facultative variation, to a [k] in [ku:l] (*cool*) but these two would belong to different allophones because it is possible to hear, perhaps with some difficulty, that the first [k] has a sound such as is usually pronounced in a comparatively front part of the mouth and

---

[18] When in this case, and in some further cases, terms are not defined and page reference not given, the reader may consult the index.

with spread lips whereas the second [k] has a sound such as is usually pronounced in a more back part of the mouth and with rounded lips. This difference is conditioned by the position in front of different vowels. An [ɪ] in [sɪt] (*sit*) and an [e] in [set] (*set*) are different and this difference persists even if both phones are thought of as being comparable as to free and facultative variation. They belong to different allophones (which belong to different phonemes).

The allophone is mainly an n-unit, and only exceptionally a b-unit, as it is usually a certain set of phones.

An allophone can be notated in [...] and abbreviated as Aph or Alloph.

The number of allophones to be established in a particular language is somewhat arbitrary. When phones of one possible allophone can be distinguished by ear from phones of another possible allophone, these two sets should definitely be established as allophones. (Note that, as a matter of fact, the number of relevant "positions", or "distributions", is the one needed to motivate the positional variants perceived.) Some of the phones of one allophone may have the same quality as some of the phones of another allophone. Only close phonetic study can reveal overlapping of this kind.

By measurements, an extremely high number of "articulatory" or "acoustic" allophones could be set up, as instruments can establish many more differences than the ear. In articulation a particular phone is influenced by every preceding and following phone (or, even, combination of phones). If these kinds of allophones are accepted, it is possible to set up subsets of allophones called diallophones, triallophones etc. E.g. the English allophone "front [k]" found in front of front vowels can be subdivided into diallophone$_1$ including all [k] in front of an [i] (*key*), diallophone$_2$ including all [k] in front of an [ɪ] (*kit*), diallophone$_3$ including all [k] in front of an [e] (*keg*) etc.

2.2. Allophones having some significant property in common could form *allophonemes*[19]. The two English "front allophones" [k] (*key*) and [g] (*give*) would belong to the same allophoneme.

3.1. *Units: phonemes. Definition* of n-phoneme: An *n-phoneme* is either (a) a set of such allophones as have complementary distribution and are felt to be sufficiently phonically similar to be grouped together, or (b) a set of one only allophone when this allophone cannot be grouped with any other allophone.

Comments: Two, or more, segments are in complementary distribution when each has a distribution which is not shared by any of the others. ("Where one finds one, one does not find the other(s).") The front and back [k] just mentioned are in complementary distribution.

The words "felt to be sufficiently phonically similar" imply that subjective judgements must be made. The front and the back [k] mentioned would be judged by an individual knowing English as phonically similar. This kind of definition implies that no universal phonic rule based on differences or similarities between sound properties can be given for assigning allophones to the same or to different phonemes.

If, for instance, in English no differences conditioned by context can be found in [s]-phones, there would be only one allophone [s] forming the phoneme /s/.

N-phonemes are required in phonic research.

---

[19] Cf. above, p. 4.

Phonemes have the functions mentioned above when the phones were described (1.1.1.1). In addition it may be noted that phonemes, and phones, may have various kinds of secondary function. A "sound symbolic" function of given vowels and consonants (particularly in poetry) has been assumed for various languages. A different case is the following. If /ɒ/ is accepted as a French phoneme, one may say that for many speakers of French the presence of an /ɒ/ in a word such as *parking* or *meeting* denotes that the word is borrowed from English.

Phonemes would be written within /.../, or more explicitly, within Ph/.../.
phoneme = {allophone$_1$, ..., allophone$_n$}[20]
allophone = {phone$_1$, ..., phone$_n$}

Definition of b-phoneme: A *b-phoneme* is a phoneme conceived as an invariant. The variants (the phones and the allophones) of the n-phoneme are excluded.

If one wishes to state that some language has a given number of phonemes, or that the phonemes can be combined in given ways, b-phonemes rather than n-phonemes would be referred to.

B-phonemes are useful in the description of longer units as consisting of phoneme sequences. If one states that the "word" (lexeme) *key* has two phonemes, b-phonemes are obviously meant. An n-phoneme /k/ would include variants of /k/ which cannot be used in front of an [i], e.g. the rounded back variant used in *cool*. It would, however, be even more appropriate to speak about b-variphones in similar cases (see next paragraph).

3.2. *Units: variphones. Definition: Variphones* are the shortest segments of lexemes (whereas phones are the shortest segments of lexes).

Variphones have usually been called just phonemes. In the terminology suggested here one would, however, say that the lexeme /ki:/ (*key*) has as its first segment the variphone /k/ rather than the phoneme /k/.

For different purposes variphones could be either n- or b-units.

It would be possible to say not only that a phoneme is a set of allophones which are sets of phones, but also that phonemes are sets of allophones which are sets of variphones which are sets of phones.

Variphones could be shown in labelled brackets: Vph/.../.

3.3. Various properties thought to be relevant could establish various *phonememes*, i.e. sets of phonemes. One phonememe would include the vowels, another the consonants[21]. Phonememes can be n- or b-phonememes.

Phonemes, or groups of phonemes, may be related through being segments of variants (allomorphs) of a morpheme (see below 1.1.4.2.1.). Such phonemes could be termed "allomorphically affiliated".

4. In some cases one feels the need for a unit that is "more than" an allophone but "not quite" a phoneme. For such a unit I have suggested the term *semi-phoneme*[22]. In certain cases one may think that a set of phones, *a*, should be an allophone which

---

[20] Read: a phoneme is a set including allophone$_1$ to allophone$_n$. In a more explicit set-theoretical formula one would write phoneme$_i$ = {allophone$_i^1$, allophone$_i^2$, ..., allophone$_i^{n_i}$}.
[21] A definition of vowels and consonants is given in *Linguistische Einheiten*, p. 31.
[22] Cf. p. 405–406 of "Über Palatographie, anatomische Bedingungen der Lautunterschiede und schwedische Vokalphoneme" (Zeitschrift für Phonetik **17**: 5, 1964, p. 397–407); p. 344 of "Sur l'inventaire des phonèmes français" (*Omagiu lui Alexandru Rosetti*, Bucharest 1965, p. 343–346); *Linguistische Einheiten*, p. 21–22.

together with another allophone, *b*, would form a phoneme because *a* and *b* are in complementary distribution and may perhaps be considered to have sufficient phonic similarity. On the other hand the difference between *a* and *b* is one that in other cases in the same language distinguishes between phonemes, and none of these allophones is conditioned by coarticulation (as is often, but not always, an allophone in complementary distribution with another allophone when both belong to the same phoneme). An example is a French [i:] as in *tige* compared with [i] in *rit*. One could let these two belong to the same phoneme. However, the difference between long and short constitutes different phonemes in other cases such as *bête-bette*. This is why the difference between [i:] and [i] seems somewhat more important than just the difference between two phones belonging to two normal allophones of a phoneme. French would have a semi-phoneme /i:/. More exactly, one could notate it Sph/i:/, i.e. use a labelled bracket rather than invent a new bracket shape. A realization of this semi-phoneme would be a semi-phone notated sph[i:]. If needed, allosemi-phones could be established.

In the case of semi-phonemes the difficulty lies not in segmentation but in establishing the units of the "system". Thus the difficulty is paradigmatic, and not syntagmatic.

The items of semi-phonemes, the semi-phones, are close to being just phones.

5. Another problem is created by those examples where the segmentation, rather than some more directly paradigmatic difficulty, is involved. In this case it is suggested that the term *quasi-phoneme* be used. The problem of many diphthongs and affricates in various languages would exemplify this.

The term *monophthongeme* is suggested for a segment that at the phonemic level is to be considered as only one, and not as two or more consecutive segments. The term is used for vowels only.

The term *monophthong* is suggested for realizations of monophthongemes, diphthongemes (see below) or, perhaps even triphthongemes (see below) that for the ear are not "segmented" or "diphthongized", i.e. they are not felt to change noticeably during the time they are being pronounced.

Ideally, the monophthongal status of a segment should be determined in listener tests. The linguist, listening himself, would, however, presumably come to results similar to those obtained in tests, which for various reasons may be difficult to administer. It seems necessary to establish monophthongs (and diphthongs, see below) at the auditory level. In normal articulation there is continuous movement of articulators and, as a consequence, in acoustic measurements the formant frequencies change continuously. Studies at the articulatory and acoustic levels cannot give results that provide us with a basis for the distinction between monophthongs and diphthongs — at least not if the sample studied is normal speech.

The term *diphthongeme* is suggested for a sequence of two segments forming the centre of a syllabeme ("phonemic syllable") or for a sequence of two segments, of which one is the centre and the other the margin within the syllabeme or, perhaps, for a sequence of two segments of which one is not alone clearly the centre and the other alone is not clearly the margin (but which combination forms a certain kind of centre). None of the two segments in question can be a consonant. I will discuss one point of this definition in some detail: It is conceivable that both centre and margin belong clearly to phonemes found also outside the diphthongeme. In this case, in the diphthongeme one clear segment would undoubtedly follow another clear segment. However, in many cases discussed in many languages by different linguists there has been no agreement about "the diphthong" containing one or two "vowels". In most cases, the adequate solution may therefore be that the diphthongeme consists of two segments, each of which has not quite the status of a phoneme but, when taken together, they are more than one phoneme at the syntagmatic level. Thus a diphthongeme would mostly be "more than one phoneme" but "less than two phonemes in sequence".

It would be of interest to try to establish exactly the criteria that, on a continuous scale from one to two, would allow us to determine that a diphthongeme is closer to being equated with one phoneme or with two phonemes in sequence.

The term *diphthong* is suggested for realizations of monophthongemes or diphthongemes that, to the listener, change noticeably during their pronunciation. The change can be such that a segment of the diphthong is heard as a contoid; i.e. not only, e.g. [ei] but also [ej] would symbolize sounds that could be diphthongs in some language. (If, however, [ej] realizes one vowel followed by a consonant, e.g. an /ej/, one would not call it a diphthong.)

We should now be well prepared for clearly formulating statements such as the following:

(a) Diphthongemes are mostly realized as diphthongs; so the English /ɔi/ realized as [ɔi] (in *boy*).

Some diphthongemes are close to consisting of two segments, or perhaps even consist of two clear segments; so /ɔi/ in *boy*. Other diphthongemes are closer to consisting of one phoneme; so /ei/ in *day*.

(b) Diphthongemes are sometimes realized as monophthongs; so the Southern Portuguese /eu/ when realized as [e] (in *eu = I*).

(c) Monophthongemes are mostly realized as monophthongs; so the English /æ/ realized as [æ] (in *hat*).

(d) Monophthongemes are sometimes realized as diphthongs (or even as triphthongs or tetraphthongs); so the English /i:/ when realized as [i:ⁱ] or [i:j] (in *feed*).

It is well known that "diphthongs" have something like a "weak" and a "strong" part and that the order of these segments can be weak-strong or strong-weak. In other words "diphthongs" are "rising" or "falling". These terms seem acceptable and can be used both for diphthongemes and diphthongs[23].

---

[23] Some attention should be given to the problem of how to show in a notation that a diphthongeme or a diphthong is rising or falling. In general, diacritics have been used to indicate either the weak or the strong segment. Another procedure is to raise the weak segment by which the English "word" *I* is written as /aⁱ/ (if a lexeme) or as [aⁱ] (if a lex).

In many notations there is nothing at all to show the weak or the strong segment. This procedure may be acceptable in either broad or phonemic notation, at least if the distribution of the phonemes in the language in question is such that the two phonetic symbols designating the diphthongeme or the diphthong can designate only segments belonging to one and the same syllable (syllabeme or syllab) when found in sequence. The procedure is less acceptable if the two symbols in sequence can, in addition, designate segments belonging to different syllables. In French a word such as *taille* can be pronounced so that it contains sounds notated [ai]. In phonemic notation this word would have /ai/ (if the second segment is thought to be the phoneme /i/ and not /j/). The same symbols would be used for the two-syllable word *haïr*. In such cases one should notate either diphthong or syllable division or both: *taille* and *haïr* would have [aⁱ] and [ai], or [ai] and [a-i], or [aⁱ] and [a-i] respectively.

Triphthongemes and triphthongs are normally weak-strong-weak as the Portuguese /ᵘɐⁱ/ in *poeira* (*dust*).

Mutatis mutandis in the definitions of diphthongeme and diphthong the terms *triphthongeme* and *triphthong* may be introduced.

A triphthongeme would mostly be realized as a triphthong but it is imaginable that it is realized as a diphthong or even as a monophthong or as a tetraphthong.

One would doubt the existence of tetraphthongemes.

Problems similar to those just discussed exist in some consonants. The affricates seem to be at the phonemic level, "more than one" but "less than two consecutive phonemes". At this level they could be called *affricatemes*. An *affricateme* would usually be realized as an *affricate* but sometimes as a simple contoid. On the other hand, a simple consonantal phoneme, e.g. a /t/, has, in some languages, variants that are affricates[24].

Each of the two segments of diphthongemes and affricatemes could be called a quasi-phoneme as each of them is, somehow, syntagmatically not a full segment. The items of quasi-phonemes would be quasi-phones. If needed, alloquasi-phones could be established. A quasi-phoneme could be denoted: Qph/.../ and a quasi-phone: qph[...].

6. Little interest has been given to what I would like to call pseudo-units. Sometimes parts of the "spoken chain" (the expression) are such that they seem to be "realizations" of well known α-units such as phonemes, syllabemes or prosodemes but in the usual description they cannot be related to any such units. The explanation of this fact is that the "rapid" listening of the normal linguist is directed exclusively towards clear, rather slow and unemotional pronunciation. This procedure provides an acceptable starting point but is not sufficient basis for a complete description as it only provides forms directly relatable to "idealized" pronunciations.

The shortest segments of the spoken chain are not always in one-to-one relation to phonemes. The Portuguese word *geral* is sometimes, under emphasis, pronounced in a way that could be written *gerali*, i.e. at the end of the word there appears an "extra" segment of the type that from the viewpoint of the sound can usually be attributed to a phoneme although in the word mentioned this does not seem meaningful. When the word written *geral* is described, it is said to end in an /l/. We suggest that a segment such as the final [i] of "*gerali*" be called a *pseudo-phone*. Even if a segment such as the one just mentioned is not what it might superficially seem to be, i.e. a segment belonging to a phoneme, it has a function on the α-level being part of a possible realization of a "longer" unit than a phoneme, namely a lexeme. Thus it can be treated less on the phonological than on the morphological level where it is considered as a segment of a lex. At the same time it is certainly part of a β-unit. (In the example given the β-value is that the word is given particular weight.) The Swedish so called supradentals, such as [s̪] in *mors* (*mother's*) are from an auditory, acoustic and articulatory standpoint comparable to phones. In the phonemic description that I prefer, however, each supradental does not correspond to a phoneme and one might be tempted to call them pseudo-phones. As, on the other hand, each

---

[24] The preceding paragraphs on monophthongemes, diphthongemes and affricatemes coincide to a considerable extent with my paper on the same topic in Linguistics 87, 1972, and Talanya 1, 1972, p. 50–53.

supradental corresponds to two consecutive phonemes ([moːṣ] — /moːrs/), it is preferable not to do so. A similar, but not altogether equal, case is constituted by a segment that occasionally (and not normally like a Swedish supradental) realizes two phonemes. "In rapid 'uncareful' speech, for example, an English vowel with a following /n/ may occasionally fuse to a single-segment portmanteau nasalized vowel [...]" (K. L. Pike, *Language in relation to a unified theory of the structure of human behavior*, II, 1955, p. 16). This type of segment, too, would not be considered as a pseudo-phone (but as an "unclear segment", see below).

In many languages, in which the orthography influences the pronunciation, spelling pronunciations, as long as they are just occasional, form a large group of pseudo-phones. (As soon as the spelling pronunciations become normal in a language, the pseudo-phones concerned become just phones.)

Pseudo-phones which phonically are such that they would have realized the same phoneme (if they had been phoneme realizations) can be considered as items of the same pseudo-phoneme. If needed, also allopseudo-phones could be established. Pseudo-phonemes would not be segments of syllabemes, morphemes or lexemes, but rather segments of syllabs, morphs and lexes, and would be n-units rather than b-units. Common to the stretches of sound corresponding to pseudo-units is:

a) They are segments of speech which usual linguistic description, being based on clear, "neutral" speech (or on the thoughts the linguist has about such speech), does not take into account. In a description where the facultative variants of α-units are included, they will, however, necessarily be considered.

b) They have different β-functions, being the expression of β-units or parts of the expression of such units. (β-units condition facultative variants within α-units.)[25]

Pseudo-phonemes could be notated: Psph/.../ and pseudo-phones: psph[...].

7. Sometimes (a) in phonetic investigation, when a test person is asked to pronounce some particular "sound", and also (b) when laymen talk about a language a vowel or a consonant may be produced in isolation. In everyday life somebody may state that he finds "the (vowel) *i*" or "the (consonant) *r*" strange, ugly or, perhaps even beautiful, in some particular geographical area, or in some particular individual. Such items could be called *meta-phones*. Meta-phones related to the same phoneme would form a particular *meta-phoneme*[26]. If needed, also allometa-phones could be established. Meta-phonemes could be notated: Mph/.../ and meta-phones: mph[...].

8. *Items: phone components. Definition:* All components which contribute to the recognition of phones by the hearer are here called *phone components*. Some are more important than others in the sense that they are easier to recognize and (or) more seldom left out than others[27].

9.1. *Units: phoneme components. Definition:* An *n-phoneme component* is a set of phone components which, in the act of communication, let the hearer recognize phones belonging to some particular phoneme and which possess phonic similarity[28].

---

[25] The paragraphs on pseudo-phones and pseudo-phonemes coincide partly with parts of my paper "Pseudo-units in phonetics" (*Proceedings of the Sixth International Congress of Phonetic Sciences*, Prague 1967, 1970, p. 411–413).
[26] Cf. *Linguistische Einheiten*, p. 22.
[27] Cf. *Linguistische Einheiten*, p. 25–28, 53, 57.
[28] Cf. *Linguistische Einheiten*, p. 26.

The phone components vary freely, facultatively and positionally (according to the position of the phoneme in relation to other phonemes). Sometimes the influence of position may be so important that it may be advantageous to establish *allophone components*. The Danish phoneme /t/ has an allophone [t] and an allophone [d][29]. The first has a component "voiceless" and the second a component "voiced". Both components would belong to the components of the phoneme /t/ but it may be of advantage to attribute them directly to different allophones of this phoneme. (Danish has also a phoneme /d/ with a [d] as one of its allophones.)

As was implied in the preceding paragraph a phone component within a phoneme component can take the value ø (zero), i.e. not be pronounced (or, perhaps, not be pronounced in an audible way).

There may be contexts where phoneme components may be considered as b-units rather than as n-units.

The common name for phoneme components (rather than phone components) is "distinctive features".

n-phoneme component = ({allophone component$_1$, ..., allophone component$_n$} =)
{phone component$_1$, ..., phone component$_n$}

9.2. If several phonemes have been grouped so as to form a set according to some phoneme component (cf. above, p. 9), for instance "voice", this set would be a phonememe. The components of all the phonemes included in the set could be called *phonememe components*, although it seems preferable to call phonememe component only the components common to the phonemes of the set. For instance, in a set /b, d, g.../ "voice" would be a phonememe component but not labiality, dentality or velarity.

10. *Paradigmatics.* Phonemes, or before the era of phonology, just "sounds", have been arranged in different ways. Sound properties, "distinctive features" or, in our terminology, phoneme components are at the base of different "tables of vowels and consonants" or "phonological systems".

Prephonological systems related to the description of some particular language, tables within general phonetics as well as Prague School systems[30] are generally two-dimensional.

C.-C. Elert has used a multidimensional display in the description of Swedish consonants[31]. In the description of vowels similar displays are more frequently used.

Under the influence of Jakobson-Fant-Halle, *Preliminaries to Speech Analysis*, many recent studies have displayed tables based on "binary features": every feature (component) used for the description of phonemes is made member of a pair of features but features arranged on a scale with more than two steps are not used. As a basic description of facts this is insufficient. It certainly provides the possibility of describing accurately certain relations: an English /d/ compared with an English /t/ has

---

[29] Cf. E. Fischer-Jørgensen, "Remarques sur les principes de l'analyse phonémique" (*Travaux du Cercle linguistique de Copenhague V*, 1949, p. 214–234), p. 224–225, and Jakobson-Fant-Halle, *Preliminaries to Speech Analysis*, Cambridge, Mass. 1951, p. 5–6.
[30] See the systems for many different languages explained by N. S. Trubetzkoy in *Grundzüge der Phonologie*.
[31] *Ljud och ord i svenskan* (Uppsala, 1970), p. 80. (For the first time this kind of display was used by Elert in 1955.)

"voice" whereas the /t/ has "no voice". In this case there is no need for an intermediate step between "voice" and "no voice". Other relations can, however, not be adequately described in this way. If a language has three, four or even more degrees of aperture in its "system of vowels" (Spanish has the front vowels /i, e, a/ and Italian /i, e, ε, a/), then the binary principle provides no adequate framework. Clearly, any basic description adequately arranging different "phonemes" according to "features" on a scale with more than two steps can so to speak be rewritten in such a way that only binary choices are used, but such a "secondary" description seems to have no relevance in linguistics although it may be useful in some technical application. It is certainly right to say that a description which conceals the basic difference between the bipolar relationship found in English /t/ — /d/ and the scalar relationship found in Spanish /i/ — /e/ — /a/ or Italian /i/ — /e/ — /ε/ — /a/ is inadequate.

Both matrices (tables) such as those used by Jakobson-Fant-Halle and multidimensional representations may be used with advantage. The former are capable of giving a clear account of a multitude of features. The latter seem to provide a representation which is close to a system of relations which is a reality for the users of the language described.

It may be noted that more recent tables are basically rearrangements of tables used for a long time by the International Phonetic Association or by many handbooks of phonetics. The older tables have usually sound features on the two dimensions and phonetic symbols fill the table itself. The more recent tables usually have phonemes on the horizontal dimension and distinctive features on the vertical dimension. The table itself is in this case filled by symbols such as + showing that a feature is present in some given phoneme.

11. *Syntagmatics*. An investigation of the distribution of (*b-*)*phonemes* starts naturally from the investigation of phones, i.e. the way they combine in given spoken texts. The aim of the investigation is to establish the distribution of (b-)phonemes within (b-)syllabemes, (b-)morphemes, (b-)lexemes and (b-)syntagmemes. In the process of this investigation, phones are first seen as belonging to some particular n-phoneme but, as n-phonemes do not usually describe syllabemes, morphemes and lexemes, instead of the n-phoneme the b-phoneme is taken and the phones are thus excluded. (Although our formulation seems sufficiently appropriate, a more precise statement of facts would have to take into account the distribution of various variphones of a given phoneme, and not just "the distribution of (b-)phonemes".)

The definition of *allophones* is based largely on syntagmatic facts, which means that already when these units are established their distribution must be established.

The same is to be said about *semi-phones*.

The distribution of *quasi-phonemes* can obviously be described. Attempts have also been made to use distributional details concerning a cluster of two quasi-phonemes, a "diphthong" or an "affricate", as a way of determining if the cluster is mono- or biphonemic[32].

The distribution of a *phoneme component* or a bundle of *phoneme components* (which can be the whole bundle of a phoneme or part of this bundle) can be studied.

---

[32] This is done by A. Martinet in "Un ou deux phonèmes?" (Acta linguistica 1, 1939, p. 94–103) and *Readings in linguistics* II, ed. by Hamp, Householder and Austerlitz, Chicago 1966, p. 116–123.

Attempts have recently been made to notate words, not as sequences of phonemes, but as sequences of bundles of phoneme components ("distinctive features"). This is hardly practical for most purposes. It is, however, an efficient technique if one really aims at a close study of how components and bundles of components can be combined syntagmatically.

A more detailed study, where more than a minimal number of perhaps partly arbitrarily chosen features are considered, would have to consider the distribution of allophone components (see above, p. 20) rather than phoneme components.

In a detailed study one will have to begin by carefully investigating phone component after phone component to establish basic facts about their syntagmatic combinability. Minor problems of how to consider and express related facts may arise. If in French the phoneme component "voice" in /b/ is not realized in a phone [b̥] found in a pronunciation of *robe teinte*, one may be tempted to say that the phoneme component "voice" is realized as ø (zero) before a voiceless consonant. On the other hand, when a voiceless consonant gets voiced before a voiced consonant, one would perhaps call voice a pseudo-component, or else one would have to say that one of the phoneme components of a phoneme such as a /t/ is "either voiceless or voiced depending largely on distribution". (If allophone components were considered instead of phoneme components, the account would be different again.)

As has been pointed out various kinds of *phonememes* can be set up. It seems interesting to investigate their distribution and such investigations have been carried out. For many languages the structure of "syllables" (i.e. b-syllabemes; see below, p. 41) has been described in terms of "vowels" and "consonants" (i.e. vowel phonememes and consonant phonememes). A language is said to have various types of syllables: V, CV, VC, CVC etc. How, for instance, voiced and unvoiced consonants, which are phonememes of another kind than those just mentioned, are distributed within "words" (i.e. lexemes; see below, p. 52–53) has also been described for various languages. For instance, in German, at the end of a word, voiceless (but not voiced) stops are possible.

12. *Glottophonemes, diaphonemes, sociophonemes, idiophonemes*[33].

12.0.1. Nobody would doubt that dialectal and sociolectal features exist and even play an important part in communication. It is, however, less certain to what extent dialects and sociolects can be established in such a way that there are clear boundaries between them (and, consequently, that they can be named and counted). In some given case one may well find a bundle of isophones or isoglosses which (almost) coincide, but then one may also find other bundles which do not at all coincide with the first and, in addition, isolated ones going in all kinds of directions. Even so, the resulting map may perhaps seem to be an acceptable representation of a dialect area. However, one should not forget that such a map is based on a handful of arbitrarily chosen features, usually either from phonetics or lexicon. One does not know what the map would be like if one added 1 000 other features chosen from all parts of the description of a language. Another complicating circumstance is that if the speakers

---

[33] What is said about glotto-, dia-, socio- and idiounits in this section, as well as in other sections below, is similar to my paper "Dialectel and sociolectal facts within the description of a language" (Language Sciences **34**, 1975, p. 13—18).

know dialectal and sociolectal features outside their own speech community, their evaluation of these features varies according to the depth of their knowledge and the characteristics of their own speech community. The practical solution to difficulties created by these circumstances seems to be (and has usually been) that one limits one's work in two ways:

(1) Places are investigated one at a time and each place is assumed to have its dialect ("the dialect of place A")[34] within which there may be sociolects, or at least sociolectal facts (which, unfortunately, are traditionally much less well studied). Thus, to begin with, the problem of extension and number of dialects does not worry the investigator.

(2) The different views of the speakers are left out and as many details as possible are described in the way they appear to the dialectologist (although unfortunately in the neogrammarian epoch there was a tendency towards selecting "old" dialects and within these "old" or "historically interesting" forms and towards studying them in isolation from more "recent" dialects or more "recent" facts within the same dialect)[35].

Thus, to begin with, the problem of how groups of speakers with some given dialect (sociolect) evaluate the dialects (sociolects) of other groups of speakers is hardly given any attention[36]. Studying in this way, place after place, nothing but dialect after dialect, each perhaps having sociolects, will be seen.

In the account given below we will accept this somewhat simplified general idea according to which a glottolect (language) has dialects, each of which has its sociolects, which have idiolects, and we choose to neglect possibilities such as dialects having no sociolects or a language having dialects but no sociolects or sociolects but no dialects or such as sociolects being common to more than one dialect. (In addition to the limitations just mentioned, problems such as to what extent some dialect as a whole has a sort of sociolectal value or to what extent different dialects may have common sociolects are left out.)

12.0.2. In comparisons between language systems, and subsequently in the establishment of units including facts from more than one system, the notion of "corresponding" is basic. For instance, a unit in one dialect may be corresponding, or not corresponding, in relation to a unit in some other dialect. Instead of "corresponding" the terms "same" or "equivalent" or "identical" are sometimes used. However, if it is accepted that two elements of two systems which are at least somewhat different cannot be absolutely the same, the term "corresponding" would seem to be preferable.

The relation of "correspondence" is consequently a relation between units which show sufficient similarity. "Sufficient similarity" would usually be established by the linguist, but speakers attempting to use a system other than their own, reveal through their mistakes where in their minds units are so similar that a correspondence is established[37].

---

[34] Cf. *Linguistische Einheiten*, p. 97.
[35] Cf. my papers "Inquéritos Linguísticos" (Revista de Portugal, Série A, 26, 1961, p. 9-32), p. 14-15, and "Dialektologiska undersökningar" (Tidsskrift for Tale og Stemme 24: 1, 1964, 27-51), p. 32-34.
[36] I have, however, given the problem some attention in "Zur soziolektalen und dialektalen Funktion der Sprache" (Zeitschrift für Mundartforschung 34: 3/4, 1967, p. 205-216).
[37] Cf. *Linguistische Einheiten* (see index).

To some extent it can be observed that laymen establish units ("glottounits") which have as variants different dialectal units which are corresponding. A speaker from Northern or Central Sweden may observe that he prefers his pronunciation of *r* (which is front) to the pronunciation of *r* (which is back) used in the south of the country. The implication seems not only to be that there are two corresponding sounds, but also that they are variants of the Swedish *r* (a kind of glottophoneme).

Also linguists have obviously often mentioned facts from more than one dialect at a time, and some have dealt with the problem in a more general way.

12.1. *Ph-glottophonemes.* If the phonological systems of two (or more) dialects (sociolects) of a language are compared, phonemes which are similar as to the place within their own system may be considered to be *phonemically corresponding*[38]. Those which are not similar in this respect are *phonemically not corresponding*. It is suggested that the prefix ph- be used to designate units based on phonemic correspondence (as defined).

Definition: A *ph-glottophoneme* (i.e. a phoneme of the whole language which is established on the basis of phonemic correspondence) is a set of diaphonemes which are phonemically corresponding. (A diaphoneme is here defined as a phoneme of some particular dialect.)

For instance, according to this suggestion, an /l/ in some English dialect and an /l/ in some other English dialect are diaphonemes belonging to the same English glottophoneme /l/.

As a traditional phonological system is based on only a minimal number of sound properties which are thought to be the "relevant" features (or the distinctive features), sound properties which may be different in different dialects are often left out. Thus it is possible for diaphonemes within a given ph-glottophoneme to have partly different allophones and different phones. If in some Swedish dialect the phoneme /r/ has no back allophone [R] and if in some other Swedish dialect the /r/ has a back allophone, it is possible for both to belong to the same glottophoneme /r/. (As, on the other hand, some Swedish dialects have a phoneme /R/ with no front allophone [r] there will be in Swedish a ph-glottophoneme /R/ in addition to the ph-glottophoneme /r/.)

If one chooses to consider allophones in a more abstract way and not exactly as the set of all their phones, or in other words, if one chooses to discard minor details, two allophones from two dialects may be corresponding even if one can establish by ear that they are not absolutely the same. For instance, the French front allophone [k̟] (as in *qui*) is more palatal in Paris than in many other French dialects, but this would not cause the description of the French glottophoneme /k/ to contain more than one front allophone [k̟].

Thus two diaphonemes of the same glottophoneme may or may not be allophonically corresponding, and they (or the allophones) may or may not be phonically corresponding.

In addition, two corresponding diaphonemes may or may not be distributionally corresponding. (The distribution to be accounted for refers to position within syllables, and not within morphemes.)

A ph-diaphoneme is usually a set of phonemically corresponding sociophonemes, i.e. ph-sociophonemes. For instance, in Australia a "low" sociolect has for /i:/ (as in

---

[38] Cf. *Linguistische Einheiten*, p. 73.

feed) a sociophoneme, which is realized with an open first segment of the diphthong, whereas a "high" sociolect has another sociophoneme which is realized with a less open first segment. Both belong to the same diaphoneme.

It is possible to let similar socioallophones from different sociophonemes of the same diaphoneme form a diaallophone. Then similar diaallophones from corresponding diaphonemes form a glottoallophone.

It may occur that a glottophoneme has more glottoallophones than any of its diaphonemes and sociophonemes as it has, so to speak, to sum up everything from the dialectal and sociolectal levels. In other words, a glottoallophone may include, among its diaallophones and socioallophones, also ⌀-diaallophones and ⌀-socioallophones.

There does not seem to be any particular difficulty in finding the appropriate phonetic symbols and labelled brackets for notating all units just mentioned.

Although linguists are naturally not very interested in individual pronunciations as such, it is clear that all units just mentioned are sets of phones pronounced by particular individuals, in other words, are realized as idiophones.

Starting from the bottom of the hierarchy the phonemes of an individual would be *idiophonemes* and the items would be *idiophones*. The allophones of an individual would be *idioallophones*.

Certain idiophonemes of all individuals belonging to the same sociolect would form a certain *sociophoneme* which would have *socioallophones*, including idioallophones, as subclasses. A sociophoneme would include phones which are sociophones, and idiophones at the same time. One could name them *socio-idiophones*. (A segment can have more than one function!)

Certain idiophones of all individuals belonging to the same dialect would form a certain *diaphoneme* which would have *diaallophones*, including idioallophones as subclasses. A diaphoneme would include phones which are diaphones and idiophones at the same time. One could call them *dia-idiophones*.

Certain idiophones of all individuals belonging to the same glottolect (language) would form a certain *glottophoneme* which would have *glottoallophones*, including idioallophones as subclasses. A glottophoneme would have phones which are glottophones and idiophones at the same time. One could name them *glotto-idiophones*. Consequently a phone is a *glotto-dia-socio-idiophone*.

As explained, two words from different dialects (sociolects) may be said to have phonemically corresponding phonemes. In this wording the use of the term phoneme is, however, imprecise, as it is clear that a phoneme with all its allophones and phones cannot be a segment of one particular word.

For a word segment, one may use the term *phoneme representative* (which I have preferred earlier) or *variphone* (which I prefer now and which I have suggested above). Variphones from different dialects (sociolects) would then correspond phonemically if they belong to corresponding phonemes. In this case they may or may not have corresponding phones. If the word *right* has a more fricative /r/ in some English dialect and a more rolled /r/ in some other dialect, these two variphones are different in quality; they have different phones or are phonically not corresponding.

Considered in one way a phoneme is a set of allophones, and considered in another way a phoneme is a set of variphones. Or, in a more complete way, it is possible to say that a phoneme is a set of allophones; an allophone is a set of variphones, and a variphone is a set of phones (as explained above). This means that a ph-glottophoneme has ph-diaphonemes which have ph-diaallophones which have ph-diavariphones.

To simplify, the term phoneme will mainly be used below even where variphone would have been more appropriate.

12.2. *M-glottophonemes*. In addition to being, or not being, phonemically corresponding, two phonemes from different dialects (sociolects) may, or may not, be morphemically corresponding.

Phonemes are *morphemically*[39] (*allomorphically, varimorphically*) *corresponding* if they occur in corresponding positions in corresponding morphemes (or in corresponding positions in the corresponding part of partly corresponding morphemes).

The Swedish word *näsa* (= nose) has in Stockholm the form /neːsa/ and in most other dialects the form /nɛːsa/. The /n/ in these and similar words are morphemically, and phonemically, corresponding. The /eː/ in one dialect is morphemically, but not phonemically, corresponding with /ɛː/ in some other dialect.

Two phonemes from different dialects are here considered to be morphemically corresponding if at least one of their variphones corresponds (i.e. if the correspondence is found in at least one pair of words). However, usually a considerable number of variphones correspond.

It is suggested that the prefix m- be used to designate units based on morphemic correspondence.

Definition: An *m-glottophoneme* (i.e. a phoneme of the whole language which is established on the basis of morphemic correspondence) is a set of diaphonemes which are morphemically corresponding.

For instance, Swedish /eː/ and Swedish /ɛː/ would be two m-diaphonemes within the same m-glottophoneme.

Mutatis mutandis one would establish m-sociophonemes which can usually be considered as variants within m-diaphonemes. The above mentioned variant of English /iː/ (as in *feed*) in a "low" Melbourne sociolect would be a sociophoneme belonging to the same m-diaphoneme as the mentioned sociolectally "high" variant of /iː/. However, these kinds of facts would mainly be dealt with at the level of ph-units (and not at the level of m-units).

Sometimes the correspondence is, not one-to-one, but one-to-many. For instance, some German dialect may have /s/ morphemically corresponding with /s/ and /z/ in some other dialect. If one thinks that the glottolect should possess the higher number of phonemes rather than the lower, German will have a glottophoneme /s/ and a glottophoneme /z/. Both /s/ and /z/ in one dialect will correspond "partly" with /s/ in the other dialect (in the sense that the variphones of /s/ and /z/ in one dialect correspond both with part of the variphones of /s/ in the other dialect). Both glottophonemes will include the "part diaphoneme" /s/ or, in other words, both glottophonemes will include part of the variphones which in the dialect where there is no

---

[39] The term morphemically is somewhat imprecise. In a more precise way allomorphs and varimorphs would be considered. The kind of morphemic correspondence referred to is established by taking not only the correspondence of morphemes, but also of morpheme sememes into account, see below p. 55—56.

difference between /s/ and /z/ belong to /s/. The German m-glottophoneme /s/ would have one diaphoneme /s/ and another diaphoneme 1/2 /s/ and the German glottophoneme /z/ would have one diaphoneme /z/ and another diaphoneme 1/2 /s/.

More generally there is sometimes a correspondence between phonemes /a/, /b/, /c/[40] in two dialects which can be shown as follows:

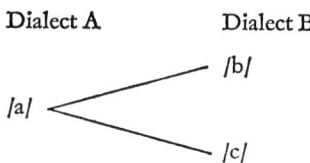

The way of accounting for these facts which we have just chosen is to establish m-glottophonemes /b/ and /c/. M-glottophoneme /b/ then includes ph-diaphoneme /b/ and ph-diaphoneme 1/2 /a/, and m-glottophoneme /c/ includes ph-diaphoneme /c/ and ph-diaphoneme 1/2 /a/. These ph-diaphonemes and 1/2 ph-diaphonemes are then also m-diaphonemes as they correspond morphemically. One may, however, also choose to establish the m-glottophoneme /a/. Then ph-diaphoneme /a/ corresponds morphemically both with ph-diaphoneme /b/ and ph-diaphoneme /c/. This means that m-glottophoneme /a/ includes ph-diaphoneme /a/ from dialect A and ph-diaphonemes /b/ and /c/ from dialect B. Ph-diaphoneme /a/ is then also an m-diaphoneme and /b/ and /c/ form together an m-diaphoneme. (In a detailed study of interference phenomena, one way of describing would suit a speaker of dialect A better, and the other way would suit a speaker of dialect B better.)

With many one-to-many correspondences in a language, the description of glottophonemes and their variants, the diaphonemes, may become very complicated. Therefore, one may choose to consider only two dialects at a time. Instead of the larger "complete" glottophoneme, one would establish "two-dialect" phonemes with diaphonemes as variants. These units are definitely needed for the description of what happens when a speaker of one dialect communicates with a speaker of another dialect. Also, "two-sociolect" phonemes can be established.

The case when some phoneme is missing in some dialect does not offer any difficulty. Within the relevant glottophoneme, or "two-dialect" phoneme, this dialect will have a ø-diaphoneme.

The most natural way of notating m-glottophonemes may be to use (as far as they go) notations relating to the dialect with the highest reputation or to the standard language if there is one.

It should be noted that a standard language, although only being loosely related to some geographical area, could be considered a kind of dialect when dialectal matters are under study, as facts of a dialect contrast not only with facts of other dialects, but also with facts of the standard language. The standard language would also have to be considered in relation to sociolects. It would also be a kind of sociolect. Among dialects the standard language would have, to some degree, the characteristics of a dialect if it were unevenly distributed over a language area, but be more clearly a

---

[40] In the specific German example just mentioned it would, however, be more appropriate to let dialect A have the phoneme /a/ and dialect B the phonemes /a/ and /b/.

"no dialect" if it had roughly the same probability of occurrence everywhere. Among sociolects the standard language is a high sociolect. Except in the more unusual case when in some dialect a word is thought to have more than one structure in terms of phonemes, a variphone in one dialect which corresponds with a variphone in some other dialect corresponds in a simple one-to-one correspondence. The particular /n/ in /ne:sa/ corresponds with the particular /n/ in /nɛ:sa/ and the particular /e:/ in the first word corresponds with the particular /ɛ:/ of the second word (etc.). (Morphemically corresponding variphones belong to morphemically corresponding diaphonemes (sociophonemes).)

Not only an m-glottophoneme, but also a "two-dialect" m-phoneme, is a set of corresponding m-diaphonemes. An m-diaphoneme (m-sociophoneme) is a set of m-variphones.

Allophones (and phones) of different kinds would generally be dealt with as ph-units rather than m-units.

12.3. In the most basic description as many diaphonemes, sociophonemes (and idiophonemes) as are presumably used by the speakers of a language would be considered. This would generally speaking mean that the overall description contains more details than those included in any given speaker's knowledge and no notice is taken of differences between speakers in their assessment of dialectal, sociolectal (and idiolectal) differences. (In an earlier paper[41] I have explained in some detail why dialectal and sociolectal differences should be considered to be "subjective".)

Glottophonemes, diaphonemes and sociophonemes are here considered as sets of α-units. Also idiophonemes are α-units. Speaking of idiophonemes just means speaking of the phonemes of an individual. The study of these could be carried out without knowledge of anybody else's phonemes. The same goes, mutatis mutandis, for the other units, i.e., phonemes relatable to the pronunciation of some particular social class or some particular geographical area can be studied without knowledge of any other class or area.

A more comprehensive study of the characteristic properties of dia-, socio- and idiophonemes provides the elements for a study of related γ-units, i.e. phoneme dialemes with phone dials, phoneme sociolemes with phone sociols and phoneme idiolemes with phone idiols[42], which this book will not deal with in detail[43].

A considerable number of further units could be obtained by adding the suffixes glotto-, dia-, socio-, idio- to phonememe, semi-phoneme etc.

Some suggestions for notations: Glottoph/.../, Glottoalloph [.../, glottoph [...]; Diaph/.../, Diaalloph [.../, diaph[...]; Socioph/.../, Socioalloph [.../, socioph[...]; Idioph/.../, Idioalloph [.../, Idioph[...].

glottophoneme = {diaphoneme$_1$, ..., diaphoneme$_n$}
diaphoneme = {sociophoneme$_1$, ..., sociophoneme$_n$}
sociophoneme = {idiophoneme$_1$, ..., idiophoneme$_n$}
diaphoneme = {diaallophone$_1$, ..., diaallophone$_n$}

---

[41] See above, p. 23, footnote 36.
[42] On this point the definitions and terminology have been somewhat enlarged since *Linguistische Einheiten*.
[43] See, however, below, p. 112–113.

sociophoneme = {socioallophone₁, ..., socioallophoneₙ}
idiophoneme = {idioallophone₁, ..., idioallophoneₙ}
glottophoneme = {glottoallophone₁, ..., glottoallophoneₙ}
glottoallophone = {diaallophone₁, ..., diaallophoneₙ}
diaallophone = {socioallophone₁, ..., socioallophoneₙ}
socioallophone = {idioallophone₁, ..., idioallophoneₙ}
idioallophone = {idiophone₁, ..., idiophoneₙ}

13. *Inventory*. It is suggested that the definition of inventory be a collection, as exhaustive as possible, of units or items, in which the units or items are enumerated according to some principle, for instance, in alphabetical order.

Inventories of phones can be established for limited texts. One cannot possibly record all phones of a language because this would imply investigating all spoken utterances of all speakers of a language. The notion seems to be of little use.

Establishing *inventories of phonemes* is, on the other hand, one of the most basic tasks in linguistics. There is hardly any danger of accidental gaps occurring in a phoneme inventory. The number of phonemes in a language is comparatively limited[44] and in a spoken text their realizations (phones) recur frequently although the realizations of some phonemes may be much less frequent than others. In the presentation of the inventory, alphabetical order may be possible but would not be particularly suitable as, obviously, notations of phonemes do not contain normal letters but phonetic symbols. If, despite this fact, one tries to order the notations of phonemes according to the alphabetical order of "related letters": /a/, /b/, /c/ etc., the principle breaks down occasionally as in English where there is no letter of the alphabet related to /ŋ/ (*thing*), or to /tʃ/ (*child*). It seems more suitable to enumerate phonemes according to the components referring to the place of articulation and start at the front part of the vocal tract and go backwards. This could first be done with the (sub)inventory of vowels. Thus, in English, the first two vowels enumerated would be /i:/ and /ɪ/. In the enumeration of the elements of the (sub)inventory of the English consonants the first two would be /p/ and /b/. In the case of the consonants it seems convenient also to take into account different manners of articulation[45].

It is also clear that inventories of phonemes, semi phonemes, quasi phonemes, pseudo-phonemes, (meta-phonemes,) and also of phoneme components can be established. By implication, what was said above of the limited value of inventories of phones and the difficulty of establishing them goes also for inventories of semi-phones, quasi-phones, pseudo-phones, meta-phones and phone components.

14. *Discovery procedures* (see above, p. 10). The existence of phones, directly, and phonemes, indirectly, can in many cases be demonstrated in a convincing way by comparing words and finding out which are the smallest segments capable of differentiating between words or "changing the meaning of words". This procedure has different names: establishing by the use of "phonological oppositions" the smallest units being capable of changing meanings of words (Prague School), making the "commutation test" (Copenhagen School) or seeking "minimal pairs" (American

---

[44] Cf. B. Sigurd, "A note on the number of phonemes" (SMIL 2, Stockholm 1963, p. 94–99).
[45] I have used this way of enumerating for Portuguese vowels and consonants in *Étude de phonétique auditive sur les parlers de l'Algarve* (Uppsala 1953), p. 41–43.

structuralists)[46]. We should like to suggest "dividing substitution" as a general name for this kind of procedure.

The way of establishing allophones, phonemes, semi-phonemes, quasi-phonemes, pseudo-phonemes and meta-phonemes is implied in the definition of these units. It is no use discussing discovery procedures in these cases.

The establishment, directly, of phone components and, indirectly, of phoneme components and phonological systems are more complicated problems which fall within auditory phonetics. It is difficult to imagine that these units and items could be discovered in articulatory phonetics. It is excluded that an acoustic investigation could establish them[47]. When phone components are established it is, however, certainly interesting to describe their relationships to articulatory and acoustic facts.

It seems that, on the whole, the auditory phone components are just the features of consonants and vowels one has always reckoned with although these are generally given articulatory names (alveolar, lateral, open, front etc.). Despite this fact, interesting auditory tests can be made. The stimuli to which the informants have to react are either real speech or synthetic speech. A particularly extensive and interesting research in this area has been carried out by G. Hanson[48]. This scholar established a phonological system for Swedish vowels which is highly isomorphous with an articulatory system (as in the Prague School) or an acoustic system (F1 versus F2).

1.1.2. Prosodemes

0. A great number of terms such as suprasegmental, intonation, contour, intonation pattern, pitch contour etc. have been used for notions that are partly or entirely the same[49]. On this point, as on so many others, a standardization of terms would be most desirable.

In the present book the two terms prosodeme and contoureme[50] will be used to the exlusion of all others for the two basic units involved.

0.1. Prosodemes are discrete units of the α-level[51]. They are either syllabeme, or morpheme, or lexeme, or syntagmeme prosodemes. The α-function distinguishes prosodemes from contouremes which are β-units.

---

[46] Cf. *Linguistische Einheiten*, p. 15, 22–23.
[47] At the best, sonagrams, and other acoustic representations, can provide suggestions to be tested at the auditory level. This is rightly pointed out by H. Pilch, „Neue Wege der englischen Phonetik" (Anglia **77**, 1959, p. 407–428), p. 427. See also *Linguistische Einheiten*, p. 27–28.
[48] Also G. Ungeheuer is a pioneer in this area. See works quoted on p. 26 of *Linguistische Einheiten* and G. Hanson, *Dimensions in speech sound perception* (*Ericsson Technics* No. 1), Stockholm 1967.
[49] In one work I counted as many as 24 different terms even without having done an absolutely exhaustive count. Cf. Phonetica **7**, 1961, p. 245.
[50] Cf. my paper "Prosodeme und Kontureme" (Phonetica **10**, 1963, p. 194–202) or *Linguistische Einheiten*, p. 8–13. See also below, p. 33, on contouremes.
[51] The α-units, which are the "central" units of linguistics (the "traditional" units of phonetics, morphology, syntax) are often discrete. Cf. *Linguistische Einheiten*, pages mentioned in the "Sachverzeichnis" (p. 105). The contouremes, being β-units, are non discrete, see below, p. 112.

The realizations of prosodemes are prosodes: syllab, morph, lex or syntagm prosodes (i.e. these terms are used for actually pronounced items). Prosodemes and prosodes have components which vary as a function of time. Articulatorily defined they are "courses" of the frequency of the vocal cords, of the force of articulation, of the form of the supraglottal cavities and of the duration. Acoustically defined they are courses of the frequency of the fundamental, of the intensity, the spectrum and the duration. Auditorily defined they are courses of pitch, loudness, quality and length.[52]

If prosodemes were exactly described in terms of these four "basic" auditory components, one would achieve a more satisfactory description than those which are now common. It seems, however, that a still more complete description would have to consider more complex components which would be based, in different ways, on the "basic" components. In this respect one would suggest:

(1) *Intonation*. If, by convention, one lets "pitch" include the sensation of "height" which is also present in whispered speech, "intonation" would hardly be different from "pitch course". One may imagine, however, that quality has perhaps some influence on the sensation of height in a prosodeme. (An /s/ is for instance "higher" than a /ʃ/.) Be this as it may and whatever the exact definition of "pitch" should be, it is here suggested that everything contributing to "height" should be included in the definition of "intonation".

(2) *Accentuation*. Although accentuated or stressed segments (usually syllables) seem often to be mainly equated with segments having great loudness, a full description of accentuated segments would usually have to take not only loudness but also pitch, quality and length into account as it must be assumed that often these four function together. Accentuation is a prosodeme pattern of accentuated and unaccentuated segments.

(3) *Rhythm*. Rhythm is the sensation of strong and weak segments following each other along the time scale so as to form given patterns. Rhythm is thus the prominent property of accentuation. However, other kinds of rhythm also occur. Long vowels may alternate with short vowels. Long words may alternate with short ones. Segments of a given kind may have certain distances in time from other given segments.

(4) *Prominence*. It is suggested that prominence be given a definition which is somewhat different from "accent" (in the meaning of stress). Syllables, words and syntactic constructions which "stand out" in relation to their context may be said to have prominence. For instance, a word with two syllables can be prominent and at the same time it has its normal accentuation (e.g. the first syllable accentuated and the second not). Boundary markers, of which pauses are part, contribute towards signalling prominence.

(5) *Tempo*. The speed with which prosodemes are said has little importance at the auditory level. It is, however, known that longer segments (hence longer prosodemes) are said with higher speed than shorter segments (prosodemes). (Tempo is more noticeable in contouremes.)

Prosodemes are sets of prosodes, or (when applicable) prosodemes are sets of alloprosodes that are sets of prosodes.

---

[52] "Prosodeme und Kontureme", p. 197–201, or *Linguistische Einheiten*, p. 8–11, 33–37. See also above, p. 7–9.

A prosodeme is either narrowly defined as the sum of its prosodes with all their properties, or broadly defined with the help of one or more typical properties that are realized in all or most of its prosodes.

Prosodeme components are sets of prosode components.

A prosodeme component is either narrowly defined as the sum of its prosode components, or broadly defined with the help of one or more typical properties that are realized in all or most of its prosode components.

Prosodemes generally have a constructive function. They may also have a distinctive function (see below, p. 35, 37).

1.1. *Items : syllab prosodes. Units : syllabeme prosodemes. Definition :* Prosodemes which have the constructive function of grouping phonemes (variphones) together so as to form "syllables" are *syllabeme prosodemes*. Realizations of these, i.e. prosodes which have the function of grouping phones so as to form "syllables" are *syllab prosodes*.

Each time a syllabeme is realized in a syllab its prosodeme is realized in a particular prosode and its prosodeme components are realized as particular prosode components. Thus the syllabeme *mean*, or more precisely, the syllabeme /miːn/ may be realized as [mɪˑʲn] and have a syllab prosode which can be described at the articulatory, acoustic or auditory level.

The syllabeme mentioned, as well as perhaps all other syllabemes in English, and in other languages, seems to have as components all four possible courses. All four, or frequently fewer than four, syllabeme prosodeme components are realized as syllab prosode components. (It seems certain that only in clear syllabs are all four realized. In less clear syllabs one or more components are not realized, or in other words realized as zero.) The first prosodeme component of a syllabeme such as /miːn/ would be (auditorily defined) a course of pitch that rises to a peak in the middle of the syllabeme and then falls. The second would be a course of loudness: the vowel is louder than the two other segments. The third would be a course of quality that would be rather clear (for /m/) followed by very clear (for /iː/) and finishing as less clear (for /n/). The fourth component would be a course of length: rather great length for /m/ (in comparison with the length of /m/ in other positions) followed by greater length for /iː/ and rather short length for /n/ in comparison with both the two preceding segments and with /n/ in many other positions[53].

Syllabs and syllab components vary "freely" and "facultatively". As pointed out above (p. 13) free variation is here defined as random variation due to the fact that speech organs are not absolutely "precise" and facultative variation is here defined as variation that is relevant at levels other than the α-level, i.e. at the β-level (level of contouremes), the γ_1-(idiolectal), γ_2-(sociolectal) and γ_3-(dialectal) level (see below, under idioprosodemes, socioprosodemes and diaprosodemes).

---

[53] As has been pointed out above (p. 19), in contradistinction to "classical" phonology that requested that only the smallest number of components capable of distinguishing the units of which they are components be accepted as "relevant", I prefer to consider relevant every component that contributes towards the listener's identification of the unit.

The components are not just "constructive" or "distinctive" but they are more or less so according to their being frequently or less frequently realized or according to their being more or less clearly perceived and therefore making a more or less significant contribution to the listener's identification (cf. *Linguistische Einheiten*, p. 35–36, and above, p. 19).

According to how something is said, i.e. according to which contour of a contoureme (see below, p. 111–112) has been used, each prosodeme will have many variants. This is true about syllabeme prosodemes as well as of other prosodemes. I have elsewhere described the difference between the Swedish word *fy* said with more, or less disgust (cf. *Linguistische Einheiten*, p. 9). In this case the contour conditions not only the syllab, but also the lex and the syntagm (as the word is said as a sentence).

1.2.1. *Units: allosyllab prosodemes. Definition:* If syllab prosodes of the same syllabeme prosodeme form groups of realizations distinguishable by the ear according to position in relation to other syllab, (morph,) lex and syntagm prosodes, each group of syllab prosodes is an *allosyllab prosodeme*. Thus an allosyllab prosodeme is a subset of a syllabeme prosodeme.

In a detailed description that takes allosyllab prosodes into account one would say that syllab prosodes vary freely and facultatively within each allosyllab prosodeme rather than within each syllabeme prosodeme.

An allosyllab prosodeme may be called a dialloprosode of a syllabememe prosodeme (see below) and an alloprosode of a syllabeme prosodeme. If so, a syllabeme prosodeme is an alloprosode of a syllabememe prosodeme.

1.2.2. Allosyllabs belonging to different syllabemes might be grouped to *allosyllabemes* if they have such common properties that it seems reasonable to do so. If this solution is chosen, also allosyllabeme prosodemes would be established. (As presently little is known about the phonic properties of syllabs, allosyllabs and syllabemes, no example will be provided here.)

1.3. A varisyllab (see below, p. 41) would have a *varisyllab prosodeme*.

1.4. Syllabemes (varisyllabs) having as segments phonemes (variphones) belonging, in the same sequential order, to vowels or consonants, would form sets of syllabemes, or syllabememes (see below, p. 41). E.g. the syllabememe CVC would include /mæn/, /hɪt/, /sæt/ etc. A syllabememe would have a *syllabememe prosodeme*. (Note that the term prosodeme can be modified by the addition of terms designating units of higher or lower order so as to show sets of prosodemes of lower or higher order. E.g. a syllabeme prosodeme is lower, i.e. includes a smaller number of elements, than a syllabememe prosodeme.)

1.5. *Pseudo-syllab prosodes and meta-syllab prosodes.* Pseudo-syllabs (see below, p. 42) will have pseudo-syllab prosodes. A "word as such", i.e. a lexeme, may have a given number of syllabemes but in the pronunciation one may sometimes hear a higher or lower number of syllabs which would be, in more precise terms, pseudo-syllabs. Such pseudo-syllabs would have pseudo-syllab prosodes.

Meta-syllabs (see below, p. 42) would have very clear meta-syllab prosodes.
syllabeme prosodeme = {allosyllab prosodeme$_1$, ..., allosyllab prosodeme$_n$}
allosyllab prosodeme = {syllab prosode$_1$, ..., syllab prosode$_n$}
syllabeme prosodeme component = {allosyllab prosodeme component$_1$, ..., allosyllab prosodeme component$_n$}
allosyllab prosodeme component = {syllab prosode component$_1$, ..., syllab prosode component$_n$}
allosyllabeme prosodeme = {allosyllab prosodeme$_1$, ..., allosyllab prosodeme$_n$}

allosyllabeme prosodeme component = {allosyllab prosodeme component$_1$, ..., allosyllab prosodeme component$_n$}
varisyllab prosodeme = {syllab prosode$_1$, ..., syllab prosode$_n$}
varisyllab prosodeme component = {syllab prosode component$_1$, ..., syllab prosode component$_n$}
syllabememe prosodeme = {syllabeme prosodeme$_1$, ..., syllabeme prosodeme$_n$}
syllabememe prosodeme component = {syllabeme prosodeme component$_1$, ..., syllabeme prosodeme component$_n$}

2. Morphemes usually have no prosodemes. If needed in some language, morph prosodes, allomorph prosodemes and morpheme prosodemes and components of these could, however, be established.

The term allomorpheme will be introduced below (p. 47) to designate a set of allomorphs that are similar in regard to their segments, which are variphones and varisyllabs. Such a set of allomorphs would have an allomorpheme prosodeme. The equally new term morphememe could be reserved for sets such as the independent (or free) morphemes and the dependent (or bound) morphemes. One might then establish the notion morphememe prosodeme but it is difficult to say how useful it would be.

If in a language no morphemes had allomorphs, it would certainly be appropriate to establish morpheme prosodemes. In a language where morphemes have allomorphs, morpheme prosodemes would often just be the sum of quite different allomorph prosodemes and therefore not really interesting. As a matter of fact, a morpheme with several allomorphs would perhaps rather be considered to have no morpheme prosodeme but there would be a prosodeme for each allomorph. In the case of a morpheme "having no allomorphs", it would then, for the sake of conformity, seem advantageous to consider that this morpheme had one allomorph and that this allomorph, and not the morpheme, has a prosodeme.

Varimorphs (see below, p. 47) would have prosodemes. A varimorph prosodeme would be an alloprosode of an allomorph prosodeme.

As will be explained, varimorphs from different morphemes could be grouped into varimorphemes whenever such a grouping was relevant. Varimorphemes would have prosodemes.

morpheme prosodeme = {morph prosode$_1$, ..., morph prosode$_n$}
morpheme prosodeme = {varimorph prosodeme$_1$, ..., varimorph prosodeme$_n$}
varimorph prosodeme = {morph prosode$_1$, ..., morph prosode$_n$}
morpheme prosodeme component = {morph prosode component$_1$, ..., morph prosode component$_n$}
morpheme prosodeme component = {varimorph prosodeme component$_1$, ..., varimorph prosodeme component$_n$}
varimorph prosodeme component = {morph prosode component$_1$, ..., morph prosode component$_n$}
allomorph prosodeme = {morph prosode$_1$, ..., morph prosode$_n$}
allomorph prosodeme = {varimorph prosodeme$_1$, ..., varimorph prosodeme$_n$}
allomorph prosodeme component = {morph prosode component$_1$, ..., morph prosode component$_n$}

allomorph prosodeme component = {varimorph prosodeme component$_1$, ..., varimorph prosodeme component$_n$}
allomorpheme prosodeme = {allomorph prosodeme$_1$, ..., allomorph prosodeme$_n$}
allomorpheme prosodeme component = {allomorph prosodeme component$_1$, ..., allomorph prosodeme component$_n$}
(morphememe prosodeme = {morpheme prosodeme$_1$, ..., morpheme prosodeme$_n$})
(morphememe prosodeme component = {morpheme prosodeme component$_1$, ..., morpheme prosodeme component$_n$})

3. If a "word" in the sense of the sum of all its realizations is called a lexeme and one particular instance of a "word" is called a lex, one would have to establish lexeme prosodemes and lex prosodes and their components.

Lex prosodes and lexeme prosodemes have in most cases a constructive function. They may, however, have distinctive function in addition as in the Chinese "tones" or as in Swedish "accent 1" versus "accent 2": *ánden* (the duck) versus *ànden* (the ghost) or as in *ímport* (noun) versus *impórt* (verb).

Lexeme and lex components would be more or less of the same kind as syllabeme and syllab components (and in the case of a lexeme having as segment only one varisyllab they would even coincide). One would, however, assume that lex components are generally more distinctively pronounced and more clearly perceived than syllab components.

Position in relation to the syntagms of the sentence conditions groups of variants within lexemes. These could be called varilexes and, obviously, they have prosodemes. Thus a varilex prosodeme is a kind of aloprosode of a lexeme prosodeme.

Varilexes from different lexemes could be grouped into varilexemes whenever such a grouping is relevant. Varilexemes would have prosodemes.

Lexemes can be grouped into sets of lexemes (i.e. lexememes) in accordance with their syntagmatic structure, particularly in terms of adherence to a given syllabememe. Lexememes will have prosodemes. Lexememe prosodemes have, as aloprosodes, lexeme prosodemes.

Lexes and lex prosodes vary freely and facultatively, which means that within each varilex there is free and facultative variation.

The notion allolex as defined in *Linguistische Einheiten* (p. 40–41, 42)[54] has not been taken into account up to this point. At least in the description of English and other "western" languages this notion is rarely necessary. It is certainly less important than the notion of allomorph (which as a matter of fact was taken into account in 2). It would be easy to make allolexes part of the above (and assign to them prosodemes) but it might be simpler to equate allolexes with lexemes in descriptions of prosodemes[55].

lexeme prosodeme = {lex prosode$_1$, ..., lex prosode$_n$}
lexeme prosodeme component = {lex prosode component$_1$, ..., lex prosode component$_n$}

---

[54] In Swedish the imperfect of the verb *betala* can be *betalade, betalde, betalte* or *betala*. These forms show "stylistic" (β-level) or regional (γ_3), sociolectal (γ_2) and idiolectal (γ_1) differences, i.e. the variation is facultative.
[55] The abovementioned allolexes *betalade, betalde, betalte, betala* can quite sensibly be thought of as four lexemes (although they are related to each other in a specific way).

varilex prosodeme = {lex prosode$_1$, ..., lex prosode$_n$}
varilex prosodeme component = {lex prosode component$_1$, ..., lex prosode component$_n$}
varilexeme prosodeme = {varilex prosodeme$_1$, ..., varilex prosodeme$_n$}
varilexeme prosodeme component = {varilex prosodeme component$_1$, ..., varilex prosodeme component$_n$}
lexememe prosodeme = {lexeme prosodeme$_1$, ..., lexeme prosodeme$_n$}
lexememe prosodeme component = {lexeme prosodeme component$_1$, ..., lexeme prosodeme component$_n$}

4. Unless the hierarchical classification is clearly worked out in syntax, syntactic prosodemes and prosodes will not be well described.

All "patterns" and sets of patterns in syntax are here called syntagmemes and their realizations in actually pronounced examples are called syntagms. In a broad definition, general patterns are emphasized. In a narrow definition, all possible characteristics of all the particular syntagms and groups of syntagms are emphasized.

Each instance of a sentence is called a "period". Syntactically similar periods form sets that are part of larger sets that may be part of still larger sets etc. The largest sets are called periodemes. If, on the other hand, one starts from periodemes and "works down", the most immediate sets are alloperiods. Subsets of these are dialloperiods. If needed the series can be continued: trialloperiods, tetralloperiods, etc.

Or another example: if one calls all possible subjects the subjecteme, allosubjects, diallosubjects etc. would be established as subsets, subsets of subsets etc. of the subjecteme. (More details are provided below, p. 66–75.)

Syntagms (such as a period or a subject) have prosodes with their components (syntagm prosode components) and syntagmemes (such as some [higher or lower] set of periods or subjects) have prosodemes with their components (syntagmeme prosodeme components).

The prosode components (auditorily defined) of the French clause *si vous parlez* [si vu parle], (*je m'en vais*) could be:

1 — course of pitch: the first three syllabs lower and the fourth syllab considerably higher;

2 — course of loudness: the first three syllabs less loud and the fourth louder;

3 — course of quality: the first three syllabs have clear quality and the fourth is particularly clear;

4 — course of length: the first three syllabs are shorter and the fourth longer[56]. (A short pause is possible after the fourth syllable.)

Although this description in terms of "basic" (see p. 8–9) components may seem acceptable, one can restate it in terms of "complex" components. The intonation would be the same as the course of pitch. The accentuation would be described as three unaccentuated syllabs followed by one accentuated syllab. The impression of more or less accentuated syllabs is certainly based on loudness and length and, in addition, to a minor degree (it seems) on quality and, perhaps, on pitch.

Syntagms, considered as elements of the set to which they directly belong differ among themselves according to (a) the structure of the lexes they include and to (b) the position of the syntagm in relation to other syntagms. Both for (a) and (b) there

---

[56] Example from *Linguistische Einheiten*, p. 45.

would be many possibilities: $a_1, \ldots, a_n$ and $b_1, \ldots, b_n$. So varying syntagms would form varisyntagms (of some syntagmeme). For designating varisyntagms one could use numbered series of a and b, e.g. varisyntagm $a_1 b_3$. Each syntagm would belong to such a set and each set would have a prosodeme, e.g. the "varisyntagm $a_1 b_3$ prosodeme" (which would be realized in syntagm prosodes).

Varisyntagm prosodemes would be alloprosodes of syntagmeme prosodemes. One might therefore prefer to call them alloprosodes, e.g. "alloprosode $a_1 b_3$" of some particular syntagmeme prosodeme. Varisyntagm prosodemes may form varisyntagmeme prosodemes.

It is not altogether clear to what extent in different languages prosodemes of syntagmemes of lower hierarchical order can be grouped together relevantly when these syntagmemes are grouped together to form sets of higher order. Nor is it known in any great detail to what extent different kinds of syntagmemes (e.g. a subjecteme versus a direct objecteme in some languages) have different prosodemes[57].

It it not clear either to what extent and in which way syntactic prosodemes should be grouped together to form prosodemes, which would be sets of other syntactic prosodemes.

Syntagm prosodes and syntagmeme prosodemes can be shown to be not only constructive but also distinctive; for instance in *old/men and women* versus *old men/and women* (see below, p. 62).

The emphatic prosodeme signals discrete differences and can in many languages mark almost any word. If one says *she hit me*, three different meanings can be expressed. If *she* is emphasized it is *she* and not somebody else who carried out the hitting. If *hit* is emphasized it means that *hit*, and not some other also possible action, was carried out. And if *me* is emphasized it means that I was hit and not another person. (The emphatic prosodeme must be distinguished from the non discrete contoureme emphasis. For instance, the word *love* in *I love swimming* can be pronounced with different emphasis and the result is that the meaning of *love* acquires different degrees of emphasis. In this case, there is not a choice between two discrete possibilities.)

To fit our overall terminological system the effect of an emphatic prosode could be called emphas and the effect of an emphatic prosodeme could be called emphaseme.

syntagmeme prosodeme = {syntagm prosode$_1$, ..., syntagm prosode$_n$}
syntagmeme prosodeme component = {syntagm prosode component$_1$, ..., syntagm prosode component$_n$}
varisyntagm prosodeme = {syntagm prosode$_1$, ..., syntagm prosode$_n$}
varisyntagm prosodeme component = {syntagm prosode component$_1$, ..., syntagm prosode component$_n$}
syntagmeme prosodeme = {varisyntagm prosodeme$_1$, ..., varisyntagm prosodeme$_n$}
syntagmeme prosodeme component = {varisyntagm prosodeme component$_1$, ..., varisyntagm prosodeme component$_n$}

---

[57] On the other hand something is known although TG-linguists (and even other linguists), who have frequently ignored syntactic prosodes and prosodemes, have too often argued as if one knew nothing. In complicated ways they have tried to disambiguate what is "ambiguous" only in their own incomplete description, i.e. as soon as one pronounces two "homonymous constructions" one hears that they are different (see below, p. 64).

varisyntagmeme prosodeme = {varisyntagm prosodeme$_1$, ..., varisyntagm prosodeme$_n$}
varisyntagmeme prosodeme component = {varisyntagm prosodeme component$_1$, ..., varisyntagm prosodeme component$_n$}
syntagmememe prosodeme = {syntagmeme prosodeme$_1$, ..., syntagmeme prosodeme$_n$}

5.1. If the study were sufficiently detailed to reveal differences in the realization of the prosodemes by different speakers, one could establish idioprosodemes, each idioprosodeme being the set of all its realizations, the idioprosodes, by one particular individual.

In such a detailed study one would need the more specific terms idiosyllabeme prosodeme, idioallosyllab prosodeme, idiosyllab prosode, idiosyllabeme prosodeme component, idioallosyllab prosodeme component, idiosyllab prosode component, idiosyllabememe prosodeme, idiosyllabememe prosodeme component, idioallosyllabeme prosodeme, idioallosyllabeme prosodeme component, etc. (cf. p. 43).

Similarly, at the morphemic level, there would be idiomorpheme prosodemes, idiomorph prosodes, etc. (cf. p. 51).

At the lexemic level, there would be idiolexeme prosodemes, idiolex prosodes, etc. (cf. p. 55).

At the syntagmemic level, there would be idiosyntagmeme prosodemes, idiosyntagm prosodes, etc. (cf. p. 82).

5.2. If more than one sociolect within a language were studied one would have to add terms such as the more general socioprosodeme, socioprosode, socioprosodeme component, socioprosode component. In addition, one would need the more specific terms sociosyllabeme prosodeme, socioallosyllab prosodeme, sociosyllab prosode, etc. (cf. p. 43); sociolexeme prosodeme, sociolex prosode, etc. (cf. p. 55); sociosyntagmeme prosodeme, idiosyntagm prosode, etc. (cf. p. 82).

5.3. If several dialects are included in the study, one can establish diaprosodemes. These prosodemes include as variants relevant socioprosodemes and idioprosodemes.

In this part of the description one would need the more general terms diaprosodeme, diaprosode, diaprosodeme component, diaprosode component. In addition one would need the more specific terms diasyllabeme prosodeme, diaallosyllab prosodeme, diasyllab prosode, etc. (cf. p. 43); dialexeme prosodeme, dialex prosode, etc. (cf. p. 55); diasyntagmeme prosodeme, diasyntagm prosode, etc. (cf. p. 82).

5.4.1. *Glottoprosodemes.* If we establish the unit glottoprosodeme, a prosodeme of a language as a whole, the relations between a glottoprosodeme and the units just described would be as follows. A glottoprosodeme would be a set of diaprosodemes, which would be sets of socioprosodemes, which would be sets of idioprosodemes, which would be sets of idioprosodes. The sound properties called idioprosodes would also be socioprosodes, diaprosodes and glottoprosodes. E.g., a glottosyllabeme prosodeme would be a set of diasyllabeme prosodemes, which would be sets of sociosyllabeme prosodemes, which would be sets of idiosyllabeme prosodemes.

The most natural way of establishing glottoprosodemes is to use functional criteria (i.e. to establish f-glottoprosodemes, see below). If, for instance, two syntactic prosodemes in two dialects signal statement (as opposed to question), they will belong to the same glottoprosodeme.

One may, however, establish four kinds of glottounits if one considers both form and function of prosodemes:

5.4.2. *Pr-glottoprosodemes*. Different diaprosodemes (socioprosodemes) which are roughly the same as to their sound properties are *prosodemically* corresponding and form a *pr-glottoprosodeme*. The differences between such diaprosodemes may, however, be sufficiently significant to be interpreted by the speakers as differences in "accent" between different dialects (sociolects). For each diaprosodeme the exact functeme (or function) can be described. It is then possible, but perhaps not so frequent that diaprosodemes of some glottoprosodeme have different functemes. For instance, what indicates a statement in one dialect may indicate a question in another dialect.

5.4.3. *Prosodemic pr-glottofuncteme*. All functions in various dialects (sociolects) (which in many cases would just mean one single function) of some particular pr-glottoprosodeme form the *pr-glottofuncteme* of this glottoprosodeme (whereby the term pr-glottofuncteme means that it is established on the basis of some particular pr-prosodeme).

5.4.4. *Prosodemic f-glottofunctemes*. Considering functemes as, so to speak, isolated from their prosodemes, one can establish *f-glottofunctemes*, which sometimes, in different dialects, could be expressed by non-corresponding pr-diaprosodemes. An f-glottofuncteme "statement", if expressed sufficiently differently in different dialects, could be expressed by non-corresponding pr-diaprosodemes. (The prefix f- obviously means that the unit is established by considering function or functeme.)

5.4.5. *F-glottoprosodemes*. In addition to pr-glottoprosodemes one may establish *f-glottoprosodemes*. All diaprosodemes having corresponding functemes form such a prosodeme.

6. It is obvious that *inventories* of all abovementioned units could be established.

7. *Discovery procedures*. To the extent that prosodemes are similar to phonemes similar discovery procedures are applicable. Both kinds of units have constructive function. In addition, phonemes usually, and prosodemes sometimes have a distinctive function. It is therefore possible sometimes to use the criterion of "opposition" or "minimal pair" also at the level of prosodemes. The Swedish sequence of phonemes written as *anden* has different meaning whether pronounced with "accent 1" or "accent 2". Thus the two words can be considered as a minimal pair which shows that there are two important word prosodemes (with distinctive function) in Swedish.

In other cases the prosodemes are not only constructive or distinctive but have direct links with the expression side. E.g. one given syntagmeme prosodeme can be said to mean "statement" and another "question". The discovery procedure will in this case be as for units which have meaning, i.e. one seeks the meaning first and then establishes what expression segment corresponds with it.

1.1.3. Syllabemes

0. Definitions of syllables have often been circular; the syllable is defined by the aid of "vowels" and "consonants" and "vowels" and "consonants" are defined through

their capacity for being margins or centres in syllables. A syllable is said to be a vowel optionally preceded or followed by a margin of one or more consonants. A word has then as many syllables as it has vowels. A vowel in its turn is defined as the centre of a syllable and a consonant is a segment found in the margin of a syllable. Also, "abstract" syllables (units) and "realized" syllables (items) are usually both just called "syllables". We shall try to avoid these two deficiencies.

1. *Items: syllabs. Definition: Syllabs* are segments which have as segments one or more phones and which, at least in clear and slow pronunciation, are pronounced and heard more or less clearly as groups of phones. Syllabs are indicated by syllab prosodes (see above, p. 32). Although syllabs have not been sufficiently described at the genetic, gennemic or energemic level, a speaker has in most cases clear knowledge of their existence. If asked, he can point them out.

One would assume that the syllabemes which are realized as syllabs are stored in the brain as segments consisting of such segments as correspond to phonemes in the description. More precisely, one would believe that the syllabemes are stored (a) as parts of words, and (b) as "syllabic patterns" not tied to any particular word (and making some contribution when the hearer interprets spoken words). However, when syllabemes are considered as parts of definite words, it may be more appropriate to call them varisyllabs (see below). It seems possible to compare syllabemes and syllabs to those groups of numbers into which one usually divides a longer telephone number in order both to remember it better and to pronounce it in a way that seems natural, although these number groups are at a higher level as each single number consists of syllabeme(s) or syllab(s).

Syllabs have (morph- and) lex-building function (see below, p. 45, 52). By using the simplicity criterion in the common inappropriate way[58] (inaugurated by the structuralists and taken over by generativists), one has had a certain tendency to neglect "syllables" because they usually have no "distinctive" function, as their length, and by implication, their boundaries, are usually automatically determined by the syntagmatic structure in terms of phones.

However, in an adequate description all details characterizing expression units and items should be described. They all contribute to correct and efficient production and understanding of speech.

It occurs that syllab (and syllabeme) length or, in other words, syllab (and syllabeme) boundaries distinguish words which are the same in terms of phones. One example is the Swedish word *lands-lag* (national team) versus *land-slag* (land battle).

Different syllabs realizing some particular sequence of phonemes may be heard to be different. I.e., a segment such as /ɪm/ in *import, impact* etc. has many variants. The following circumstances must be taken into account: (1) There is *free variation* (see above, p. 13). (2) There is *facultative variation* at the β- and γ-levels (see above, p. 2, 13). In other words, there are different *syllab contours* (β-variation). There is γ_1-*variation* as each individual has his *idiosyllabs* (see above, p. 3). There is γ_2-*variation* as different groups within a society may differ in that they have *sociosyllabs* (see above, p. 3). There is γ_3-*variation* as different *diasyllabs* may exist (see above, p. 3). (3) Also *positional variation* conditions differences. For instance, the position can be determined

---

[58] Cf. *Linguistische Einheiten*, p. 24–25 (with reference to two of my earlier papers).

in relation to "stress". An unstressed item of /ɪm/ in the verb *impórt* is different from a stressed item in the noun *ímport*.

Syllabs are notated by appropriate phone symbols within square brackets, e.g. [ɪm]. For a higher degree of explicitness the bracket can be labelled s[ɪm].

2. *Units: allosyllabs. Definition:* Syllabs realizing some particular sequence of phonemes and differing between themselves only through *free* and *facultative* variation (points 1 and 2 above) form a set called *allosyllab*.

A "stressed" [ɪm] and an "unstressed" [ɪm] belong to different allosyllabs. (In this example the difference between the two allosyllabs is conditioned by position.)

Not only position within words, but also position within syntactic constructions provides variation. The syllab prosode makes [ɪz] different in *it is* when said as a statement, and when said as a question. This kind of variation could be accounted for by the establishment of diallosyllabs within allosyllabs. (See syllab prosodes, p. 32).

It is suggested that allosyllabs and diallosyllabs be numbered and notated by symbols for phonemes within labelled brackets; for instance: $\text{Allos}_1 /\ldots/$, or $\text{As}_1/\ldots/$, and $\text{Diallos}_1 /\ldots/$. Another suggestion would be to use phonetic symbols sufficiently detailed to indicate each allosyllab or diallosyllab in a specific way, whereby the numbering would be less necessary: Allos /.../ and Diallos /.../.

3.1. *Units: syllabemes. Definition of n-syllabeme:* An *n-syllabeme* is a set of allosyllabs relatable to the same sequence of phonemes.

The "stressed" and "unstressed" /ɪm/ just mentioned belong to the same syllabeme.

An n-syllabeme would be notated by symbols for phonemes within a labelled bracket; thus: n-S/.../.

n-syllabeme = {allosyllab$_1$, ..., allosyllab$_n$}
allosyllab   = {syllab$_1$, ..., syllab$_n$}

Definition of b-syllabeme: A *b-syllabeme* is a syllabeme conceived as an invariant. The variants (syllabs and allosyllabs) of the n-syllabeme are excluded.

B-syllabemes may be used in the description of longer units as consisting of syllabeme sequences. If one states that the word (lexeme) *import* has /ɪm/ as one of its two syllabemes (varisyllabs), a b-syllabeme would generally be meant. All the syllabs of the n-syllabeme /ɪm/, which appear in a great many words and in different positions within words and syntactic constructions, would not be taken into account.

A b-syllabeme would be notated by symbols for phonemes within a labelled bracket; thus: b-S/.../.

3.2. *Units: Varisyllabs. Definition:* A *varisyllab* is an "abstract" syllable of a given word. Varisyllabs are usually called just syllables.

For different purposes varisyllabs could be either n- or b-units. B-varisyllabs would have no items, but n-varisyllabs would have syllabs as items.

Varisyllabs would be written within /.../, or more explicitly within Varis/.../.

3.3. Various works have dealt with types or categories of syllables. Such units could suitably be called *syllabememes*. B-syllabemes having in the same order, segments belonging to either the set of the vowels or the set of the consonants form a syllabememe. Consonant followed by vowel followed by consonant would form a syllabememe CVC, to which, in English, *man, hat, dog* etc. would count.

Syllabememes seem mainly to be interesting as b-syllabememes and the notion n-syllabememe would be of less importance.

b-syllabememe = {b-syllabeme$_1$, ..., b-syllabeme$_n$}
n-syllabememe = {n-syllabeme$_1$, ..., n-syllabeme$_n$}

4. The notions of *semi-syllabemes* and *quasi-syllabemes* may be of doubtful use. It could possibly be argued that some languages have syllabemes in which a consonant is the centre, and which are often realized as zero, as a phonically weak syllab or as part of another syllab. They could be considered as being "less" than a full syllabeme or syllab, and called, perhaps, semi-syllabemes and semi-syllabs. If so, they should perhaps also be considered as quasi-syllabemes and quasi-syllabs. According to a solution that I have already suggested[59], French consonants can form centres of syllabemes and syllabs. A lexeme such as *atteler* would have three syllabemes: /a-t-le/. Lexes could have three syllabs: [a-t-le], [a-tᵊ-le] or [a-tə-le]. In more rapid speech they could have also two syllabs (the first of which a pseudo-syllab): [at-le] (or [a-tle]?).

The French *pauv(re) garçon* would contain a syllabeme which can be realized as zero.

5. *Pseudo-syllabs* are items which are pronounced and heard as syllabs but which do not belong to any syllabeme. The Portuguese "word" (lexeme) *geral* is generally considered to possess two "syllables", i.e. two syllabemes, but if the word is pronounced with much weight it may have three syllabs, "ge-ra-li". Of these three, the first is clearly a syllab because it can be attributed to a syllabeme. The second is a somewhat complicated case. The syllabeme is /ral/ but the syllab is [ra] and must be considered as a pseudo-syllab. The third is more clearly a pseudo-syllab. Pseudo-syllabs which consist of phones which phonically are such that they would have realized identical phonemes (if they had realized phonemes) can be considered as items of the same *pseudo-syllabeme*. Pseudo-syllabemes would not normally be segments of lexemes and they would perhaps be n-rather than b-units.

6. The notions of meta-syllabs and meta-syllabemes can be established. The definitions would be obvious. (See above, p. 19, under meta-phones and meta-phonemes.)

7. *Items: syllab prosodes. Units: syllabeme prosodemes and syllabememe prosodemes.* Syllabs have *syllab prosodes*, see above, p. 32. Syllabemes have *syllabeme prosodemes*, see above, p. 32. Syllabememes have *syllabememe prosodemes*, see above, p. 33.

Syllabs, syllabemes and syllabememes are described in terms of the segments that build them, and of prosodes or prosodemes.

8. *Paradigmatics.* The most important *paradigmatic* fact seems to be that syllabememes can be described in terms of segments, and then compared (opposed) to one another. Some language may possess the syllabememes V, CV, CCV, VC, VCC, CVC, CCVC, CVCC, CCVCC. The systematic aspect seems to imply nothing more elaborate than enumerating the syllabememes in some reasonable order (as we have just done).

---

[59] In "Sur l'inventaire des phonèmes français" (*Omagiu lui Alexandru Rosetti*, Bucharest 1965, p. 343–346), p. 345.

9. *Syntagmatics*. Syllabs consist of phones, alone or in different combinations. Syllabs, alone or in different combinations, build (morphs[60] and) lexes. Syllabemes, alone or in different combinations build (allomorphs[60] and) lexemes (allolexes[61]). Although most syllab boundaries are evident some are unstable and more difficult to determine. In the Swedish word *svenska* it seems to be normal that the boundary between the two syllabs is either after [n] or after [s], or even in the middle of [s]. Such *moving boundaries* occur perhaps generally in sequences of consonants which contain a segment such that it can end a word (in the Swedish example given compare with the word *hans*) and a partly overlapping sequence such that it can begin a word (in the example given compare with *skal*).

A moving boundary occurs perhaps also generally when a sequence of two consonants is such that it can both begin and end a word. For instance, the Swedish *kasta* can be compared with *kast* and *stad*.

In case moving boundaries exist in syllabs, they should also be made part of the description of syllabemes (if one thinks that the units should be as directly as possible relatable to the items).

Syllabs and syllabemes can be said to have constructive function.

10.1. *Glottosyllabememes, glottosyllabemes, glottoallosyllabs, glottosyllabs; diasyllabememes, diasyllabemes, diaallosyllabs, diasyllabs; sociosyllabememes, sociosyllabemes, socioallosyllabs, sociosyllabs; idiosyllabememes, idiosyllabemes, idioallosyllabs, idiosyllabs* would mutatis mutandis have definitions similar to those given above in 1.1.1.12.

10.2. *Ph-glottosyllabemes*. Syllabemes from different systems are phonemically (variphonically) corresponding if they contain in the same order phonemically corresponding phonemes. If one English dialect has the syllabeme /pɪn/ and another English dialect has also /pɪn/, then these two syllabemes are phonemically corresponding.

Definition: Phonemically corresponding diasyllabemes form a *ph-glottosyllabeme*. A ph-diasyllabeme is usually a set of corresponding ph-sociosyllabemes.

Dialects with a higher number of phonemes in the inventory will automatically have more syllabemes, or at least different syllabemes, in relation to dialects with a lower number of phonemes. Any diasyllabeme in any dialect (sociolect) will be the basis for the establishment of a glottosyllabeme. Thus a glottosyllabeme may have ∅-variants in some dialects (sociolects).

10.3. *M-glottosyllabemes*. Syllabemes from different systems may be considered as *morphemically corresponding* if they occupy a corresponding position in corresponding morphemes. Syllabemes may correspond morphemically although they do not correspond phonemically. If in a Scottish dialect *arm* has three phonemes (having an /r/ in the middle) and in some English dialect is considered to have only two phonemes, the two words have not only corresponding morphemes but also morphemically corresponding syllabemes (which are not phonemically corresponding). In a more precise way, the two words should be said to have corresponding varisyllabs.

---

[60] As in many languages morph and allomorph boundaries sometimes do not coincide with syllab or syllabeme boundaries (see below, p. 45) it does not always seem quite adequate to say that syllabs "build" morphs and syllabemes allomorphs. It would, however, be more adequate to say this in a language where the two kinds of boundaries always coincide.

[61] "Allolex" is here the more rigorous suggestion but as allolexes (see below, p. 52) are so rare, it may be practical to mention "lexeme" instead.

It is possible that diasyllabemes such as the Scottish and the English ones just mentioned include some varisyllab which has no correspondence in the other dialect (because it does not exist in this dialect). By the term morphemically corresponding syllabemes is meant (more exactly) that at least one of the varisyllabs of the syllabemes corresponds.

As phonemes can correspond morphemically in different and complicated ways, also morphemically corresponding syllabemes, which have morphemically corresponding phonemes as segments, will correspond in complicated ways.

Definition: Morphemically corresponding diasyllabemes (diavarisyllabs) form an *m-glottosyllabeme*. An m-diasyllabeme is usually a set of corresponding *m-sociosyllabemes*.

11. *Inventories.* For *inventories of syllabs* the comments given above concerning inventories of phones are, mutatis mutandis, applicable. (See 1.1.1.13.)

Establishing *syllabeme inventories* is obviously of interest. One connected problem is the one of the "gaps". In English, e.g., there are the syllabemes (forming the words) *bill, pill, sill* etc., but there is no *yill*.

As a systematic order of syllabememes is a linear arrangement (see above, 1.1.3.8.), an inventory of *syllabememes* coincides with this system. *Inventories* of (*semi-syllabs* and) *semi-syllabemes*, of (*quasi-syllabs* and) *quasi-syllabemes*, of (*pseudo-syllabs* and) *pseudo-syllabemes*, (*meta-syllabs* and *meta-syllabemes*) can be set up. Also *inventories* of *idiosyllabememes, idiosyllabemes, idioallosyllabs* (and *idiosyllabs*), of *sociosyllabememes, sociosyllabemes, socioallosyllabs* (and *sociosyllabs*), of *diasyllabememes, diasyllabemes, diaallosyllabs* (and *diasyllabs*), of *glottosyllabememes, glottosyllabemes, glottoallosyllabs* (and *glottosyllabs*) can be set up. For comments compare above 1.1.1.12.

12. *Discovery procedures.* The most adequate discovery procedure for syllabs would be either introspection by the linguist or tests with informants by which syllabs and boundaries of syllabs would be directly pointed out.

If one knew better the articulatory and acoustic description of syllabs, it could be of interest to compare examples having uncertain boundaries with those having unquestionably established boundaries and thus, perhaps, to cast some light on the former.

1.1.4. Morphemes

0. Phonemes (phones), syllabemes (syllabs) and (in most cases[62]) prosodemes have no meaning in the normal sense of the word. The shortest units and items having meaning are the morphemes and the morphs. The word "meaning" in this context has a wide sense including (a) clear meaning, (b) unclear meaning and (c) grammatical function. It should be noted that a morph or a morpheme has sometimes two or more "simultaneous meanings" (as the -s in *he hits*, see below). Instead of the word "meaning" the following two more adequate terms may be used: *morph seme* and *morpheme sememe* (see below, p. 86, 92), the more exact use of which will be explained in the next paragraph.

---

[62] *Some* prosodemes have a kind of meaning or contribute to meaning. E.g. the prosodeme with final stress indicates 'verb' in *import*.

1. *Items: morphs. Definition: Morphs* are expression items having as segments (a) phones, (b) unclear segments and (c) syllabs. The length of a morph in terms of these "shorter" segments is the one which corresponds with one, but not with two, consecutive semes. Thus the morph is defined in complete dependence on the morph seme and we assume that such semes can be established by the linguist alone or by the linguist's asking informants appropriate questions.

The most important comments on morph segments would be:

(a) They are generally phones. The realization of the morpheme (see below) (and lexeme) written *man* may, e.g., be [mæn].

A morph may also be described, when applicable, in terms of semi-, quasi-, pseudo- and meta-phones.

(b) They are sometimes unclear segments, by which we mean certain segments that are not realizations of some particular phoneme. Such segments could be "vocal murmurs" realizing two or more phonemes, perhaps in such a way that one does not know exactly to which phonemes one should relate them[63]. (Thus their status may be unclear in two different ways.) They could also be occasional assimilations. If the second and third segment in the word written *man* fuse so as to give one nasalized segment [æ̃], the morph [mæ̃] would contain one clear and one unclear segment.

(c) They may be syllabs (including semi-, quasi-, pseudo-syllabs) but this sort of segment would perhaps only be fully relevant in a language where morpheme boundaries always coincided with a syllabeme boundary. This is, e.g., not the case in English where a word such as the one written *boys* would most often be realized as [bɔɪz]. In this example it does not seem to be very meaningful to say that the first morph [bɔɪ] would have as segment the first part of a syllab and the second morph [z] would have as a segment the last part of a syllab. For further discussion, see below, p. 45.

In a more precise way a morph could be written within a labelled bracket, thus: m[mæn].

Some comments on morph semes would be:

(a) Clear meaning can constitute a morph seme. There is one clear meaning in the morph written *black*. (It is not important, in this context, to consider "shades" or variants of a "meaning".)

(b) Unclear meaning can constitute a morph seme. If *cranberry* and *blackberry* are compared it appears that both have a meaning expressed by the morph corresponding to the written form *-berry*. This has a clear meaning. Although *black-* has a clear meaning, *cran-* has not a clear meaning because one cannot explain what it means in the same direct way as in the case of *black*. However, it can be said that *cran-*, when combined with *-berry*, does indeed contribute to the meaning of the whole word *cranberry* (which is different from the meaning of *berry* alone). This sort of meaning is here called unclear[64].

---

[63] See below, p. 52, where it is explained how a certain segment [ə] cannot be related to any particular phoneme or sequence of phonemes in the language under consideration.

[64] It is assumed that, e.g., in *blackberry* one recognizes the meaning 'black' and the meaning 'berry' although the combination of the two does not mean a berry which is black (see below, p. 52, 87).

Although *cran-* has unclear meaning the whole word *cranberry* has a clear meaning.

(c) Grammatical[65] function can constitute a morph seme. An [s] in *he hits* has the function of signalling third person singular, present tense (and also indicative although this in a marginal way as the subjunctive is rare in present day English).

Although some more complicated cases will be dealt with below, in most cases the morph semes are simply consecutive, which means they just follow each other and there is no overlapping between the morphs they are related to. In *blackberry*, the first four phones have one meaning and the next four phones have another meaning.

A seme can consist of more than one grammatical function, as the seme of the just mentioned [s] in *hits*. These functions are then simultaneous, and not consecutive. They are simultaneously related to the same phone or sequence of phones.

In the kind of phonetic studies usually carried out, morphs are of little importance. The exact quality of phones is described with reference to distribution in relation to other phones and with reference to their place within syllabs and items longer than syllabs, but they are not described in relation to morphs. Actually, nothing in the morph structure seems to condition anything in the segments of the morph[66]. Nor do morph prosodes seem to be very common (but morph contours may be more common, see below, p. 88).

2.1. *Units: allomorphs. Definition*: Different morphs which realize a particular sequence of phonemes (variphones) and which have semes belonging to some particular sememe[67] form an *n-allomorph*. The differences between morphs of the same n-allomorph are accounted for exclusively by free and facultative variation. E.g. all pronunciations of the plural ending /s/ in *hats, caps* etc. belong to the same n-allomorph. /z/ in *hands* would be another allomorph with the same kind of variation.

To each *n-allomorph* a *b-allomorph* can be related. For the establishment of this kind of unit, the morphs of the n-allomorphs should be discarded. The b-allomorphs would have phonemes (variphones) as segments. Also semi- and quasi-phonemes could be segments.

In the definition, mention was made of morphs having "semes belonging to some particular sememe". Although a definition of sememe is given below at the present stage it is sufficient to let the expression in quotation marks mean "roughly the *same* meaning or grammatical function".

For reasons similar to those given above (p. 44) it would not be equally relevant to consider syllabemes (varisyllabs) as segments of allomorphs. Although it may be of some interest to state that a particular allomorph has one syllabeme in contradistinction to some other allomorph which has, e.g., two syllabemes, in some cases, e.g., in the case of the plural allomorph /z/ (as in *boys*) this kind of segment would not be a syllabeme but just the last part of a syllabeme.

N-allomorphs and b-allomorphs could be written within labelled brackets: n-Am/.../ and b-Am/.../ or n-Allom/.../ and b-Allom/.../.

Some further explanations on allomorphs are given below in connection with morphemes (1.1.4.3.1.).

---

[65] If we choose not to include phonology in grammar, "grammatical function" will not include "distinctive function".
[66] The problem of the Swedish word *mör*, and some other examples, could be more or less isolated exceptions, cf. *Linguistische Einheiten*, p. 18.
[67] Exact definition below, p. 92.

2.2. As has been briefly mentioned above (Introduction, point 8), terms formed by *allo-*, *diallo-*, *triallo-* etc. stand for sets of variants that are generally felt to be the basic ones for the unit under consideration as in the case of the widely accepted term allomorph. If, however, a subset is established by criteria that are sufficiently different from those on which the "basic" set with its subsets was based, then the series *allo-*, *diallo-*, *triallo-* etc. should be broken. When the new criterion is used, it is therefore suggested that the series of terms *vari-*, *divari-*, *trivari-* be introduced.

If one faces the task of grouping morphs belonging to some particular allomorph into sets conditioned by different contexts one would choose, not the term diallomorph, but rather *varimorph*. Thus morphs in some given context could be grouped to form a varimorph. For instance, all morphs of all realizations of the first part of *blackbird* would form a varimorph which would be different from the varimorph /blæk/ in *blacksmith* or in *black*.

From the viewpoint of phonics *varimorphemes* could be established on the basis of phonic similarity. The context conditioning the different varimorphs would be other preceding or following phones in the same lex. Varimorphs may thus form sets, i.e. varimorphemes. For instance, the varimorphs of the allomorph /s/ as a plural ending can form sets determined by their exact phonic quality. The varimorpheme including all varimorphs with a very fronted [s] as in *hats*, the varimorpheme including all varimorphs having a slightly less fronted [s] as in *packs* etc. could be established. The establishment of such varimorphemes seems to be of little use and the facts concerned will be taken care of in the description of phones and allophones.

2.3. The *allomorpheme* is a set of allomorphs that are similar in regard to their segments, which are (b-)phonemes and (if applicable) (b-)syllabemes. The /s/ of *hats* and the /s/ of *writes* would belong to the same allomorpheme, equally the /ɪz/ of *churches* and the /ɪz/ of *teaches*. (Note that the allomorphs concerned belong to different morphemes.)

Also the allomorphememe could be introduced. This unit, being a set of allomorphemes, would have as segments (b-)phonememes ("vowels" and "consonants") and (b-)syllabememes. E.g. an allomorphememe VC, i.e. any vowel followed by any consonant forming a syllabeme, would include /ɪz/ (as in *teaches*), /ən/ (as in *oxen*) etc.

It may be of some interest to take position within the lexeme ("the word") into account. In this case the allomorph /ʌp/ (*up*), although it has structure VC, would not be grouped with the endings /ɪz/ and /ən/ just mentioned. (It is assumed that *up*, having no variation at the level of allomorphs, possesses all the same *one* allomorph.) Instead *up* would be grouped with *in*, *at* etc.

Another kind of allomorpheme could be established from the viewpoint of the distribution and function of the allomorph. Allomorphs beings stems, prefixes, infixes, suffixes etc. would form as many allomorphemes.

It seems, however, usually possible and appropriate to take care of similar sets under the morphememe (see below, 1.1.4.3.2.).

Allomorphemes and allomorphememes could both be considered either as b- or n-units.

b-allomorphememe = {b-allomorpheme$_1$, ..., b-allomorpheme$_n$}
b-allomorpheme = {b-allomorph$_1$, ..., b-allomorph$_n$}

n-allomorphememe = {n-allomorpheme$_1$, ..., n-allomorpheme$_n$}
n-allomorpheme   = {n-allomorph$_1$, ..., n-allomorph$_n$}

3.1. *Units: morphemes. Definition*: Allomorphs having the same sememe form a *morpheme*[68]. Allomorphs within one morpheme have often complementary distribution. (In *clot* the plural ending is /s/ and not /z/. In *clod* it is /z/ and not /s/.)

It occurs that allomorphs within one particular morpheme, although having per definition the same sememe, may have different β- and (or) γ-functions. The Swedish form *betalade* (= paid) is the "careful" pronunciation in contradistinction to the more "casual" *betala* (β_2-level). The latter form, in addition, is used in definite parts of the country (γ_3-level). Such differences between allomorphs are usually not phonemically conditioned (see next paragraph).

Allomorphs within a morpheme may be "phonemically conditioned", in which case particular phonemic contexts require particular allomorphs: after /t/ in *clot* the plural is /s/ and after /d/ in *clod* the plural is /z/. Allomorphs may, however, also be "morphemically conditioned", which means that no prediction can be made from the phonemic context but knowledge of the particular morphemic pattern of the case under consideration is needed. The plural of *ox* is *oxen* but without sufficient knowledge on this point one would have predicted **oxes*.

When a morpheme has only one allomorph there is no difficulty in finding a way of designating it. E.g. the morpheme of *hat* would be written M/hæt/. In this case the morpheme has just the same segments as the allomorph. When a morpheme has more than one allomorph the problem is more complicated (see p. 46).

Morphemes as well as allomorphs can be considered as b-units or as n-units.

b-morpheme = {b-allomorph$_1$, ..., b-allomorph$_n$}
n-morpheme = {n-allomorph$_1$, ..., n-allomorph$_n$}
n-allomorph = {morph$_1$, ..., morph$_n$}

3.2. One might attempt to establish *morphememes*, i.e. sets of morphemes, on the basis of morpheme segments (which are of the same kind as allomorph segments). Morphememes would be appropriate for a language which had only morphemes and no allomorphs. In languages which have allomorphs the notion of allomorphememe (see above) would be sufficient. However, even in such languages it could be of interest to establish a slightly different kind of morphememe and let all morphemes having one allomorph form only one set, all morphemes having two allomorphs form another etc.

Morphememes of another kind could be established from the viewpoint of the distribution and the function of the morpheme. *Table*, *walk*, *red* etc. would form the morphememe of stems. Other morphememes would be those of prefixes, infixes and suffixes.

In many languages it is also adequate to let all morphemes form two large sets: the *independent* and the *dependent morphememe*. An allomorph, a morpheme or a morphememe are independent (or "free") when they can form alone allolexes, lexemes and sets of lexemes respectively. Dependent (or "bound") segments can only be segments of allolexes, lexemes or sets of lexemes if an independent segment is also included.

---

[68] It is assumed that there are no true synonyms (see below, p. 91). If true synonyms did exist, two different morphemes could have the same sememe.

E.g. the allomorph *table* (the notion allomorph being used here although this lexeme has only one allomorph) is independent but in *tables* the plural ending is dependent.

4. *Units : semi-morphemes. Items : semi-morphs*. In some cases a word seems to have two consecutive "unclear meanings" and no other segment of meaning. As such a word has no segment with "clear meaning" or "grammatical function" both segments distinguish themselves less clearly. They may then be considered to be "less" than morphs or morphemes and be semi-morphs at the level of lexes or semi-morphemes at the level of lexemes. In Swedish *hallon* (raspberries) and *lingon* (cranberries) are words for different kinds of berries. One is tempted to split them up into /hal/ followed by /ɔn/ and /liŋ/ followed by the same /ɔn/ but no speaker would know the meaning of the segments. The segments of each word could be semi-morphs or semi-morphemes.

In *why, when, where*[69] etc. one may establish a segment /w/ with the meaning "question". But is it as "much" as a morph or morpheme? If this segment is a semi-morph or semi-morpheme, what then is the rest of the word? Is, e.g. the vowel in *why* a semi-morph or semi-morpheme? Should it perhaps be assumed that a word can have a segment without function at the morphemic level? Such a segment of one or more phonemes would, however, contribute to the structure of the lex or the lexeme.

This solution is certainly more natural for *why* than for *when*, which can be compared with *then*, or for *where*, which can be compared with *there*. The latter words would more clearly consist of two segments.

5. *Units : quasi-morphemes. Items : quasi-morphs*. Seen from a syntagmatic viewpoint quasi-morphs and quasi-morphemes seem adequately to account for facts which should be described.

The lexemes corresponding to the forms written *stand* and *stood* would have the allomorphs /st-nd/ and /st-d/ which would belong to the same morpheme. It would be adequate to consider these as quasi-units (quasi-morpheme and quasi-allomorphs) as, although they have the major part of the meaning "stand", they have not the whole of this meaning. On the other hand they also contribute to the meanings "present" and "imperfect" through the fact that /st-nd/ has an /n/ and /st-d/ when combined with a particular vowel forms a "short" imperfect (no ending). /æ/ and /ʊ/ have a great part of the meanings 'present' and 'imperfect', respectively, but they also make a contribution to the meaning 'stand'. Both /stænd/ and /stʊd/ consist thus of two quasi-allomorphs. Similar solutions apply to *take — took* or *man — men*. At the morphemic level they have so to speak more than one but less than two full segments in sequence.

A word such as *children* may offer problems which would perhaps not be completely solved by the introduction of the notion quasi-morpheme. The introduction of "vague boundaries" might also be indicated. The word mentioned would have as its first morphemic segment the allomorph /tʃɪld/. Next segment would be a grammatical morpheme, a "stem-formative" /r/. The third segment could be the same plural allomorph /ən/ as one finds in *oxen*. However, the boundary between the second and third could be considered as vague: /r/ is, partly, stem-formative and, partly, part of the plural allomorph; the plural allomorph has one segment /r/, which

---

[69] Note that in spoken language *who* does not belong to this group. See below, p. 115, about written language, where in some cases morphemic facts could be considered to be different.

is only partly part of it and one part /ən/ that is exclusively plural ending. If this solution is adopted /(r)ən/ could be called an allomorph with a vague boundary[70].

6. There does not seem to be any need for pseudo-units and items at the morphemic level.

7. The definitions of meta-morphs and meta-morphemes would be self-evident but these units and items do not seem to be really interesting.

8. *Paradigmatics*. All cases where different allomorphs or different morphemes are felt to have some relevant paradigmatic relation to one another are certainly worthy of study.

One such relevant relation is the one grouping certain allomorphs into one morpheme. The English plural morpheme has a considerable number of allomorphs and could be given a notation showing all of them: M/s, z, ɪz, ən[71], ∅[72], "vowel difference"[73]/. By the use of some arbitrary symbol, instead of the enumeration of all the allomorphs, or even by just saying "the plural morpheme", one would give a more condensed name to the morpheme.

The lexeme related to the written form *courage* has an allomorph with the vowel /ɪ/ and the one related to the written form *courageous* has an allomorph with the vowel /e^1/. These two allomorphs would show an interesting relationship.

The Latin cases in e.g. *servus, servi, servo, servum, servo, serve* are related morphemes which also show an interesting relation.

When such relevant relations are described there is no reason for using any technique involving "processes" or "transformations" unless one is convinced that one unit is actually basic and the other, or the others, are derived (in the traditional sense of the word). Nor is there any need for deriving anything from strange "underlying abstractions".

In the case of the different plural endings it is difficult to see why one should be the basic one. The relation between them is nothing more complicated than their being allomorphs of the same morpheme.

In the case of *courage* — *courageous* it seems possible to think that the more common substantive is basic and the adjective is derived. This could be shown by a labelled and directed arrow: *courage* — subst. — adj. → *courageous* or concentrating on the change in vowel: /ɪ/ — subst. — adj. → /e^1/. If one were convinced that neither of the two forms was basic, or if one were perhaps doubtful, it is suggested that a labelled double arrow be used: ← subst. — adj. →.

If more than two units are to be related and none is more basic than the others, one could use a double arrow in a somewhat different way. In the case of the Latin example one could use the formula M/us/ : M/i/ : M/o/ : M/um/ : M/o/ : M/e/ ↔ nom. : gen. : dat. : acc. : abl. : voc.

Problems of the kind just described are often said to belong to morphophonemics, which is sometimes thought of as constituting a part of linguistics comparable to

---

[70] For words such as *stand, stood; take, took; man, men; child, children* etc. various solutions have been suggested, cf. C. Hockett, "Problems of morphemic analysis" (Language **23**, 1947, p. 321–343 or *Readings in Linguistics* I, ed. M. Joos, p. 229–242).
[71] *oxen*.
[72] *sheep*.
[73] *men*.

phonetics or morphology. It would, however, seem more natural to let morphophonemics form part of morphology.

9. *Syntagmatics*. The way the segments are combined to form morphs, allomorphs and morphemes belongs to morphemic syntagmatics.

The context of morphs, allomorphs and morphemes is sometimes of importance. The context conditioning different plural endings, e.g., would have to be described. However, in many cases no context can be stated. Instead one would have to include words such as *oxen*, *sheep*, *men* in lists to be added to the allomorphs the form of which is conditioned by context.

10. The terms *morph*, *allomorph* and *morpheme* could be prefixed in a meaningful way by *glotto-*, *dia-*, *socio-* and *idio-* (cf. below 1.1.5.11.4.).

11. Inventories of *morphs*, *allomorphs*, *morphemes* and *morphememes* could obviously be set up.

12. *Discovery procedures* are implied in the definitions above. The most important point is that the linguist, or informants, find the number of consecutive "meanings" or "grammatical functions" of the sample under consideration; i.e. the semes or sememes are first sought. Then, or perhaps at the same time, the sequences of phones or phonemes (which ever is applicable) to be related to each seme or sememe are established[74].

1.1.5. Lexemes

0. It seems difficult to give to the notion of "word" a fully satisfactory definition.

In many written languages the words are shown by spaces between them. Except for a low number of cases which may seem doubtful the spoken words correspond exactly with these written words. The written word could thus be taken as starting point in a definition which would be almost satisfactory.

Sometimes one has thought that boundaries between words can be established by showing that a word can, or cannot, be introduced where the hypothetical boundary is situated. This procedure is circular in the sense that words are required for use in the procedure which is thought to establish words. If, however, the procedure is only meant to be an auxiliary one to be used in some difficult and doubtful cases after the bulk of the words has been taken for granted it is more acceptable. On the other hand the procedure is not very efficient. French has a word *te* and a word *le* but in *je te le dis* no word can be inserted between *te* and *le*. Portuguese has a word *farei* (I shall do) but another word can be inserted in the middle: *fá-lo-ei* (I shall do it).

One may think that words are segments such as to contain one or more morphemes (or morphs) and to form directly the segments contained in syntactic constructions. This would, however, again be circular as words would probably be used in the definition of syntactic constructions. In many languages words have such prosodic features that they can be more or less clearly heard, particularly in slow and clear

---

[74] I have profited from reading H. Pilch's paper "Modelle der englischen Wortbildung" (*Festschrift H. Marchand*, The Hague 1967, pp. 160–178), although I have not directly taken over anything from this author.

speech. This is the case in e.g. English, German and Swedish but it is only true for French in a much lower degree.

Whatever the difficulties of definition may be, it is the case that in almost every single example the words can just be taken for granted. One can assume that nobody would deny that *table, too, go* etc. are words in English.

One may, however, attempt a definition based on content units. It has been assumed above that it is possible to discover the morphs of a sentence by finding first the shortest content items and then letting the morphs be the expression segments which express these content segments. Considering the content segments, the morph semes, one can establish that (a) some are just juxtaposed and that (b) some are not only juxtaposed but also "amalgamated" so as to form together a content segment. In a sentence such as *this is a blackbird* the first three morph semes are unamalgamated but the last two are amalgamated so as to form the meaning "blackbird". (In this particular case it can be easily shown that the two unamalgamated meanings ("black", "bird") are different from the amalgamated one. The meaning of *black bird* is not the same as the one of *blackbird*.)

1. *Items: lexes. Definition*: An unamalgamated morph seme or a series of amalgamated morph semes form a lex seme. The expression segment corresponding with a lex seme is a *lex*. (*Black* and *blackbird* are lexes.)

Lex segments may be constituted by morphs of which each lex has one or more. At another level phones including semi-, quasi-, pseudo-phones and syllabs (including semi-, quasi-, pseudo-syllabs) are also lex segments. In addition unclear segments can form lex segments in rapid and less careful speech. If in a pronunciation of the Swedish word *naturligtvis* a [naəs] is recorded the [ə] is not a phone attributable to any phoneme but just an unclear segment of the lex as a whole[75].

Lexes would be notated in labelled brackets. E.g., *sun* would be l[sʌn].

2. *Units: allolexes. Definition*: As has been pointed out (p. 35), in some cases allomorphs may differ by facultative variation only. Each such allomorph is segment of an allolex, which it constitutes.

In the example given above (p. 48) one allolex corresponds to each of the two forms *betalade* and *betala*.

Allolexes can be notated in labelled brackets. *Sun* would, e.g. be Al/sʌn/ or Allol/sʌn/. (It is not implied that there are other allolexes of *sun*. A lexeme has mostly just one allolex; see next paragraph. In this case the establishment of the allolex is of little interest.)

3.1. *Units: lexemes. Definition* of n-lexemes: Generally, an *n-lexeme* is a set of lexes, each of which has a morph belonging to some given morpheme or has a sequence of morphs belonging to a sequence of morphemes the sememes of which are amalgamated.

This definition accounts for the general case, where the lexeme has no different allolexes.

In the less frequent case where a lexeme has different allolexes the definition would read: An n-lexeme is a set of allolexes, each of which has an allomorph belonging to some given morpheme or has a sequence of allomorphs belonging to some given sequence of morphemes the sememes of which are amalgamated.

---

[75] Cf. *Linguistische Einheiten*, p. 44, footnote 110.

N-lexemes can be notated in labelled brackets. E.g. *sun* would be n-L/sʌn/.
n-lexeme = {n-allolex$_1$, ..., n-allolex$_n$}
n-allolex = {lex$_1$, ..., lex$_n$}

Definition of b-lexemes: *B-lexemes* are established on the basis of n-lexemes in such a way that to each n-lexeme corresponds a b-lexeme. The b-lexemes have, however, no lexes but they may have b-allolexes.

B-lexemes have as segments (b-)phonemes and (b-) syllabemes or, more precisely, variphones and varisyllabs. They can also be said to have as segments (b-)morphemes or (b-)allomorphs.

B-lexemes can be notated in labelled brackets. E.g., *sun* would be b-L/sʌn/.
b-lexeme = {b-allolex$_1$, ..., b-allolex$_n$}

3.2. *Units: varilexes.* All lexes of a lexeme which are found in some given context can be called a varilex. Varilexes would be of particular interest when they have characteristic phonic qualities conditioned by the particular context. A given phonic property may establish a set of varilexes, a varilexeme (see varimorphemes, above p. 47). A varilex would thus be a variant of the lexeme. A varilex would usually be an n-unit. However, also b-varilexes can be established.

3.3. *Units: lexememes.* One way of establishing sets of lexemes is to consider the segments, i.e. (1) the (b-)phonemes and (b-) syllabemes or (2) the (b-)morphemes or (b-)allomorphs. E.g., *man, dog, cat,* etc. would form a set as they have the same number of phonemes and syllabemes. Such a lexememe would usually be a b-unit but, mutatis mutandis, there is a possibility of considering it also as an n-unit.

It is a more complicated problem to establish those lexememes which are usually called "word classes". In the discussion of these lexememes three kinds of criteria have been used:

(1) Distribution within syntactic constructions may be considered. In *the tall premier* and *the young premier, tall* and *young* have the same distribution. (The syntactic construction is in this case "determiner — attribute — head".)

It is obviously possible, and desirable, to set up sets of lexemes, i.e. lexememes, letting distribution alone determine the sets. The result would, however, not be the traditional word classes (adjectives, verbs, adverbs, etc.), at least not in any direct and simple way. To the two examples just provided one may add *the then premier*. At least here the "adverb" *then* has the same distribution as the "adjectives" *tall* and *young*.

If one again added the observation that adjectives can also have another distribution: *the premier is tall, the premier is young,* the example *the premier is ill* could be added and found similar. *Ill* could then be thought to be just an adjective but further comparisons show that it has not the same distribution as *tall* and *young* because *the ill premier is not usually said. Lexememes established on the basis of distributional criteria could be called *d-lexememes*.

(2) Paradigmatic sets based on endings (or similar morphological facts) can be established. *Boy, girl,* etc. would form a set because they can take the forms *boys, girls* etc. *Tall* and *then* would for instance certainly not belong to this set. *Small* and *young* would be elements of another set as the endings *-er* and *-est* can be added to both. As *sheep* has no plural ending it would not belong to the same set as *boy* and *girl*. *Beauti-*

ful, to which one cannot add *-er* and *-est*, would not belong to the same set as *small* and *young*.

Lexememes based on this kind of criteria should certainly be established. They could be called p-lexememes and they would obviously not coincide with the traditional word classes.

(3) Semantic criteria may be used in establishing the sets. The words *book, table* etc. would possess the semantic feature 'thing', *white, young* etc. the feature 'quality' and *go, run* etc. the feature 'action'. This kind of sets could be called *s-lexememes* and they would not coincide with the "word classes" either. The feature 'quality' exists e.g. also in *the white* or *the youth* (in the sense "the state of being young", excluding the sense "the young man"). The feature 'action' exists also in *action* or *murder* etc.

To sum up: the possibilities just mentioned under (1), (2) and (3) must all be thoroughly investigated if the aim is a detailed description of a language. In our account only English has been considered but in many other languages the facts would be similar. This means that none of the three criteria mentioned would generally provide the "word classes".

If one wishes to retain the traditional "adjectives", "verbs", "adverbs" etc., one would best define them on the basis of criterion (1); i.e. they would have to be d-lexememes. One would, then, perhaps prefer to discard many possible subsets: *tall* and *ill* would perhaps just belong to the adjectives and not to different sub-sets of the adjectives. One would also have to make statistical considerations: *then* can be used in *the then premier* and in *then he came*. The latter use is more frequent than the former. Consequently, *then* is called adverb rather than adjective.

For the purpose of a detailed description of "syntactic constructions" (syntagmemes) the three kinds of lexememes (d-, p-, and s-lexememes) must be kept apart (see below 1.1.6.). They would all be b-lexememes rather than n-lexememes, i.e. they may have relevant lexemes but lexes are usually not taken into consideration. They would, however, have various subsets.

4. In some examples lexemes (lexes) have segments which seem to be "more than" morphemes (morphs), i.e., they are "almost" lexemes. These segments could be called *semi-lexemes (semi-lexes)*. In *instead of* the segments *in* and *stead* would be such segments. The Swedish *idag* (today) is a similar case. In both cases it occurs that a writer breaks up the word and spells *in stead of* and *i dag*, which seems to indicate that the English *in* and *stead* and the Swedish *i* and *dag* in these cases are more "prominent" than just morphemes (morphs) within lexemes. In "enclitics", e.g. when in Latin *cum* is added to *vobis* to give *vobiscum*, one would also have a case of a semi-lexemes (semi-lexes). The Spanish word *contigo*, which is somehow felt to consist of *con* followed by *ti*, would have two semi-lexemes (semi-lexes). (Cf. p. 93.)

5. *Quasi-lexemes* and *quasi-lexes* would be words which are less clearly distinguished than is normally the case in the language under consideration. (Would some languages have only words which are more or less clearly quasi-words?)

In French, e.g., *me* and *le* in *l'enfant me le donne* may be considered to be words in a "weaker" sense than most others (although they are complete words if the semantic criterion is used as they have each an "unamalgamated" seme, see above). Between *me* and *le* no other word can be inserted to "break up" the sequence. In addition, these words (and a handful of similar ones) don't include any of the "full" vowels, of which most other French words have at least one. (This is said notwithstanding the fact that *all* French words seem to be less "detached" than words in many other languages.)

In cases where there may be some sense in saying that two words have "amalgamated" but where there is no trace at all of two segments, as in the French /o/ (*au*) (in some sense = *à* followed by *le*), it seems preferable just to speak about one single lexeme (with four simultaneous semantic components: 'to', 'masculine', 'singular', 'definite').

6. It is doubtful if the notions of pseudo-lexemes and pseudo-lexes can be used in an interesting way. One may perhaps feel that utterances such as [ə:] (for hesitation) or [pst] may be similar to words without being really words. If so, they would be pseudo-lexes.

7. The notions of meta-lexemes and meta-lexes are obviously useful. Phoneticians have often studied words in isolated or "lexical" pronunciation.

8. *Items: lex prosodes. Units: lexeme prosodemes.* These items and units, which are of considerable interest in various languages, have been explained above (1.1.2.3.). Certain *lexeme prosodemes* could also be of interest.

9. *Paradigmatics.* All the sets of lexemes just mentioned are defined by paradigmatic criteria.

Also, when two, or more, morphemes (morphs) are paradigmatically related to each other (as was explained above in 1.1.4.8), two, or more, lexemes (lexes) containing such segments are paradigmatically related. In *courage — courageous*, not only the segments /ɪ/ — /eᴵ/ are related, but also the whole words.

10. *Syntagmatics.* Considerations about the way the segments (see above, 1.1.5.1., 1.1.5.3.1., 1.1.5.3.3.) combine to form lexemes and lexes would fall within the field of syntagmatics.

The way lexemes and lexes combine is a syntactic problem to be treated below in 1.1.6.

11.0. The terms *lexeme*, and *lex* (etc.) can be suffixed by *glotto-*, *dia-*, *socio-* and *idio* to express meaningful units and items.

11.1 *Ph-ph-glottolexemes.* Lexemes may correspond "phoneme by phoneme", i.e. have in the same order phonemically corresponding phonemes (variphones). Lexemes from different dialects which correspond in their lexemic structure in regard to ph-phonemes (ph-variphones) could be named ph-ph-dialexemes. An English lexeme /tʃɑ:ns/ in one dialect would correspond with the same form in another dialect, but not with /tʃæ:ns/. Corresponding ph-ph-dialexemes may have corresponding, partly corresponding or non-corresponding sememes.

Definition: Corresponding ph-ph-dialexemes form a *ph-ph-glottolexeme*.

11.2. *M-ph-glottolexemes.* Lexemes may also correspond in a more complicated way. In a group of lexemes in one dialect, given variphones may correspond with given variphones in a group of lexemes in another dialect and the correspondence, which is not necessarily a ph-correspondence, is discovered by the fact that pairs of lexemes have corresponding sememes (meanings).

Lexemes from different dialects which correspond in this way can be named m-ph-dialexemes as they have morphemically corresponding phonemes. Not only /tʃaːns/ and /tʃaːns/ from different dialects are corresponding m-ph-dialexemes, but also /tʃaːns/ and /tʃæːns/. Corresponding lexemes from different dialects (sociolects) may have different numbers of phonemes (variphones) as in /hɔt/ versus /ɔt/ (*hot*).

Definition: Corresponding m-ph-dialexemes form an *m-ph-glottolexeme*.

11.3. *Se-glottolexemes*. The "same meaning" can be expressed in different dialects by different words. In English, "bucket" can either be expressed by *bucket* or *pail*. These two words have consequently corresponding diasememes.

Definition: Dialexemes which have corresponding diasememes form an *se-glottolexeme*.

The most convenient way of notating this unit seems to be to choose a lexeme from the standard dialect (if there is one). For instance, one would say that the English se-glottolexeme *bucket* has the se-dialexemes *bucket* and *pail*.

11.4. As the problems connected with morphemes and lexemes (words) are very similar, for the sake of brevity, we have only dealt in detail with lexemes. However, most lexemes mentioned above (1.1.5.11.1.—1.1.5.11.3.) are single morphemes, which means that everything said about them holds also for morphemes (if some terms are changed).

12. *Inventories* of *lexes, allolexes, lexemes, lexememes, semi-lexes* and *semi-lexemes, quasi-lexes* and *quasi-lexemes, pseudo-lexes* and *pseudo-lexemes, meta-lexes* and *meta-lexemes, lex prosodes* and *lexeme prosodemes*, and of *glotto-*, *dia-*, *socio-* and *idio-items* and *units* can be set up. *An inventory of lexemes*, usually together with their meanings, is called a vocabulary, glossary, lexicon or dictionary.

13. Some possible discovery procedures are implied in what was said above (p. 51–52).

In most cases the problem does not seem to be difficult: the words can just be taken for granted, as has already been stated. (Who would doubt that *table, too, go* etc. are words in English?) The comparatively low number of doubtful and more complicated cases could be picked out and judged by the linguist or by informants. From their answers conclusions with reference to lexemes or semi- and quasi-lexemes could be drawn.

1.1.6. Syntagmemes

0. Syntagms, syntagm functions, syntagmemes and syntagmeme functions (definitions below) may be considered as the major parts of syntax.

1. *Items: syntagms*. *Definition*: A *syntagm* is an item which has as segments one or more lexes and which has some definite function at the level of syntax. Some syntagms are indicated by specific prosodes.

This means that, in order to establish a syntagm, e.g. a subject, a syntactic function, i.e. a subject function, must be sought. It may be difficult and unnecessary to try to define any further the term syntactic function or, in this case, "syntagm function"[76].

A syntagm, e.g., *the little boy (did it)*[77], is often equal to what has been called a syntactic construction, but not always, as a syntagm, e.g., *I (did it)* may consist of just one word.

A syntagm can be a segment of a longer syntagm: The syntagm *I* is part of the syntagm *I did it*.

Syntagms are often, but not always, indicated by a particular prosode, see above p. 30–32 and 1.1.2.4.

It should be noted that the most immediate syntactic functions that one would find by analysis, are sufficient to establish the syntagms as such, but not until the particular kind of segment and the distribution of the segment has been considered in more detail is it possible to label it the way one usually does. A somewhat informed first consideration of the functions of *the boy* in *the boy hit the girl* and *by the boy* in *the girl was hit by the boy* could give as its only result that both segments have the same function, that of 'agent' or 'actor'. This would be sufficient to establish the segments but would make them seem more similar than they are. For further discussions see below p. 64–66.

If one considers the syntagm *the little girl always liked him*, the first observation may be that it consists of six consecutive lexes. These are the "ultimate constituents", i.e. the shortest segments which are usually[78] considered in syntax.

Each shortest segment can, to start with, be considered as belonging to some particular "word class". One would have classes such as *adjectiveme, adverbeme, auxiliareme, cardinaleme, determinereme, conjunctioneme, indefinite pronomineme, interrogative pronomineme, interrogatoreme, ordinaleme, personal pronomineme, possessive pronomineme, prepositioneme, relative pronomineme, substantiveme, verbeme* etc. and the elements of these sets would be *adjectives, adverbs, auxiliaries, cardinals, determiners, conjunctions, indefinite pronouns, interrogative pronouns, interrogators, ordinals, personal pronouns, possessive pronouns, prepositions, relative pronouns, substantives, verbs* etc. These traditional word classes are d-lexememes of the kind described above (p. 53) for the establishment of which some distinctions have been discarded and a statistical criterion has been added: Firstly, one establishes a number of large sets within which all elements have roughly the same distribution. Secondly, it is found that some words have distributions corresponding

---

[76] It seems advantageous to choose this sort of function as a starting point for defining syntagms and syntagmemes and admit that it is immediately given rather than well defined. It is certainly less acceptable to provide a circular definition as Gleason (*An Introduction to Descriptive Linguistics*, p. 132) who says: "A construction is any significant group of words (or morphemes)". In this context "construction" means "syntactic construction" and "significant group of words" must mean "syntactically significant group of words", which obviously equals "syntactic construction". Also C. H. Borgstrøm is circular (*Innføring i sprogvidenskap*, Oslo 1958, p. 69) when saying (in translation): "By 'syntagm' we understand here a sequence of word forms which is formed according to given rules, e.g. *a new bike*, or *the bike is new*. We can then say that syntagms are the subject matter of syntax." Unfortunately the rules for the syntagms must be syntactic rules. I.e. syntactic constructions (syntagms) are those constructed according to syntactic rules, which hardly means more than that syntactic constructions are syntactic constructions.
[77] Note that in this chapter examples are given in normal orthography although phonic notation within [...] would have been more exact.
[78] Morphs and morphemes have, however, also been thought of as segments of syntactic constructions.

to the distributions of two or more of the already established sets. These words are, however, then attributed to the set they most frequently belong to. E.g. (as has been explained above, p. 53, 54) *then* has most often the distribution of an adverb but in some cases it has the distribution of an adjective (*the then premier*). Therefore, call *then* an adverb. However, the information lost in this process can be recovered, if subsets are set up. E.g., within the adverbs, i.e. the adverbeme, the adverbs which can also be used in front of a substantive as in *the then premier* would form a particular allo-adverb[79]. The syntagm *a Melbourne doctor* shows the substantive *Melbourne* in a position where one usually finds adjectives.

Returning to our example, the six lexes mentioned would be determiner (*the*), adjective (*little*), substantive (*girl*), adverb (*always*), verb (*liked*), personal pronoun (*him*).

Generally, a lex or a sequence of lexes which is a syntagm or a segment of a syntagm can be considered as an *adverbial, appositive, attribute, direct object, finite verb, includer, indirect object, object complement, predicate, subject, subject complement* etc.

The "longest" syntagms are *periods* (or sentences).

A *clause* is a syntagm having typically a subject and a predicate (and possibly complements to these segments). (A period such as *sit down!* would also consist of a clause although no segment which could be called a subject is present.) It is in principle shorter than a period as a period sometimes has clauses as segments: *the boy came and the girl went*. Sometimes the clause has the same length as the period of which it is a segment: *the boy came*.

Phrases are certain frequent syntagms which either have a head with or without a complement, or are a syntagm introduced by a preposition. *The little boy* or *the boy* or *John* are substantive phrases. *Has come* or *came* are verb phrases. *With you* is a preposition phrase. Phrases are, in principle, shorter than clauses as they are usually segments of clauses.

It occurs that the hierarchical order period — clause — phrase is broken in the sense that a higher level unit is found in a position where a lower level unit is usually found. In *that he drank the whole bottle worried me*, the clause *that he drank the whole bottle* is used in a position where substantive phrases are much more frequent. In this case the period consists of a clause (which can be said to function as a phrase) and a phrase whereas the more common similar period type (*his attitude worried me*) consists of one clause which consists of two phrases.

Let us consider in detail the period *the little girl always liked him*. It has the two syntagms of subject (*the little girl*) and predicate (*always liked him*). The subject is a substantive phrase which has a determiner (*the*) as a complement to a head (*little girl*), which consists of an attribute (*little*) followed by a head (*girl*). The predicate consists of a head (*always liked*), which is a verb phrase, and a complement (*him*), which is a direct object. The verb phrase has a complement, which is an adverbial (*always*), and a head, which is a finite verb (*liked*). The adverbial is a single adverb and the finite verb is a single verb. (In some other period the adverbial could have been the sequence

---

[79] Note that *then* is one single lexeme, which occasionally partly shares the distribution of adjectives. It is not to be compared with, e.g. *love* because there seem to be one lexeme *love* as a substantive and one lexeme *love* as a verb. Note also that *then* as an attribute does not behave completely as most adjectives. A syntagm such as **the very then premier* (cf. *the very old premier*) is not possible.

on a hot day (which would have had another position than *always* in the period) and the finite verb could have been the sequence *would have liked*.) The direct object (*him*) is a syntagm but has only one segment, which is a personal pronoun.

Everything said about the period mentioned could be summed up in a box diagram, where at the bottom the individual lexes are given:

			period			
			clause			
	subject			predicate		
	substantive phrase			verb phrase		substantive phrase
complement	head		head			complement
			complement	head		
	attribute	head	adverbial	finite verb		direct object
determiner	adjective	substantive	adverb	verb		personal pronoun
the	little	girl	always	liked		him

As has already been mentioned a syntagm can have (shorter) syntagms as segments. In the example given, the period (which is a clause) consists of a subject and a predicate.

By definition one may consider every lex in a period to be a syntagm. However, it would perhaps be better not to class certain lexes as syntagms. This could be the case of the determiner *the* in *the little girl*. This phrase would then be a syntagm consisting of the lex *the*, which is a complement which would not be a syntagm, followed by the syntagm *little girl*. Generally one would say that if a lex belongs to a set of lexes of which no element can be expanded, it should not be called a syntagm. Although the direct object *him* cannot be expanded it belongs to a set which has expandable elements, and therefore *him* would be a syntagm. Instead of *him* one could have said *men* or its expansion *old men*.

When a syntagm is divided only once, the segments are *direct segments* of that syntagm. In the period given, the substantive phrase *the little girl* has the direct segments *the* and *little girl*.

The term direct segment corresponds to the more common "immediate constituent".

Segments of a syntagm which are established by more than one division, are *indirect segments* of that syntagm. If *the little girl* is first divided into *the* and *little girl* and if then *little girl* is divided into *little* and *girl*, *little* and *girl* will be indirect segments of *the little girl* (but direct segments of *little girl*).

The term indirect segment would correspond to "constituent which is not an immediate constituent" (or "mediate constituent").

When a box diagram shows a subdivision of a syntagm, the direct segments appear on the next lower level. Indirect segments appear at still lower levels[80].

The most basic facts about the structure of a period can be explained in different ways:

(1) Plain words can be used. The period *the little girl always liked him* has a subject *the little girl* and a predicate *always liked him*. The subject is a substantive phrase, which consists of a determiner as complement of a head consisting of an adjective and a substantive etc.

(2) The information given in plain words under (1) can be abbreviated in different ways. Using a notation similar (but not equal) to devices used by tagmemicists, the most basic facts about the period given could be written $Pe = S: s.ph + P: v.ph + d.o.$ (where Pe = period, S = subject, $:$ = consisting of, $s.ph.$ = substantive phrase, $+$ = followed by, P = predicate, $v.ph.$ = verb phrase, $d.o.$ = direct object). Using "rewrite rules" one could write: $Pe \to S + P$, $S \to s.ph.$, $P \to v.ph. + d.o.$ (where the arrow means "to be rewritten as" or, more exactly, "being" or "consisting of").

(3) A box diagram, as above, can be used. The simplified description of the period under discussion would be

period		
subject	predicate	
subst. phrase	verb phrase	direct object

(4) A "tree" can provide the same information as the box diagram. In the centre of each box a dot can be imagined. Then connect the dots (the "nodes") and take away the boxes. The diagram under (3) would thus be transformed into:

Or using the labels as above:

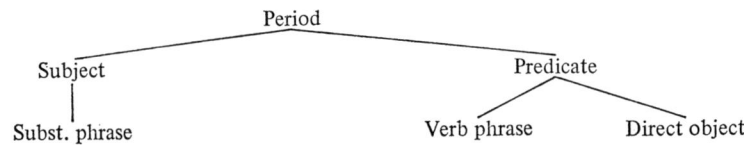

Discontinuous syntagms could be shown by some convention such as shaded boxes. For instance, *saw ... frequently* in *saw him frequently* could be shown as

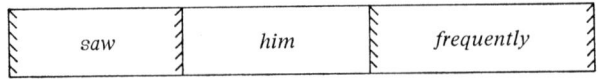

---

[80] The kind of analysis of a sentence just provided may seem very intuitive. The explicit use of the substitutions suggested below, p. 67–68, may, however, contribute to making the procedure less unsatisfactory. Besides, there seems to be little doubt about the result of the analysis. At least most linguists would do roughly the same thing.

A corresponding tree would show the segments of the discontinuous syntagm by shaded branches:

(5) Labelled brackets, which are somewhat complicated to read but which can be more readily represented as they do not need any graph to be drawn, can be utilized:
period[subject[subst. phrase[ ]] predicate[verb phrase[ ] direct object[ ]]].

In the situation of communication several facts underlie the signalling of boundaries between syntagms (or lack of boundaries between lexes which in other contexts could have formed separate syntagms), function of syntagms and relationships between syntagms:

(1) *Word order* often shows which kind of syntagm is involved. In *Elaine likes Paul*, *Elaine*, coming first, is subject (and cannot possibly be direct object) and *Paul* is direct object (and cannot possibly be subject). It is obvious that a more or less fixed word order is as such more efficient than a freer word order in showing what kind of syntagm is involved.

(2) Syntactic relationships between two or more lexes can be signalled by *agreement*, i.e. the lexes related by agreement show some given expression feature. Usually they have particular morphs with semes containing one or more common features. E.g. there is agreement between *the boy* and *eats* in *the boy eats snails*. The lack of ending at the end of *boy* as well as the *s* at the end of *eats* signal both third person singular, which is the common feature. (Cf. *the boys eat snails*.) In this example the agreement does not make any significant contribution to the meaning of the period. It is even redundant in the sense that *the boy *eat snails* and *the boys eat snails* would also have shown the relevant distinction. In other examples agreement may be more important. E.g. the Latin syntagm *dominus bonus servi* (the slave's good master) has the two direct segments *dominus bonus* and *servi* but *dominus boni servi* has the two direct segments *dominus* and *boni servi* (the good slave's master), i.e. the agreement efficiently signals syntactic structure. (Word order is in Latin less efficient in this respect.)

Agreement can be shown by some appropriate symbol, e.g. some device connecting the two items in agreement: *dominus bonus servi*.

(3) By *government* (or *rection*) one lex determines the form of some other lex or lex combination. In this case one cannot say that the determining lex and the determined lex have any semantic feature in common (as in the case of agreement). The German preposition *mit* is followed by dative: *mit seinem Freund(e)*. The German preposition *ohne* is followed by accusative: *ohne seinen Freund*. In similar cases the government makes a contribution towards signalling that the lexes belong to a syntagm (a preposition phrase in the two German examples).

(4) *Knowledge of word-classes*, d-lexememes, and their role in syntactic constructions, helps the listener interpret utterances. So called function words, i.e. words which partly or exclusively have the meaning of showing some grammatical function, are particularly efficient in this regard. E.g. the English articles *the* and *a* have, in addition to other features of meaning, the function of signalling the beginning of a substantive

phrase. In *he wants to do it*, the lex *to* seems to have no other function than the one of showing that a verb in the infinitive is following.

Also lexes which are not "function words" are to be considered. If a syntagm starts with the lexes *a very* the next lex will probably be an adjective and this adjective will not usually be the end of a syntagm. The adverb *very* after an *a* does certainly not signal the end of a syntagm but that the syntagm is still to be completed. In *I saw a bear* the lexes *saw* and *a* cannot form a syntagm because there is no syntagm consisting of a verb followed by an article.

The fact that certain lexes have structure which, more or less clearly, indicates word-class may be remembered here although this circumstance belongs directly to morphology and is only indirectly of importance in syntax. In English, lexes containing certain dependent morphs have this kind of structure. A word ending in *-ish*, as *boyish*, is most probably an adjective. A word ending in *-ly*, as in the case of *nicely*, may belong to various word classes but most frequently it is an adverb.

(5) *Frequency* of a syntagm is of importance as one is inclined to interpret in accordance with the most frequent pattern. This is so either generally or for some particular context. Generally one might be inclined to divide *Old Light Church* into *Old* and *Light Church* in the same way as one would divide *old light house*. However, if this syntagm is found in a context, where already *Old Light movement* or *Old Light preacher* has occurred one would instead be inclined to divide it into *Old Light* and *Church*[81].

(6) *Knowledge of the "things"*, i.e. kowledge which is not part of one's practical knowledge of language, may help one's interpretation. In *the shooting of the elephants* one understands naturally that the elephants were shot (as this has often occurred) and not that the elephants had been shooting (as this is not a normal event).

(7) *Syntactic prosodes* alone may show syntactic structure. Through different pronunciations it is possible to differentiate between *old men/and women* (i.e. the women are not necessarily old) and *old/men and women* (i.e. both men and women are old). In similar cases one often makes the difference clearer by adding some appropriate kind of emphasis (which as such belongs to the β-level). It seems even reasonable to assume that sometimes the most common prosodes within the relevant prosodemes are not at all capable of showing some syntactic difference but that some particular prosodes, e.g. those conditioned by emphasis, signal the difference. The possibility that β-facts may have, so to speak, a secondary function at the α-level would need to be investigated.

As a suggestion for abbreviation the most essential facts about the period *the little girl always liked him* would be symbolized:

P(c(subj(subst phr) pred((v phr) (d o)))).

I.e. this period consists of a clause. The clause has the two segments subject and predicate (in this order). The subject consists of a substantive phrase. The predicate consists, in this order, of a verb phrase and a direct object.

If one wanted a phonic notation of syntagms seen as sequences of lexes, one would use labelled brackets: synt[...].

---

[81] The example is borrowed from H. A. Gleason, *An Introduction to Descriptive Linguistics*, p. 135-136.

2. *Units : varisyntagms. Definition :* A *varisyntagm* is the set of syntagms which have, in the same linear order, given lexes with given functions. The segments of a varisyntagm are the relevant varilexes. Some varisyntagms have prosodemes.

If the period *the little girl always liked him* is conceived as a series of lexes it is a syntagm; if conceived as a series of varilexes, it is a varisyntagm.

It would perhaps not make much difference if, in the definition, "lexeme" were used instead of "varilex". However, if in a detailed study it is found that different contexts condition different sets of lexes within the same lexeme, the lexeme itself with all its lexes will be too large a set to be a segment of the varisyntagm. Instead a varilex will have to be established, as suggested.

The difference between syntagms and varisyntagms would have to be constantly borne in mind in a detailed study of realizations but in the kind of syntactic study usually carried out this difference is of little consequence. In a loose sort of way it is perhaps permissible to say that syntagms are grouped into syntagmemes and thus forget about "the intermediary step" of varisyntagms.

In a more precise way varisyntagms are, however, the elements directly forming the syntagmemes. (Varisyntagms will not be called syntagmemes.)

In the study of many syntactic problems b-varisyntagms, for which syntagms would not be considered, would be the only interesting ones. In detailed studies of realizations n-varisyntagms, including all the variants, i.e. the syntagms, would be appropriate.

B-varisyntagms would have b-varilexes as segments and n-varisyntagms would have n-varilexes as segments.

n-varisyntagm = [syntagm$_1$, ..., syntagm$_n$].

3. *Items : syntagm functs. Definition :* A syntagm has a *total meaning* which is mainly made up of the function of the syntagm, in the following called *syntagm funct*, and the lex semes, or the lex seme, in the following called *syntagm seme* (cf. below, p. 87–88).

Variations between syntagm functs (belonging to some particular varisyntagm functeme) and syntagm semes (belonging to some particular varisyntagm sememe) are conditioned by distribution, i.e. position in relation to other syntagms, and by expresses and emphatic prosodes (see below, p. 88–89, 111–112). Thus distribution, expresses and emphatic prosodes make also a contribution to the total meaning of a syntagm.

In the period (the syntagm) *the girl hit the boy* the subject funct of *the girl* and the direct object funct of *the boy* contribute to the total meaning: *the girl* is the one who acts and *the boy* is the target of the action. This is not given by the semes of *the girl* and *the boy*. These semes, however, also contribute to the total meaning of the period.

The relevance of the position of a syntagm is shown in the difference between *I know this* and *this I know*. In initial position the direct object *this* becomes more emphasized. (At the same time, the whole period gets a particular shade of meaning, which may be difficult to explain, but could be something like a somewhat impatient protest that one really knows the fact under consideration although somebody has shown some doubt about this fact.)

If in *the girl hit the boy*, *the girl* is said with an emphatic prosode the period means that the girl, and not someone else, hit the boy (cf. below, p. 88). The effect of the emphasis would, however, concern the seme of *girl* no less than its funct.

If, on the other hand, one "stresses" in a particular way *high* in *the tree is high*, the seme of *high* is influenced so as to be not just "high" but "very high". This β-problem would however, hardly be syntactic but concern the seme of the *high*.

By comparing the syntagms having the same sequence of semes but being differently divided into shorter syntagms one sees in a striking way how syntagmic structure alone can change the meaning of a syntagm. Two examples would be:

(1) *light house keeping*,
(2) *they don't know how good meat tastes*.

Such examples have sometimes been considered as "homonymous"[82] or showing "ambiguity"[83]. If, however, syntactic prosodes and prosodemes are taken into account, these terms are often not adequate. The two different syntagms under (1) and the two under (2) are usually distinguished by different pronunciation.

There is "vertical" interselection between lex semes in given syntagms and syntagm functs of the same syntagms. There is also "horizontal" interselection between syntagm functs following each other. Also "diagonal" interselection must be considered. These interselections will be explained below (p. 77–79, 85).

4. *Units : varisyntagm functemes. Definition :* a varisyntagm has a *total meaning* which is made up of the functs of its syntagms, i.e. the *varisyntagm functeme*, and by the varilex sememes, or the varilex sememe, i.e. the *varisyntagm sememe* (cf. below, p. 89).

In other words, any syntagm, e.g., the period *the little girl always liked him* (p. 59) or *the tree is high* (above), repeated a number of times on different occasions, would be

---

[82] H. A. Gleason, *An Introduction to Descriptive Linguistics*, p. 136.
[83] N. Chomsky, *Current Issues in Linguistic Theory*, p. 42. *Topics in the Theory of Generative Grammar*, p. 14.

I have taken over the example *John does not know how good meat tastes*, as well as some other examples on the following pages, from N. Chomsky. I find that these examples and problems discussed by Chomsky are good and relevant. It has, however, not been possible to take over any of his solutions as I find (a) that they consist partly of elements known before, (b) that they often lack relevant pieces of information and (c) that the original elements are mostly inadequate and meaningless.

I disagree with the idea of "deep structure", as this sort of structure cannot be accepted as the structure of any specific language (and this is the kind of structure we have in mind in this book) as long as it cannot be supported by any reasonable assumption, intuition or knowledge about the language in question.

Deep structure, seen as a universal system to which all specific language could be related, is another problem again. Establishing in an unprincipled way bits and pieces of so called deep structure for a couple of languages cannot advance this problem in any significant way. A thorough discussion on principles would be more welcome. It should be noted that this sort of deep structure would not necessarily have to be directly adequate for any specific language. Its only condition would be that it should function well in its capacity of universal system to which specific languages could be economically related.

The assumption that at some deeper, or higher (i.e. some "abstract") level human languages have similarities which linguists should detect is also interesting. But this would be yet another problem. Little explicit and coherent knowledge seems to be available in this field. B. Sigurd believes in *Frågor och svar i lingvistiken* (p. 95 of *Vetenskapliga Perspektiv*) that (in translation) "the transformational revolution" has had the effect that "considerable similarities in the abstract deep structure has been demonstrated between various languages". As the suggested deep structures are unacceptable as structures for these particular languages the only thing demonstrated so far is, however, that various linguists influencing each other are capable of imagining similar things about different languages. It is certainly possible to relate, through "rules", structures of rather different languages to an imagined common "deep" structure. The real problem is if this game is meaningful.

different, even if only slightly, as to functs and semes. These variants would add up to the total meaning of the varisyntagm. For instance, subject functs within the same varisubject (e.g. the functs of *the boy (did it)* said on different occasions) would form a varisubject functeme which would be a subset of a subjecteme allofunct (viz. the allofunct called below number 2).

It is not easy to say exactly what the functs of a varisyntagm functeme are. It could even be doubted if they are really acceptable and relevant. However, one could, for instance, believe that a subject is not only a subject but more or less clearly so in different contexts. "Subfunctions" (or "additional meanings") such as target seem to be capable of being more or less emphasized: *The* boy *was hit (and not the girl)* versus *the boy was hit*. It is easier to imagine different semes of the sememe of a given word. In one context *boy* may mean a quite small boy and in some other context a bigger boy. (See above, 3.)

varisyntagm functeme = {syntagm funct$_1$, ..., syntagm funct$_n$}.

5. *Units: syntagmeme allofuncts, syntagmeme functemes.*

Below, it will be shown that syntagms, or varisyntagms, should be grouped together according to their function. I.e. syntagmemes will be established on the basis of functemes.

Definition of syntagmeme functeme: A *syntagmeme functeme* is a unit which groups together all syntagm functs, or varisyntagm functemes, having the same basic meaning.

For instance, all functs of subjects establish the subjecteme functeme as they have the basic meaning "that which something is said about" (or something of this kind). This is true about *the sky (is blue)*, *the boy (came)*, *John (is easy to please)* etc. However, the subject functs in these have not just the basic meaning but also an "additional meaning" but this fact is not taken into account at this stage.

Definition of syntagmeme allofunct: Syntagm functs are grouped together so as to form *syntagmeme allofuncts* on the basis of their additional meaning. Syntagmeme allofuncts form syntagmeme functemes on the basis of their basic meaning.

The functs of the subjects[84] just quoted belong to three different allofuncts within the subjecteme[85] functeme. In *the sky is blue* the additional meaning could perhaps be called zero as nothing is really added to the basic function ("that which something is said about"). This could be a funct of subjecteme allofunct$_1$ (additional meaning ∅). In *the boy came* the additional meaning is "agent". This could be a funct of subjecteme allofunct$_2$ (agent). In *John is easy to please* the additional meaning is "target". This could be a funct within allofunct$_3$ ("target, goal, aim or similar")[86].

---

[84] Being obviously syntagms or varisyntagms.
[85] Being obviously a syntagmeme.
[86] The structure of this sentence has been compared by Chomsky to the one of *John is eager to please* (cf. *Current Issues in Linguistic Theory*, p. 34–35, 61–62; *Language and Mind*, p. 37).
As in all other cases I cannot see that the introduction of "underlying structures" or mysterious "deep structures" adds anything of value. In this latter example *John* is a subject with a funct belonging to the subjecteme allofunct$_2$. This means that the most basic difference between *John is easy to please* and *John is eager to please* is the one between a funct belonging to one allofunct (target) and a funct belonging to another allofunct (agent).
It could be added that, although it has been thought that these two sentences have the same "constituent structure" ("box structure" or "tree structure"), it seems reasonable to think that they are different in this regard. Using brackets the difference would be [[*John*][*is*] [*easy to please*]]] as against [[*John*][*is eager*] [*to please*]]].

It is not difficult to see that in English most subjects are actually defined by the "basic" meaning ("that which something is said about"). There are, however, cases such as *it rains*, where the definition is less acceptable. There seem to be three ways of solving this difficulty: (1) redefine the basic function, (2) agree that *it* is so different that it should be called something else than subject, (3) accept that one single basic meaning of a functeme does, exceptionally, not define *all* allofuncts.

If possibility (3) is accepted some additional criterion would have to be added in order to make it possible to establish *it* as a subject. This criterion would be similarity of syntagms and their distribution: *it rains, money rains over the rich, the boy goes, he goes, it goes*, etc. would have such similarities on the expression side that one would be inclined to think that they all started with a subject. (One may add that also periods introduced by *there is* ..., *there are* ... would have to be dealt with in some specific way.)

It could possibly be advantageous to distinguish, in some discussions, between n- and b-allofuncts and n- and b-functemes.

6. *Units: syntagmemes and their subsets*. Although what was said at the end of the preceding paragraph implies that one may doubt whether it is possible to establish syntagms and sets of syntagms on the basis of functemes only, we shall assume that this is feasible.

Definition: A *syntagmeme* is an expression unit established (as stated above) on the basis of a syntactic functeme. All syntagms (varisyntagms) having functs belonging to some given syntagmeme functeme belong to the same syntagmeme.

Syntagmemes have *allosyntagms* as subsets. If needed, an allosyntagm can be subdivided into *diallosyntagms, triallosyntagms* etc. These subsets are established on the basis of their syntagmatic structure: *the little boy, the older man, the young wife* etc. would belong to the same subset (see further explanations below)[87].

Some syntagmemes have prosodemes (see above, p. 36-38).

Syntagmemes may have shorter syntagmemes as direct and indirect segments. The syntagmeme (an alloperiod) of which *the boy came* is a syntagm has as direct segments the syntagmeme (an allosubject) of which *the boy* is a syntagm and the syntagmeme (an allopredicate) of which *came* is a syntagm.

A syntagmeme may have as segments a lexeme which is not a syntagmeme, and a syntagmeme. *The little girl* (cf. above, p. 59), *a tall boy, the old man* etc. would be syntagms belonging to such a syntagmeme, viz. the one which has as first segment a determinereme[88], which is no syntagmeme, and a syntagmeme consisting of an alloadjective[89] followed by a substantiveme[90]. (Note that the segments of "longer" syntagms are "shorter syntagms" or lexes and "shorter syntagms".) It seems advantageous to use, in a general way, the term syntagmeme for all "syntactic constructions" which have as segments "word classes", d-lexememes, or subsets of these and syntag-

---

[87] See also my paper "On linguistic terminology" (Actes du Xe Congrès international des linguistes, Bucharest 1969, p. 321-325).
[88] Assuming that all determiners can appear in this position. Otherwise allodeterminer would be the appropriate label.
[89] Assuming that not all adjectives can appear in this position. Otherwise adjectiveme would be the appropriate label.
[90] Assuming that all substantives can appear in this position. Otherwise allosubstantive would be the appropriate label.

memes (in contra-distinction to "syntactic constructions" consisting of "particular words", i.e. the syntagms and the varisyntagms). This means that what is in a general way called a syntagmeme may well be an allosyntagm of some particular syntagmeme.

A number of substitution tests[91] may be used in order (a) to divide longer syntagms into segments, on which the establishment of syntagmeme segments can be based, (b) to establish directly if a lex alone is a syntagm and, by implication, if a lexeme alone is a syntagmeme, (c) to group syntagms into syntagmemes, (d) to establish subsets of syntagmemes, (e) to establish heads of syntagms and, by implication, of syntagmemes.

(1) The problem under (a) is elucidated to some extent by "dividing substitutions". Such substitutions require that one single lex be substituted for two or more lexes. In the new and shorter version the syntactic functions (the functs) are similar in some essential way. (The exact meaning of this requirement is somewhat obscure but when an example of the test at work is shown, one may feel that it is not completely unsatisfactory.) The syntactic structure of the syntagms containing the substitutes is less complicated and the content, also, usually becomes less detailed than in the original syntagm.

The starting point, which it may be necessary just to take for granted, is usually a period. Considering again the period analyzed on page 59, the lexes imagined during the test could be those shown in the box diagram under the original sentence:

the	little	girl	always	liked	him
she			came		
		girl	liked		

First *she* is substituted for *the little girl* and *came* for *always liked him*. This establishes two syntagms or, in other words, divides the period into two segments. *Girl* may be thought of as saying *little girl* in a less detailed way. It would certainly be less natural to believe that something could be substituted for *the little*. *Liked* is then substituted for *always liked*. If the knowledge of lexes is taken for granted and if the subdivision is required to show also the structure in terms of lexes, the establishment of the lowest level of the box diagram just requires some automatic cuts.

It may certainly be said that the dividing substitutions, as well as the substitutions explained below, are of limited value.

(2) The problem under (b) may be elucidated by the use of "expansion substitutions". A lex which can be expanded in such a way that the new longer segment has essentially the same function as the shorter original one, is a syntagm. In the period *the girl always liked him*, *girl* can be expanded to *little girl* and is therefore a syntagm. The lex *the* on the other hand cannot be expanded and is therefore no syntagm (but *the little girl* is obviously a syntagm). As *him* has the same distribution and function as expandable syntagms it is a syntagm.

---

[91] As one may expect, these tests do not mechanically provide unquestionable solutions. They may, however, be of help to a linguist wanting to make things somewhat clearer to himself and other linguists. They could also be used to test laymen. (See above, p. 10.)

(3) "Identity substitutions" may help establish syntagmemes (c). If in *the little girl always liked him*, *the old man*, *the young boy* and similar syntagms are substituted for *the little girl* the new period has exactly the same syntactic structure as the original one. These syntagms should therefore belong to the same syntagmeme.

(4) In "similarity substitutions" segments different in syntactic structure but having essentially the same function are tried out in order to establish subsets of a syntagmeme (d). Instead of saying *the little girl always liked him* one can say *the girl always liked him* or *she always liked him*. This shows that *the little girl*, *the girl* and *she* are three syntagms belonging to three different subsets of some given syntagmeme.

(5) In "compression substitutions" the head of a syntagm (and, by implication, of a syntagmeme) can be found (e). *He spoke very well* can be compressed to *he spoke well* but not to *he spoke very*. This means that the suppressible *very* is complement and the non-suppressible *well* is head of *very well*.

As was said above, it is assumed that syntactic functions can be discovered and that they can be used for subdividing longer syntagms into shorter syntagms. In a somewhat less "mentalistic" way "dividing substitutions" achieve the same goal. In a slightly more mentalistic way one can say that all syntagms having the same funct(ion) form a syntagmeme or, in a way perhaps appearing more rigorous, one can say that all syntagms which can be substituted for each other in similarity substitutions belong to some particular syntagmeme[92].

A syntagmeme such as the set of all subjects, the subjecteme, will include syntagms, or varisyntagms, of different "length": *he*, *the man*, *the old man* etc. In identity substitutions it will be found that *he*, *she* etc. as in *he did it*, *she did it* etc. belong to one allosyntagm (an allosubject); *the man*, *the woman* etc. as in *the man did it*, *the woman did it* etc. form another allosyntagm. In a similar way *the old man*, *the young woman* etc. form yet another allosyntagm. In the process the d-lexememes are also established, as lexemes are grouped into d-lexememes on distributional criteria. These d-lexememes are labelled (as above, p. 57) and constitute the segments of syntagmemes.

In the description of the syntagmeme including *the little girl*, *a tall boy*, *the old man* etc. (mentioned above p. 66) terms such as alloadjective and substantiveme were used. Assuming that this syntagmeme is an allosubject and using italics to indicate the name of the syntagmeme, colon to mean "which has the segments" and dash to mean "followed by" one would write:

allosubject : determinereme — alloadjective — substantiveme[93].

Using labelled brackets (and abbreviations for the labels) in the way suggested above (p. 61) for syntagms one would write instead:

Asubj (Det Aadj Subst).

It is suggested that the set of all periods be called *periodememe*. If really all possible periods were thought of, one could speak of n-periodememe being a set of n-periodemes having as elements n-variperiods (which include periods). If, however, one felt that a less "detailed" statement was more appropriate one could speak of b-periodememe being a set of b-periodemes having as elements b-variperiods (which do not include the periods).

---

[92] The formulation avoiding substitutions and basing the argument only on "basic" functions (e.g. subjecteme functeme) seems preferable in the sense that the problem of various "restrictions" on the combinability of various segments is avoided at this stage.

[93] If the conditions assumed p. 66, footnotes 88–90, were true.

Each *periodeme* would include periods (variperiods) having, as direct segments, clauses belonging to the same clauseme or to some particular arrangement of clausemes in sequence. (By "arrangement" is here meant the way clausemes are co-ordinated or subordinated.) As the clauses are direct segments, the clausemes also would be considered as direct segments. (The point is emphasized as it occurs that segments which usually are direct segments of some comparatively "long" segment are occasionally used as segments so "short" that they are indirect segments of the "long segment". See p. 58: *that he drank the whole bottle worried me*.) In some language, periodeme$_1$ could just consist of a clauseme (or some alloclause). Periodeme$_2$ could consist of a subordinate clauseme (or alloclause) followed by a main clauseme (or alloclause). Periodeme$_3$ could consist of a main clauseme (or alloclause) followed by a subordinate clauseme (or alloclause) etc.

As abbreviations for these three periodemes one may suggest: P_1: MC, P_2: SC — MC and P_3: MC — SC.

Each periodeme can be subdivided into alloperiods. Each alloperiod has, in some particular order, a specific number of segments such as adverbialeme, appositiveme, attributeme, direct objecteme, includereme, indirect objecteme, object complementeme, predicateme, subjecteme, subject complementeme etc., or, perhaps, in most cases of most languages, subsets of these: alloadverbial, alloappositive etc. (or still "lower" sets). An alloperiod of some language could be "adverbialeme — subjecteme — predicateme" but this formula would imply that *all* adverbials, *all* subjects and *all* predicates could be combined in the periods forming the set. If the language were English the periods *yesterday I told a lie, today my brother is coming, on a Sunday few people are here* etc. would belong to this alloperiod. If, e.g. only *some* adverbials could be followed by subjects and predicates the alloperiod would contain some particular alloadverbial and not an "adverbialeme". Alloperiods can be divided into dialloperiods by taking subsets of the alloperiod segments into account. One dialloperiod of the alloperiod just quoted could be "alloadverbial$_1$ — allosubject$_1$ — allopredicate$_1$," and include *yesterday he came, here I go, generally we sleep* etc. (but not *on Sundays he sleeps, yesterday the man came* or *today I should have gone*). This means that periods included in the same dialloperiod are required to be so similar that they have lexes belonging in the same order to the same d-lexemes. The dialloperiods could conceivably be counted and numbered but their number would be very high. To count them one would have to establish some symbol meaning that a segment can be repeated a number of times that cannot be exactly determined and count only once each dialloperiod containing that symbol. Otherwise it would not be possible to reach a definite number of dialloperiods. As alloperiods are so much more restricted in number than dialloperiods, they could be more easily counted and numbered.

If it seemed appropriate to divide the sets forming the segments of dialloperiods into smaller sets (alloadverbials into dialloadverbials, allosubjects into diallosubjects etc.) then one would have to establish trialloperiods. If needed, tetralloperiod, pentalloperiods etc. could be established.

Differences between adverbials of time, place, manner etc. would not as such establish different syntagmemes but different allofuncts within the adverbialeme functeme.

It was just said about some syntagmemes that they can be n- or b-units. This goes obviously for all syntagmemes.

As has been implied above, b-syntagmemes can be considered as having variants at one level but n-syntagmemes have variants at two different levels:

(1) Each b-syntagmeme is usually a very large set of b-varisyntagms. *A man came, the girl went* etc. would be b-varisyntagms belonging to one syntagmeme; *he said it, I believed it* etc. would belong to another syntagmeme etc.

(2) Each n-syntagmeme includes n-varisyntagms in number corresponding to the b-varisyntagms of the corresponding b-syntagmeme. This means one kind of variation. Another kind of variation stems, however, from the fact that each n-varisyntagm is realized in the form of many different syntagms due to positional, free, β- and γ-variation. (Syntagms have lexes, prosodes and contours.)

In the "syntactic system" there is "economy" in a sense similar to the one often discussed in phonology. Segments, and in many cases rather long ones, are used in more than one syntagmeme. This is particularly true for clausemes and phrasemes (and parts of phrasemes). In English "noun phrases" or substantive phrases occur in several syntagmemes. In a period such as *on this beautiful morning the boy gave a good book to a very pretty girl* there are few lexes outside the substantive phrases. First a preposition phrase consists of a preposition and a substantive phrase. Then the subject is a substantive phrase. After the finite verb the direct object is a substantive phrase and the last phrase is a preposition phrase containing a substantive phrase.

In an economical description of a language sets of recurring segments can be described once with all their subsets and thereafter all the subsets will not have to be written out when the whole set is part of some longer syntagmeme. This economy is actually enormous. It explains that the periodemes with all their subsets, all "syntactic patterns" of a language, can be learnt and used in communication. A comparatively small number of high level patterns and (in addition) the "recurring subpatterns" (such as the substantive phraseme) must be learnt from experience. When learning a language in a "natural way", as in the case of a child learning his native language, these "patterns" are abstracted from periods heard.

It is here suggested that the term syntactic pattern be used in reference to the speaker's and the hearer's activity. Rather than saying that syntagms are produced and understood in relation to syntagmemes, one would say that patterns are used.

More exactly, a pattern would be equal to the description of a syntagmeme, using its distinguishing features, but leaving out an explicit statement of its subsets (and items). (In a sense a pattern would be a kind of b-unit of a unit (the syntagmeme) which from another view point may already be a b-unit.) To distinguish patterns from syntagmemes one could use the terms suggested for syntagms, put them in quotation marks and let them be preceded by the word "pattern". Patterns for periods would be "the pattern subj — pred", "the pattern subj — pred — direct object" etc. Subpatterns would be "substantive phrase", "verb phrase" etc. It is assumed that these patterns are stored in the brain and that in the speech act they are easily available to the communicators.

In the speech act the speaker constructs many of his periods according to patterns. Of these, certain have never been uttered before[94]. Either this is true for the speaker only, or it is even true for the language as a whole. There are, however, also periods which are not constructed at all as they are directly available to the speaker. As a

---

[94] How this is possible has been particularly well described by H. Paul in *Prinzipien der Sprachgeschichte*, chapter V ("Analogy").

matter of fact it must be assumed that periods which have often been repeated are stored in the brain in their "full form". Examples would be *nice weather today, isn't it?* or *I beg your pardon.*

One would assume that between "constructed" periods and the "directly available" periods there are many mixed ones. Both procedures may often be at work when sentences are produced or understood.

One may believe that individuals with poor capacity for expressing themselves use syntactic means only to a minor degree when producing periods.

In the way explained, it is not necessary to learn the enormous number of dialloperiods (trialloperiods, tetralloperiods) of a language. Periods according to patterns never heard or produced by the speaker can be understood and produced. Many complicated patterns for periods, such as patterns having many substantive phrases, each containing unusually many segments, may hardly ever be used but would immediately be recognized as possible. The pattern according to which *the extremely little, fat and redhaired boy gave this very beautiful, old and valuable book to a horribly ugly, thin and stupid girl* is formed, may never have been used or heard by some speaker of English, but it would still be immediately recognized as an acceptable, though perhaps somewhat ridiculously complicated pattern as the "over all pattern" as well as the "subpatterns" are known.

If the number of the "ultimate" most detailed patterns, or, in other words, the lowest level syntagmemes, is extremely high, this number is obviously very low in comparison to the number of the b-varisyntagms (let alone the periods of the n-varisyntagms). Even if a comparatively simple pattern such as "a subject consisting of a determiner and substantive followed by a predicate consisting of a verb" were chosen, in a language where it is applicable one would have one or a couple of determiners, any one of which could be combined with a high number of substantives, which could be combined with a high number of verbs, all of which taken together would give an extremely high number of varisyntagms[95].

The suggested classification of all periods in a language would describe the most basic syntactic facts. It would also show many of the most important relations between constructions as it would give a survey of all constructions having subject and predicate, all periods having only one clause as opposed to those having more than one, etc.

Although what has just been said may take care of the most basic facts, we have not as yet mentioned several problems arising as soon as one tries to go into more detail. Some suggestions in this regard would be:

(1) In the choice between establishing one or more syntagmemes, one could opt for one only if the main difference between the syntactic patterns under consideration were only that they can be differently expanded. The patterns for *I agree, he knows* and

---

[95] Whatever this number may be, it is finite and not infinite, cf. my *The problem of nonsense linguistics*, p. 105. Again, I should like to stress that there is no need for any mysterious "deep structure". Speakers produce sentences according to known syntagmemes or "syntactic patterns".

B. Collinder (*Noam Chomsky und die generative Grammatik*, p. 26) says about a certain syntactic construction: "Den heutigen Benutzern des Englischen steht aber diese Konstruktion sozusagen automatisch zur Verfügung, und in diesem Fall kommen sie sowohl bei der Erlernung der Sprache wie im täglichen Gebrauch ohne Transformationen und Derivationen aus." He also says (p. 27): "[...] können wir sagen, daß die sprachrichtigen Sätze nach üblichen Mustern gebildet sind."

I came may be considered as being basically the same and as belonging to the same alloperiod despite the fact that they can be expanded in different ways. They can all be described as "personal pronoun as a subject and a simple finite verb as a predicate". The first period can be expanded into *I agree with this*, the second into *he knows it*, the third into *I came here* and the kind of expansion is specific for each period. If needed, one could provide the alloperiod taking care of these three periods with three subsets called a, b, c rather than let them belong to three different alloperiods (or perhaps to one alloperiod with one dialloperiod for each).

The example *I disapprove of John's drinking*[96] is slightly different. Let us assume that this period has two interpretations although (as pointed out by B. Collinder[97]) said without context, the period is actually hardly ambiguous.

In one interpretation a possible expansion would be *I disapprove of John's horrible drinking* but not **I disapprove of John's horrible drinking beer*. In this case the present participle is "highly substantivized". Syntactically it is used in a way close to the one of many substantives: it can, among other things take an adjective as an attribute. It refers to "the activity of drinking" and has a seme belonging to the alloseme "consume alcoholic liquor". (The highly substantivized present participle selects this alloseme of this verb.)

In another interpretation a possible expansion would be *I disapprove of John's drinking beer*. In this case the present participle is "less highly substantivized". It retains e.g. the capacity of the verb *drink* for having a direct object. It refers to "the act of drinking, possibly just once".

It is obvious that many other verbs can be (a) highly, (b) less highly substantivized. This is a fact to be described in syntax. It is, however, suggested again that this fact should not give rise to different syntagmemes but just to special subsets within the same syntagmeme.

It should perhaps be noted here (although similar cases are mentioned above, p. 64) that syntagms may have the same words in the same order and still be syntactically very different. *Flying planes (can be dangerous)*[98] is a syntagm belonging to one syntagmeme if *planes* is direct object to the verb and a syntagm belonging to another syntagmeme if *flying* is an attribute to the following head.

It is suggested that different allofuncts alone do not establish different syntagmemes (cf. above, p. 69), or, in other words, that if two syntagms have functs belonging to different allofuncts they can still be included in the same syntagmeme if the allofuncts in both cases belong, in the same order, to the same functemes[99]. This would mean that both interpretations of *the shooting of the hunters*[100] would belong to the same syntagmeme but to different "special subsets"[101]. In both interpretations

---

[96] Cf. N. Chomsky, *Current Issues in Linguistic Theory*, p. 47–50.
[97] *Op. cit.*, p. 14–15.
[98] Cf. N. Chomsky, *Syntactic Structures*, p. 87; *Current Issues in Linguistic Theory*, p. 42.
[99] According to this suggestion *John is easy to please* and *John is eager to please* would perhaps be included in the same syntagmeme, had it not been for the different "constituent structure" assumed above (p. 65).
[100] Cf. N. Chomsky, *Syntactic Structures*, p. 88.
[101] In a non-technical way a paraphrase can make things clear to a beginner: In one interpretation, the hunters shot something (most likely an animal) or, perhaps (which is somewhat different), the hunters carried out a (possibly wild and purposeless) shooting. In the other interpretation, the hunters are shot.

of the hunters a preposition phrase is functioning as an attribute. It is, however, assumed that the attributeme functeme (which would be something like "saying something about the substantive, or "substantivized" word, which is the head") has different allofuncts.

In the first interpretation the syntagm *of the hunters* has the funct "agent" belonging to the allofunct "agent" (within the attributeme functeme). (This function is also the one of many subjects.) In this case the meaning of *of* is such that it belongs to an alloseme "by" or "through the action of". (No wonder that it is also possible to say *the shooting by the hunters*.)

In the second interpretation the allofunct which includes the funct of *of the hunters* is "target" (which is also the main function of direct objects). In this case the meaning of *of* is such that it belongs to an alloseme "directed against". The hunters are the target of the action expressed by the substantivized present participle.

It could be noted that, said without context, there does not normally seem to be any signal showing which interpretation to give to *flying planes can be dangerous, I disapprove of John's drinking* and *the shooting of the hunters*. It is, however, possible that one can use special contours (see below, p. 111–112) — certain kinds of emphasis — in such a way that a listener has some chance of understanding which interpretation is meant.

The analysis of *the picture was painted by a new technique* and *the picture was painted by a real artist*[102] is similar to the one just given. In both periods the phrase beginning with *by* is an adverbial. Adverbials in general would have the function of "adding to the head, which is mostly a verb, an adjective or an adverb, some circumstance". The adverbialeme functeme has the allofuncts "manner", "agent", "time", "place" etc. In the first example *by* has a seme belonging to the alloseme "by the use of" and the adverbial is of manner. In the second example the alloseme is "through the action of" and the adverbial is an agent adverbial. (There is interselection between the seme of the first *by* and the seme of *technique* as this latter seme belongs to some set of sememes which have the common component 'manner'. There is interselection also between the seme of the second *by* and its head, *artist*, which has a seme belonging to some set of sememes having the common component 'capable of acting, working, producing an effect' or something comparable.)

Giving account of the various syntagmemes of a language, after having "named" them by the use of numbers as indices, one can use devices partly similar to those suggested above (p. 60–61) for the description of syntagms.

Let us assume for convenience that the language under consideration has one periodeme, which has three alloperiods. These alloperiods could be (1) "verb in imperative" (as *come!*), (2) "subject — verb as predicate" and (3) "subject — verb as part of the predicate — direct object as part of the predicate". To describe these facts:

(1) Plain words can be used: There is one periodeme and it has three alloperiods.
(2) A set-theoretical formula can be used as a kind of abbreviation:
periodeme = {alloperiod$_1$, ..., alloperiod$_3$}
(3) A box diagram can be used:

periodeme		
alloperiod$_1$	alloperiod$_2$	alloperiod$_3$

---
[102] Cf. N. Chomsky, *Syntactic Structures*, p. 89–90.

(4) A tree can provide the same information as the box diagram:

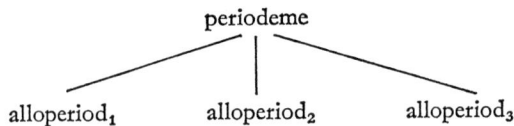

The term syntagmeme can be abbreviated as Synt.

b-syntagmeme = {b-varisyntagm$_1$, ..., b-varisyntagm$_n$}
b-syntagmeme = {b-allosyntagm$_1$, ..., b-allosyntagm$_n$}
b-allosyntagm = {b-diallosyntagm$_1$, ..., b-diallosyntagm$_n$}
b-allosyntagm = {b-varisyntagm$_1$, ..., b-varisyntagm$_n$}
n-syntagmeme = {n-varisyntagm$_1$, ..., n-varisyntagm$_n$}
n-syntagmeme = {syntagm$_1$, ..., syntagm$_n$}
n-syntagmeme = {n-allosyntagm$_1$, ..., n-allosyntagm$_n$}
n-allosyntagm = {n-diallosyntagm$_1$, ..., n-diallosyntagm$_n$}
n-allosyntagm = {n-varisyntagm$_1$, ..., n-varisyntagm$_n$}
n-allosyntagm = {syntagm$_1$, ..., syntagm$_n$}
n-varisyntagm = {syntagm$_1$, ..., syntagm$_n$}

7. *Units : syntagmememes.* It is of interest to establish sets of syntagmemes, i.e. *syntagmememes*. Of these the following three are among the most important:

(1) *Nexsyntagmememe.* All syntagms having a subject and a predicate can be called nexsyntagms. These can be grouped into *nexsyntagmemes.* E.g. *I came, he left* etc. would belong to one (which could be allonex$_1$); *the boy came, the girl left* etc. to another such syntagmeme (which could be allonex$_2$). All nexsyntagmemes would form the nexsyntagmememe.

(2) *Hypotactical syntagmememe.* All syntagms having a head and a complement can be called *hypotactical.* These can be grouped into syntagmemes. E.g. *very often, quite recently* etc. would belong to one such syntagmeme and *beautiful garden, old man* etc. to another. All hypotactical syntagmemes would form the *hypotactical syntagmememe*.

(3) *Paratactical syntagmememe.* One segment is sometimes added to another segment by means of some function word, or just by juxtaposition, in such a way that none of them is head or complement. This is the case in co-ordination[103]: *the boy and the girl.* Even more than two segments can be co-ordinated: *the boy, the girl and the woman.* It is obvious that this kind of syntagms can be grouped into syntagmemes, which can be grouped into the *paratactical syntagmememe*[104].

There are, however, several other kinds of syntagmememes. For instance all "active" clauses could form the "active clauseme" opposed to all "passive" clauses forming the "passive clauseme".

As each of these particular clausemes groups together certain (but not all) subsets (being syntagmemes) of the overall, "basic" clausemes, it would be convenient to consider them as syntagmememes.

---

[103] Co-ordination is here considered to be a subdivision within the paratactical constructions.
[104] Some of the most basic parts of the preceding pages have already been explained in *Linguistische Einheiten*, p. 44–51, and in "On linguistic terminology".

It should be noted that all syntagmememes just mentioned are sets which are established on the basis of the overall, "basic" classification of all syntagmemes of a language.

8. *Affiliation. Definition*: Two (or more) syntagms (varisyntagms), syntagmemes or syntagmememes are *affiliated* if they have some functional feature(s) in common or if they are different in some given functional feature(s) in such a way that the difference relates them in some relevant way (positive versus negative, statement versus question etc.). The features forming the basis for establishing an affiliation may themselves be called affiliated.

We shall first consider "active" clauses together with affiliated "passive" clauses.

These active clauses have typically:

(1) a subject with the funct subject (agent)[105],
(2) a finite transitive verb in "active" and
(3) a direct object with the funct direct object (target).

The passive clauses have:

(1) a subject with the funct subject (target),
(2) a finite transitive verb in "passive" and
(3) an adverbial with the funct adverbial (agent).

As the active clauses are affiliated with the passive clauses one can also say that the active and the passive clauseme are affiliated. They have important common or, at least, similar segments. Both have the functions 'agent' and 'target' and also a verb expressing an action (or similar). The order in which these three common elements are provided is here considered to be immaterial. (Using transformations or a "deep structure" and derivations to show the relation between "active" and "passive" just adds unnecessary complications[106].) Further explanations would state that in "active" the subject has the agent function but in "passive" this function is taken over by the adverbial; in "active" the direct object has the target function and in "passive" the subject has this function; the verb is in "active" in the first case and in "passive" in the second case.

One may consider in detail the syntagmemes which are hierarchically between the active syntagms and the active syntagmememe and between the passive syntagms and the passive syntagmememe.

Any active syntagmeme, allosyntagm, diallosyntagm etc., i.e. any subset of the active clauseme such as the one to which *the boy hit the girl* and *the man saw the woman* belong, is affiliated with any passive syntagmeme, allosyntagm, diallosyntagm etc., i.e. any subset of the passive clauseme such as the one to which *he was hit by a terribly strong man* and *she was seen by an extremely beautiful woman* belong. At the level of the syntagms the clause (variclause) *the boy hit the girl* is affiliated with *he was hit by a terribly strong man*.

---

[105] Using a convention according to which on the "basic function" "the additional function" (see above, p. 66) follows in brackets.
[106] Even if one believes that transformations are of little importance in the description of a language, this does not imply that it may not be acceptable, and efficient, to let students transform "active" into "passive" (in such languages as German or Latin) or "positive" sentences into "negative" sentences (in a language such as English) in language learning drills.

It is possible to think that affiliation is graded. The more similar the comparable segments would be the higher would be the degree of affiliation. If some active syntagmeme would include subjects such as *the little girl, the old man* etc. (but not *he* or *the very old man*) and if some passive syntagmeme would include "agents" such as *the little girl, the old man* etc. this would raise the degree of affiliation. Considering syntagms (varisyntagms), although (as has just been mentioned) *the boy hit the girl* is affiliated with *he was hit by the terribly strong man*, *the boy hit the girl* and *the man was hit by the girl* are affiliated to a higher degree.

At the highest possible degree of affiliation between syntagms (varisyntagms) it may occur that the total meaning (see above, p. 63) of the two (or more) variperiods is *roughly* the same: *the boy hit the girl* and *the girl was hit by the boy*. In such cases also semantic affiliation occurs.

Labelled two-way arrows can be used to show affiliation and the segments possessing the similarities can be indicated by numbered brackets. At the level of syntagms (varisyntagms) one example could be:

1 (*the boy*) 2 (*hit*) 3 (*the girl*) ← act. — affil. — pass. → 3 (*the girl*) 2 (*was hit*) 1 (*by the boy*)

At the level of syntagmemes one example would be (if written in the somewhat simplified form of a "pattern"):

subj. (1 agent) — 2 act. verb — direct obj. (3 target) ← act. — affil. — pass. → subj (3 target) — 2 pass. verb — adv. (1 agent)

N. Chomsky provides various sets of interesting examples of the kind which here is called affiliated. In *Aspects of the Theory of Syntax*[107] we are given *for us to please John is difficult, it is difficult for us to please John, to please John is difficult for us, John is difficult for us to please*.

These four have almost the same total meaning and are syntactically affiliated. (The difference in meaning would be that different segments are focussed in each case.) For the sake of the argument let us simplify our task and deal with only two of these four periods. The affiliation could be shown as: *it* 1 (*is*) 2 (*difficult*) 3 (*for us*) 4 (*to please*) 5 (*John*) ← affil. → 4 (*to please*) 5 (*John*) 1 (*is*) 2 (*difficult*) 3 (*for us*).

Such formulae, although abbreviated and far from explicit, explain in a simpler and clearer way relations which also are thought to be shown to be derivations from "underlying abstractions".

However, the interest of explaining affiliation between such syntagms (varisyntagms) is obviously subordinated to the more general interest of explaining affiliation between syntagmemes. The four periods quoted would belong to four different syntagmemes and the affiliation between these four would have to be described. The affiliation between the two syntagmemes to which the two syntagms (varisyntagms) belong for which an affiliation formula has just been given would be:

it 1 (alloverb$_a$) 2 (alloadjective$_a$) 3 (*for* followed by the substantive allophrase$_a$) 4 (*to* followed by the transitive alloverb) 5 (substantive allophrase$_a$) ← affil. → 4 5 1 2 3.

---

[107] P. 125. See also *Current Issues in Linguistic Theory*, p. 34.

In this case it has been possible to abbreviate to the right of the two-way arrow: a sequence of figures is enough. Even to the left of the two-way arrow several possible explanations are left out[108].

If everything has been well explained in the text a still more abstract formula can be used:

1 2 3 4 5 ← affil. → 4 5 1 2 3

In the definition above it was mentioned that being "different in some given functional feature(s)" could be the basis for affiliation. One may think of cases such as "positive" clauses against "negative" clauses, which obviously could also be shown in affiliation formulae (although we shall not attempt to show one here).

If we abbreviate *affiliated* as a-, we can write:

a-syntagmememe = {a-syntagmeme$_1$, ..., a-syntagmeme$_n$}
a-syntagmeme   = {a-varisyntagm$_1$, ..., a-varisyntagm$_n$}
a-varisyntagm   = {a-syntagm$_1$, ..., a-syntagm$_n$}

An affiliated syntagmememe is, for instance, the "active syntagmememe" (including all active syntagmemes), which together with the "passive syntagmememe" forms a particular "set of a-syntagmememes".

9. *Interselection. Definition*: In a general way it will be said that syntactic functional units (or items)[109] and semantic units (or items) interselect each other if they can be related in some syntactically or semantically relevant way[110].

Sometimes the expression units (items) of the interselected units (items) signal overtly the interselection (see below, agreement) but often there is no overt signal.

It is suggested that, metaphorically, semantics is thought of as being at a higher level than syntax (although, for our purpose, it could equally well have been put at a lower level). These two levels are the basis for the terms (a) "horizontal", (b) "vertical" and (c) "diagonal" used below.

---

[108] *It* is an "extra" anticipatory subject.
"Alloverb$_a$" means finite forms of a special set of verbs (*be, become* etc.) as predicate.
"Alloadjective$_a$" means a set of adjectives such as *easy, difficult* etc. for which one could most probably find one or a couple of common semantic components such that they could define the set. The alloadjective is subject complement.
"*For* followed by the substantive allophrase$_a$" functions as adverbial. By "substantive allophrase$_a$" is meant a subset of all substantives including *me, the boy, the charming man, the very charming women* etc. The "transitive alloverb" means the set of all transitive verbs. The substantive allophrase$_a$ following the transitive alloverb is a direct object to the preceding alloverb.
To followed by the transitive alloverb and the direct object form together the subject.
[109] Not expression units (items).
[110] As is well known L. Hjelmslev distinguishes between selection (specification) (*a* does not presuppose *b* but *a* is presupposed by *b*), solidarity (complementarity) (*a* and *b* presuppose each other) and combination (autonomy) (*a* and *b* do not presuppose each other). (Cf. p. XIV–XXI of E. Fischer-Jørgensen's Introduction to H. J. Uldall, *Outline of Glossematics*, Travaux du Cercle Linguistique de Copenhague. 2nd ed., 1967).
Similar distinctions could establish subdivisions within our general notion of interselection but we have not elaborated on this point.
As our account is supposed to be essentially "neutral" in relation to encoder and decoder (see above, p. VI), we will not consider here the fact that sometimes it is possible to assume that some given item is in the encoder's mind before some other item or that the decoder interprets one item first and uses the knowledge of it at the decoding of some other item.

The possible relations can be shown as follows:

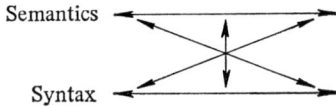

(a) If only syntax (or only semantics) is involved the interselection can only be *horizontal*, which means that the units (items) in interselection follow each other at the same level.

The interselection between the functions of the two *-us* in the Latin syntagm *dominus bonus* (a good master) is *horizontal* and overt. The same is to be said about *the boy eats* (sing.) or *the boys eat* (plur.). In each of these two syntagms there is interselection between the singular and plural functions of the substantive and the verb.

In "ambiguous" cases one would say that for at least one of the parts in interselection one has a choice between at least two units (items). This is the case of *flying planes can be dangerous* where one could speak of "multiple interselection". To this written sentence correspond two different variperiods, which have syntactically different subjects in interselection with the same predicate. The use of either *is* or *are* instead of *can*[111] provides two syntagms each showing the much more frequent "simple" interselection.

(b) Interselection is *vertical* if both semantic and syntactic levels are involved and if both the semantic and the syntactic unit (item) involved are related to the same expression segment (unit or item).

In the example *this picture was painted by a real artist* (which has been explained in some detail above, p. 73) there is interselection between the seme of *artist* and the agent funct. If *a new technique* is substituted for *a real artist*, a different kind of interselection occurs which does not involve agent. However, in both cases the interselection is vertical.

(c) Interselection is *diagonal* if both semantic and syntactic levels are involved and if the semantic and the syntactic unit (item) involved do not belong to the same expression segment.

The interselection is *descending diagonal* if the semantic unit (item) precedes the syntactic unit (item). (The relation can be thought of as being between a point "to the left" at the higher semantic level and a point "to the right" at the lower syntactic level.)

In English a rather short list of verbs with a semantic component 'wish', 'want' or such like, or being at least capable of having in certain contexts such a component, can take a subjunctive as in *I recommend (suggest etc.) that he be appointed*.

French is similar: *Je veux (je désire, j'exige etc.) qu'il vienne*. (The number of verbs containing a component 'wish' or 'want' and taking the subjunctive is much higher in French. However, as *all* verbs with similar semes take the subjunctive they are better defined and there is less need for presenting the whole list. There is also less need for the speakers to store the list in their minds.)

---

[111] N. Chomsky says in his review of B. F. Skinner, *Verbal Behavior*: "*Struggling artists can be a nuisance* has the same frame as *marking papers can be a nuisance*, but is quite different in sentence structure, as can be seen by replacing *can be* by *is* or *are* in both cases." (P. 574 of reprint in *The Structure of Language*, ed. J. A. Fodor and J. J. Katz. The review was first published in Language **35**, 1959. See also p. 237 of *The Structure of Language*.)

The interselection is *ascending diagonal* if the syntactic unit (item) precedes the semantic unit (item). Because of the meaning of the rest of the period *flying gliders* would be syntactically different in *flying gliders could be made a useful part of the training of pilots* and in *flying gliders could be a beautiful sight for the spectators at the airshow*.

It does not seem correct to say that given syntagmemes and given prosodemes interselect each other as particular prosodemes are part of the complete description of particular syntagmemes.

We have already assumed (p. 62) that it is possible that some contouremes disambiguate an "ambiguous" construction. There might be particular ways of pronouncing *the shooting of the hunters* or *flying planes* such that the listener understands what is meant. This means that there may be interselection between contouremes (contours) and syntagmeme functemes (syntagm functs).

In a somewhat complicated way idiolectal, sociolectal and dialectal characteristics of speakers may be said to enter interselections. In an act of communication where more than one variety of a language is involved a communicator may use knowledge of the other variety to interpret a construction which would have been less clear, perhaps ambiguous, in his own variety.

It is possible to establish interselection between personal characteristics outside language and syntactic (or semantic) facts although this kind of interselection is not very efficient when used in communication. If it is known about somebody that he is a keen pilot and also that he thinks flying is very dangerous, then one would be inclined to give one interpretation only to *flying planes can be dangerous* said by this particular person. This kind of interselection could be established not only for particular speakers but also for sociolectal or dialectal groups of speakers.

The context outside given periods may enter interselections with segments inside these periods. If somebody has just explained how the hunters had been shooting all night so that it had been impossible to sleep, and if he ends his utterance with *yes, the shooting of the hunters was terrible* there cannot be any doubt about the meaning of his words.

There is also interselection where knowledge of the situation is relevant. If at an air show a plane has flown too low and removed the floral decorations from a distinguished lady visitor's hat, an utterance *flying planes can be dangerous* would be interpreted in one rather than in the other of the two possible ways.

10. *Units: semi-syntagmemes. Items: semi-syntagms*. If the quasi-syntagmemes (quasi-syntagms) described below are thought to be something between "fully grammatical" syntagmemes (syntagms) and stretches of words in just some arbitrary order, they will be semi-units (semi-items) in addition to being quasi-units (quasi-items).

11. *Units: quasi-syntagmemes. Items: quasi-syntagms*. The syntactic constructions usually studied are "well-formed". The linguist either invents his examples and intends them to be "grammatically acceptable" (although it may occur that he is mistaken in the sense that an example thought to be acceptable is not really so, or an example said to be unacceptable actually is acceptable). Or the linguist obtains his examples from a corpus which is usually a normal written text where all constructions

are "grammatically acceptable", or at least meant to be so. The corpus can also consist of notations of tape recordings[112].

Assuming that we can establish all "well-formed" constructions, the other constructions in actual use could be called quasi-syntagms or semi-syntagms. In the first instance these terms should refer to all those "incoherent", anacoluthic or interrupted syntagms which are much more usual in spoken texts than one may imagine. They are often not felt as ill-formed and they may be as efficient in communication as well-formed constructions. It can even be assumed that they have particular functions which should be studied and determined. It is, however, noticeable that quasi-syntagms (semi-syntagms) cannot be found with certainty and to any extent by the linguist searching in his own mind but must be studied in a corpus consisting of texts written down from tape recordings of natural speech.

It is obvious that a spoken sentence should not be called ill-formed just because it has a form which would not be accepted as well-formed in a written text.

In one of my publications one finds comparatively early (1953) two texts containing real spoken language[113]. As the informants have little or no schooling they have possibly a more "incoherent syntax" than more cultivated people but one would imagine that also the most cultivated person would sometimes use constructions similar to theirs.

A combination of quasi-lexemes (-lexes) or semi-lexemes (-lexes) (see above, p. 54) would form quasi-syntagmemes (-syntagms) of a different kind.

Both semi- and quasi-syntagmemes can be thought of as b- and n-units.

12. *Units: pseudo-syntagmemes. Items: pseudo-syntagms.* The usual syntactic analysis is based on clear, unemotional speech (which is one of the range of possibilities of the β-level). The resulting syntagms are pronounced and heard as groups of lexes. Under given β-conditions the lexes are grouped in a way that does not correspond with the usual syntagms of the sentence. These groups of lexes can be called *pseudo-syntagms*.

Pseudo-syntagms can split up the basic syntagms (pronounced and heard in most cases). They can also join together lexes usually belonging to separate syntagms, i.e. given syntactic means, which usually group together the lexes of a given syntagm, are used by the speaker to group this syntagm and one or more adjacent syntagms into a

---

[112] For most purposes it would be good if the linguist used both his own knowledge and a corpus. On the one hand it does not seem possible to make one's mind produce all interesting material relevant to a particular problem. On the other hand it is practically impossible to enlarge the corpus to the point where all interesting examples would have been found. Each of these techniques will leave gaps in the description which will sometimes be easily filled by also using the other technique.

[113] See *Étude de phonétique auditive sur les parlers de l'Algarve* (Uppsala 1953), p. 56–57 and 110–112.
In "Inquéritos Linguísticos II" (Revista de Portugal, Série A, vol. 26, 1961, p. 9–32, I said: (p. 27) "Os textos seguidos anotados segundo o método indirecto que já foram publicados revelam coisas interessantes. O que salta mais aos olhos são as repetições, as interrupções, as frases que começam de uma maneira e acabam de outra, as partes dificilmente compreensíveis. É um facto interessante e espantoso, o de que quem participa directamente na conversação registada repara muito pouco nestes detalhes. Só os descobrimos usando a anotação indirecta. O que quer fazer um estudo de sintaxe original só tem que utilizar o método indirecto. Uma multitude de problemas interessantes espera-o."
This same passage is to be found on p. 45–46 of the Swedish translation of the paper, "Dialektologiska undersökningar" (Nordisk tidsskrift for tale og stemme 24, 1964, p. 27–51).

"long" pseudo-syntagm. An example of this possibility is offered by a tape recording that I made of a French speaker some years ago. The three consecutive periods *Il est trop petit. Ce n'est pas pour lui. C'est pour les grandes personnes* are usually pronounced so that the end of each period is clearly indicated (i.e. mainly through falling pitch) but the speaker in question grouped the three periods into one pseudo-period. This was indicated i.a. by rising pitch at the end of the first two periods. The result is a stylistic (β-)effect: The three periods become closely tied together. The first two periods enumerate two closely related facts and the third closely related fact of the third period is added in a particularly conclusive way.

Syntagms are characterized by syntagm prosodes belonging to syntagmeme prosodemes but the pseudo-prosodes of pseudo-syntagms do not correspond to such prosodemes.

Pseudo-syntagms relatable to the same syntagmemes form *pseudo-syntagmemes*. If the French pseudo-period just mentioned had been repeated the resultant pseudo-periods would have belonged to the same pseudo-unit (a pseudo-varisyntagm)[114].

13. *Units : meta-syntagmemes. Items : meta-syntagms*. When laymen or linguists speak about language, or even sometimes in a normal situation of communication, syntagms may be "quoted" or otherwise said outside their usual context. These may be *meta-syntagms*. Meta-syntagms, on the one hand, retain the description of their syntactic structure which they had in the original period, but, on the other hand, as a whole they fulfil some syntactic function in the period within which they are quoted.

If a speaker says: *I do it on occasions*. A listener may ask back: *did you say "on occasions"*? In this example the adverbial *on occasions* of the first period, when quoted in the second period, is as a whole a direct object. The use of the expression "as a whole" implies that it is not meaningful to try to divide up the direct object into the kind of segments that usually form a syntagm. The only segment which is directly a segment of the direct object is the whole adverbial. Consequently in meta-use the distribution of a syntagm is often not the usual one. Within a period it functions, as other meta-items, as a substantive. Like other meta-items it is characterized by a clear, "detached" pronunciation (a β-feature).

In phonetic experiments, instead of reading lists of "isolated words"[115] a test person may say the words as periods or within "a frame" as part of a period[116]. Meta-syntagms relatable to the same "original syntagm" (in the case of "quotations") or, in general, "having the same words" and "being the same construction" form a meta-varisyntagm. All meta-syntagms "*on occasions*" would form the meta-varisyntagm "*on occasions*". Similarly constructed meta-varisyntagms would form a meta-syntag-

---

[114] Cf. p. 412–413 of my paper "Pseudo-units in phonetics" (Proceedings of the Sixth International Congress of Phonetic Sciences, Prague 1967, p. 411–413. Prague 1970).

[115] In order to avoid reading a long list of "isolated" words I have used for the study of phonetic problems the technique of having the words on small pieces of paper, asking the question "What is on the paper?", and then reading the word as an answer. The lex is thus a period. (See p. 11 of "Sur la durée des phonèmes en suédois", Revista do Laboratório de Fonética Experimental da Faculdade de Letras da Universidade de Coimbra 1, 1952, p. 9–27).

[116] Others have used "test sentences" containing the word(s) to be studied. In "Spectrographic Study of Vowel Reduction" (The Journal of the Acoustical Society of America **35**, 1963, p. 1773–1781) B. Lindblom puts the words to be investigated in the frames *så är det ...* or *... är det så* (of which the second unfortunately does not have any understandable meaning while the first seems to mean: *now it* [= the word?] *is ...*).

meme. (If they were needed, one could establish meta-syntagmememes and, perhaps, sets of meta-syntagmememes.)

Meta-syntagmemes, as well as pseudo-syntagmemes, are interesting as n-units rather than as b-units, i.e. it would be of particular interest to study in detail their phonetic properties.

14. *Paradigmatics.* Establishing syntagms by comparison and grouping them together in sets (syntagmememes, syntagmemes, allosyntagms etc.) are operations within paradigmatics. The sets themselves are basically paradigmatic ones in the sense that syntagms with similar distribution and function are grouped together although distinctions according to syntagmatic structure are also taken into account.

Finding syntagm functs and syntagmeme functemes is also essentially within paradigmatics.

15. *Syntagmatics.* The study of the structure of syntagms and syntagm sets in terms of their segments and the study of how syntagms and syntagm sets are combined are obviously syntagmatic.

The combinability of syntagm functs and of syntagmeme functemes is also a syntagmatic problem.

16.1. *Units: glotto-, dia-, socio- and idiosyntagmemes. Items: items thereof.* It is clear that glottosyntagms are the syntagms of a glottolect (language), diasyntagms are those of a dialect, sociosyntagms those of a sociolect and idiosyntagms those of an idiolect. Grouping various kinds of syntagms into glotto-, dia-, socio- and idiosyntagmemes is a possible task for linguistics although one usually describes only one particular sociolect of a dialect or perhaps one particular dialect with some indications of sociolectal variation within it.

As far as different dialects (and sociolects) have the "same" syntagmemes, perhaps even with the "same" functemes, there is no real problem. In this case syntagmemes from different dialects are easily grouped together so as to form glottosyntagmemes. However, some dialects may have more or fewer syntagmemes than others. If so, one would attribute to the glottolect all the kinds of syntagmemes found in all dialects. Thus the glottolect would probably have more different glottosyntagmemes than any particular dialect has diasyntagmemes. Some given glottolect could have a glottoperiodeme$_1$ having as subsets the diaperiodemes of all the dialects: diaperiodeme$_1$ of the first dialect, diaperiodeme$_1$ of the second dialect etc. Glottoperiodeme$_2$ could have subsets in only some dialects (and be ∅ in the others). Similar remarks could be made about glottoalloperiods, glottodialloperiods etc., glottosubjectemes, glottopredicatemes etc.

All this could be described without much attention being given to functemes. If, however, these units were also studied in detail, one could provide all syntagmemes with their exact functemes and then establish to which extent corresponding syntagmemes in different dialects have, or have not, corresponding functemes. Have, for instance, all diasubjectemes of some given glottosubjecteme similar, or different, functemes? This would provide a possibility of grouping together all syntagmemes (whether similar or not) which have corresponding functions.

Mutatis mutandis, what has just been said about diasyntagmemes can be said about sociosyntagmemes if they are to be related to diasyntagmemes and about idiosyntagmemes if they are to be related to sociosyntagmemes.

It would seem that in many languages the syntax is not so different in various dialects and sociolects. Also, comparing individuals, one would possibly find an extensive "central" part more or less common to all of them. Comparative statements could therefore concentrate on the differences and, in addition, specify that all other aspects follow the normal. (Is this true to a higher or lower degree in morphology and phonetics?)

On the basis of these considerations one may establish *sy-glottosyntagmemes* and *f-glottosyntagmemes*.

16.2. *Sy-glottosyntagmemes*. If in different dialects syntagmemes (syntactic constructions) have as segments corresponding word classes in the same order and have the same immediate constituent structure, they may be considered as syntagmemically corresponding diasyntagmemes or corresponding sy-diasyntagmemes. Such diasyntagmemes would most often have corresponding functemes (functions) or be homofunctemic, as dialects of the same language seem usually to be syntactically rather similar. They may, however, be different or partly different in function, or in other words be completely or partly heterofunctemic. Two English dialects may both have a diasyntagmeme to which syntagms such as *is he?* belong. With the same functeme (function), the one of being a question, in both dialects, the two diasyntagmemes would be homofunctemic.

Definition: Corresponding sy-diasyntagmemes form an *sy-glottosyntagmeme*. Dialects will probably have some syntagmemes which do not exist in all other dialects of the language. Thus, there will be more glottosyntagmemes than there are diasyntagmemes in any particular dialect, and dialects may possess ø-diasyntagmemes.

16.3. *F-glottosyntagmemes*. It is also of interest to consider which diasyntagmemes express some given syntactic function.

Definition: Diasyntagmemes (which may be syntagmemically corresponding or not) which express some given f-glottofuncteme (see below 17.3.) form an *f-glottosyntagmeme*. (Note that under 16.2.—16.3. part correspondences have not been considered.)

17.1. *Units: syntagmemic glotto-, dia-, socio- and idiofunctemes. Items: items thereof.* It is clear that glottofuncts are the functs of a glottolect (language), diafuncts are those of a dialect, sociofuncts those of a sociolect and idiofuncts those of an idiolect.

Basing oneself on principles explained in the preceding paragraph (16) one could attempt to group functs together so as to form idio-, socio-, dia- and glottofunctemes. One would have to establish enough glottofunctemes and glottoallofuncts in the glottolect for all dia- and sociofunctemes and allofuncts to be covered. This procedure could involve considerable difficulties and it is too early to see all its implications.

It is, however, clear that one can start from the glottofunctemes and glottoallofuncts and establish which exist or do not exist in the different dialects and sociolects of a language, or in what way these functemes and allofuncts are expressed (in syntagmemes).

As an example, some language could have a dialect$_1$ with an alloperiod$_1$ "subj. — pred." and an alloperiod$_2$ "pred. — subj.". A dialect$_2$ of this language could have the same alloperiods and, in addition, an alloperiod$_3$ "interjection adverb — subj. — pred.".

Let us assume that alloperiod$_1$ has the same functeme ('statement') in both dialects and that alloperiod$_2$ has a functeme 'question' in dialect$_1$ and that this alloperiod has two functemes, 'question' and 'interjection' in dialect$_2$ (as in English *is he beautiful*). Starting from the functional side, the glottofuncteme 'statement' has a diafuncteme in each dialect (and the expression is the same in both dialects). The glottofuncteme 'question' has a diafuncteme in each dialect although the expression is somewhat different in the sense that in dialect$_1$, diaalloperiod$_2$ is unambiguously question but in dialect$_2$ diaalloperiod$_2$ is question or interjection. If we assume that two kinds of somewhat different 'interjections' are involved (one could be stronger and one weaker), there would be a glottofuncteme 'interjection' with glottoallofunct$_1$ and glottoallofunct$_2$. Dialect$_2$ would have diafuncteme 'interjection' with two diaallofuncts. This glottofuncteme would be represented by $\emptyset$ in dialect$_1$,[117].

17.2. *Syntagmemic sy-glottofunctemes.* It is certainly of interest to consider which diafunctemes are expressed by a given syntactic construction.

Definition: Syntagmemic diafunctemes which are expressed by some given sy-glottosyntagmeme form a *syntagmemic sy-glottofuncteme*.

17.3. *Syntagmemic f-glottofunctemes.* An sy-glottosyntagmeme may be mono- or polyfunctemic. Corresponding syntagmeme functemes can be called corresponding diafunctemes of syntagmemes. Corresponding diafunctemes may be homosyntagmemic (if they have corresponding syntagmemes) and heterosyntagmemic (if they have non-corresponding syntagmemes).

If an imagined language has two dialects and if in each there is a diafuncteme 'question' and if the first dialect has one syntagmeme for question (*is he?*) and if the other dialect has another syntagmeme for question (*does he be?*) this language has corresponding diafunctemes 'question' which are heterosyntagmemic.

Definition: Corresponding syntagmemic diafunctemes form a *syntagmemic f-glottofuncteme*. (The prefix f- means that the functeme is established on purely functemic grounds.)

An f-glottofuncteme may be mono- or polysyntagmemic.

(Note that in the definitions of 17.2. and 17.3. part correspondences have not been taken into account.)

18. *Inventory.* An inventory of syntagms is any collection of syntagms. It could be the syntagms of a tape recording to be notated by the linguist with the purpose of using them in a study of spoken syntax.

The complete (or near complete) inventory of syntagmemes of a language could be established. Although this may be a painstaking work, it can certainly be carried out within a reasonable amount of time. (While being perhaps very high in all languages, the number of syntagmemes is in no language infinite.)

19. *Discovery procedures.* To a great extent the linguist does not use any other discovery procedure than searching in his own knowledge of the syntactic domain of the language under study. Doing this he finds directly the description which he thinks appropriate. Fortunately in a great many cases other linguists agree about basic facts. ("This is the subject". "This is the direct object". Etc.)

---

[117] One would have to assume that in dialect$_1$ one never felt the need for using 'interjections' (which is unlikely) or that 'interjections' were expressed by non-syntactic means.

For certain problems some tests may be of use: dividing, expansion, identity, similarity and compression substitutions (see above p. 67–68), as well as tests of other kinds.

Some studies have tested informants as to their views on syntactic problems. Thus one has treated the problem of determining the acceptability of different syntactic facts[118]. More studies of this kind would seem desirable.

1.1.7. Sememes

0. Sememes, allosemes and semes, and components of these are the most important part of what is usually called semantics. They belong to the study of meaning in the narrow sense of the term. In a wider sense of the term, meaning can include syntactic functions, the effect of some prosodemes and prosodes (see above p. 64), β-facts and γ-facts (because how something is said as well as idiolect, sociolect and dialect mean something to the listener). Even the context of situation, when in interselection with language facts, contributes to meaning.

Laymen, and sometimes even experts, are inclined to think that words (obviously in the sense of units of the expression side of a language) stand directly for things, actions, qualities, relationships etc. which exist in a universal way. As soon as one has realized that each language has a content side which is to a great extent "arbitrary" and specific for that language this assumption becomes untenable. Saussure[119], among others, has already warned against this kind of mistake. Not only do meaning units of different languages have different relations to the "things" (the "referents") but also the same language can usually say the same "thing" in different ways. If the name of somebody's husband is *John*, in some context expressions such as *John, her husband, her spouse, her old man* may refer to the same person but in a linguistic description these expressions are different whether the content side or the expression side is considered.

It is clear that the content side must be carefully studied for each language. As, however, the meanings of a language certainly refer to things, actions, qualities, relationships etc., one would ideally relate the whole content side to things, actions, qualities, relationships etc. which would have to be described in a way not specific to any natural language. In other words the "referents" would have to be described in a universal way. (The term content side is here meant to include the meanings of α- and β-units but exclude γ-facts.)

The idea of a universal meaning system seems attractive (cf. above, p. VI). Theoretically (if not practically) all languages could be tied up to such a system and a translation, which could be automatic (more or less), from one language into another language could go over the universal system.

In this context it may be of interest to note that a good translator seems to take the following steps: (a) read or hear something in one language, (b) extract the

---

[118] Cf. Quirk, R. and Svartvik, J., *Investigating linguistic acceptability*. The Hague 1966. Cf. review by A. A. Hill in Language 45, 1969, p. 622—624.
[119] *Cours de linguistique générale*, p. 98: "Le signe linguistique unit non une chose et un nom, mais un concept et une image acoustique."
See also E. Coseriu, "Les structures lexématiques", p. 3 (Zeitschrift für französische Sprache und Literatur, Beiheft, Neue Folge, Heft 1, p. 3–16).

meaning of it and keep it so to speak floating without being tied to the expression side, (c) find the corresponding meaning in another language, (d) combine this meaning with the appropriate expression (although it may be agreed that the steps are not quite as clear cut as this in real life). The two languages may have words and constructions which seem very similar as to meaning but the skilled translator may translate a sentence of the source language in such a way that no word or construction in the target language is similar. (A bad translator makes a "literal" translation where words and constructions are "matched", which sometimes works and sometimes not.) See below, footnote 125.

A syntagm may, on the one hand, be thought of as having basically a syntactic function. It "realizes" a certain construction or, in other words, belongs to some syntagmeme. On the other hand, considering everything realized when a syntagm is produced, one may say that it has also a much wider meaning, a total meaning (see above, p. 63). The syntagm in this sense could be called "total syntagm". If one uses this term one would say that a total syntagm has a meaning rather than saying that it has a total meaning (as it would be unnecessary to repeat the word "total").

The total meaning of a syntagm, perhaps abbreviated as T. M., would include the syntagm funct(s), the syntagm seme (consisting of the lex seme[s]), emphas[120] (of the kind produced by emphatic prosodes) and express(es). It could also include variants brought about by different "reference" (see above, p. 65). In addition idiolectal, sociolectal and dialectal features would usually be part of the T. M. Considering all these variables it is obvious that even syntagms belonging to the same varisyntagm may have different T.M.s. The opposite case is the one where roughly the same meaning (roughly relatable to one particular "referent") is expressed by different varisyntagms (see above, p. 85).

As no hierarchically higher syntagms than periods are dealt with in this work, the "longest" T.M.s are those of periods. It is, however, clear that a text or a part of a text containing more than one period would also have a T.M. and that the T.M. of given syntagms (including periods) is influenced by the T.M. of surrounding syntagms.

1. *Items : semes*. Semes are the meanings of morphs and lexes. Semes are also the meanings — in a narrow sense (not equal to T.M.) — of syntagms.

(a) *Morph semes. Definition :* The seme of a morph is either (a) its clear meaning, or (b) its unclear meaning, or (c) its grammatical function (as stated above, p. 45–46). A morph may also have (d) two (or more) simultaneous semes belonging to two different allosemes, of which usually one refers to meaning and one to function.

Morphs are segments of lexes (except for meta-morphs) and morph and lex semes are closely related. When a lex has only one morph, the morph seme is the same as the lex seme. When a lex consists of two or more morphs, two or more morph semes make up the lex seme (see below).

The indefinite article in English has two simultaneous allosemes (semes) as it has meanings such as 'one particular' or 'any' and at the same time the function of contributing to signal the beginning of a substantive phrase. (The first kind of

---

[120] See above, p. 37.

meaning would be found in *we saw a man* and the second kind of meaning in *a man is easily charmed by an attractive woman*[121].)

Some details about variation between morph semes will be given below under syntagm semes.

As an abbreviation for a morph seme the square brackets already used for certain expression units could be suggested. The first-mentioned kind of seme of the indefinite article could be written [one particular]. A more redundant way would be ["one particular"]. The most precise way would, however, be m. seme[one particular] (although the "simultaneous" syntactic function of signalling the beginning of a substantive phrase is not notated).

(b) *Lex semes. Definition :* The seme of a lex is its meaning which can be (a) meaning in the narrow sense of the word, (b) grammatical function or (c) meaning and function simultaneously, (d) meaning, function or meaning-function in a sequence, i.e. each tied to a morph within the lex (in the case of given lexes which have two or more morphs as segments [example: the plural *boys*]).

All lex semes seem to be "clear". Although the lex seme of *cranberry* contains the morph *cran-*, which has an "unclear" meaning, the lex seme as a whole is a clear meaning. A speaker who is familiar with cranberries might not know exactly what *cran-* is, but he would know clearly what a *cranberry* is.

A lex seme such as "blackberry" consists of two morph semes, which amalgamate. Although the two morph semes do not "disappear" (as they exist as morph semes), they constitute a "new" meaning, the lex seme, which is not just one meaning added to another meaning but which exists as a whole (see above, p. 52).

It is obvious that in cases where a morph simultaneously has meaning and function (as the indefinite article just dealt with) the lex containing it also has meaning and function.

If a morph seme has "grammatical" function and if the morph constitutes a lex, then the lex seme is obviously also "grammatical". In *I want to leave* the lex *to* has only a grammatical function (the one of signalling that an infinitive is coming).

When a lex contains a "grammatical" morph together with one or more other morphs, this morph is "added" to the rest. Often it can be substituted by another form of a paradigm (Latin *servus, servi* etc.) or it can be taken away without the word being destroyed (*blackberries — blackberry*). In a constituent analysis, *blackberries* would first be divided into *blackberry* and *-s* and in a second 'cut' *blackberry* would be divided into *black* and *berry*. This "morphological" description seems to be just a reflection of facts related to lex semes. In *blackberries* the two first morph semes *amalgamate*[122] and the third segment is *added* to these as a whole. (It is not *black*, nor *berry* which is in the plural, but *blackberry*.)

A lex seme could be notated similarly to morph semes. The seme of l[blæk] would be l. seme[black].

(c) *Syntagm semes. Definition :* A *syntagm seme* is the meaning of the lex semes related to the sequence of lexes of a syntagm (or to the lex of a syntagm if the syntagm contains only one lex).

---

[121] Note that each of these meanings is in intersection with the rest of the period within which it is found. There is no ambiguity.
[122] *Blackberries* are not *black berries*. One can meaningfully say: *these blackberries are still red*.

A study of the meanings of syntagms includes various kinds of amalgamation and interselection between lex semes. E.g. in the period *the guest had a mini-skirt*, the correct interpretation is normally that the *guest* is female because of the lex seme of *mini-skirt*.

A syntagm seme would be labelled "synt. seme". To synt[bɪg blækberɪz] corresponds synt. seme[big blackberry + plural], where the seme of the grammatical morph has been separated from the amalgamated part in the second lex.

The possible role of an emphas or an express was hinted at above (p. 86). It seems that both can be related to a morph, a lex or a syntagm seme. It seems also that an emphas is relatable to a funct (see above p. 63, 65).

The emphatic prosode expressing the emphas may concern a morph only. If a speaker realizes that somebody has mistakenly heard "hat" when he said "hats", he may say *I did not say hat, but hats* giving the emphas to the plural ending.

A lex may receive an emphatic prosode, which produces an important change in meaning. *It is mý hat* is different from *it is my hát*. The following example may be worth a detailed explanation: Instead of pronouncing *glass is elastic* in the most common way, the first word can be emphasized. In this case it could be an answer to a question such as: *do you know some elastic substance?* The kind of emphasis used implies that the word under emphasis is opposed to one or more other words. In our case, *glass* is elastic but many other substances are not. It is comparable to saying *mén are like that* implying that *wómen are not like that*.

In *glass is elastic*, and similar cases, it has been suggested that the predicate, *is elastic*, is first in the thought and is actually something like a "psychological subject" and that *glass* has rather the function of a predicate[123]. There may be some truth in this thought but it does not seem appropriate to make use of it in the most immediate description of the period. It seems to be rather part of the explanation of why the speaker chose the expression he did, or perhaps even part of an explanation of how an "amorphous thought" takes the shape of a syntagm in the mind of a speaker. It should be noted that the problem as understood here is not syntactic but semantic.

An emphatic prosode would not usually stretch over a whole period but could well concern a syntagm of some length: *This is mý hát, not yoúr cát*.

Expresses, on the other hand, are related to syntagm semes, including period semes, and to lex semes, but less often to morph semes [124]. A period such as *this is beautiful* can be said with an express "delight" stretching over the whole or just concerning the last lex.

It seems natural to think that a seme and the simultaneous express (which is obligatory) amalgamate or, perhaps, rather that the express selects the particular seme (within the lexeme). The occasional emphas is rather something "added".

Some further details on the variation of semes are given in the next paragraph (2)[125].

---

[123] N. Chomsky suggests a similar explanation (*Aspects of the Theory of Syntax*, p. 163), but does not seem to be quite satisfied.

[124] One may, however, imagine a happy Minister of Trade who puts all his delight into one syllable when reporting to the Prime Minister: *we have got an éxport surplus at last*.

[125] The problem of translation, which was mentioned above (p. 85–86), can now be stated in the following more explicit way. A *syntagm* and its *meaning* of a source language is given, e.g. *I am hungry* — "I am hungry". The corresponding meaning in the target language is sought and found, e.g. "j'ai faim". The relatable syntagm *j'ai faim* is established. Although this

2. *Units: varimorph, varilex and varisyntagm sememes. Definition:* All semes of a varimorph form its sememe. All semes of a varilex form its sememe. And all semes of a varisyntagm form its sememe.

If a period such as *this is my hat* were repeated a number of times, each of the four varimorphs and varilexes would, to start with, have many different semes conditioned by different emphases and expresses. In addition, one may consider the referents: *this* and *hat* could refer to an enormous number of different hats and *my* could refer to any speaker of the language. Each reference would make the seme vary somewhat in a particular speaker. A further variation still would be caused by the fact that each speaker has to some extent his individual semes (and sememes). Even simple notions such as *pen, table, cold, hate* would not be exactly the same in each speaker. All this would increase the number of semes in the extreme[126].

As all lexes of the variperiod quoted are also morphs, the variperiod (a varisyntagm) would have not only four varilex sememes but also four varimorph sememes. All the meaning variants of the whole variperiod would be included in its variperiod sememe, which is a varisyntagm sememe.

If varimorphs, varilexes and varisyntagms are considered as "total", they have total meanings (see above, p. 86).

A varimorph sememe can be considered as a subset of a given morpheme alloseme and it cannot possibly belong to more than one such alloseme.

A varilex sememe is little different from a varimorph sememe in case the varilex has only one varimorph (and not two or more consecutive ones). Whether the varilex has one, or two or more amalgamated varimorphs, its sememe belongs to some given lexeme alloseme. If the varilex contains also one or more functional ("grammatical") varimorphs (e.g. a plural ending), it seems convenient to treat this added segment separately. At the level of varilexes *blackberry* has one sememe but *blackberries* would be described as having two segments although, in a sense, they do make up a varilex sememe.

The three units could be notated: varim. sememe/.../, varil. sememe/.../ and varisynt. sememe/.../.

varimorph sememe = {morph seme$_1$, ..., morph seme$_n$}
varilex sememe = {lex seme$_1$, ..., lex seme$_n$}
varisyntagm sememe = {syntagm seme$_1$, ..., syntagm seme$_n$}

3. *Units: allolex varilex sememes.* In the less frequent case where a lexeme has allolexes, varilexes of allolexes or allolex varilexes belonging to some given lexeme, would have sememes. Thus the allolexes *betalade* and *betala* (cf. above, p. 52) would each have a group of varilexes with given sememes.

allolex varilex sememe = {lex seme$_1$, ..., lex seme$_n$}.

4. *Units: morpheme allosemes.* In many instances the semes of a morpheme seem to fall naturally into sets to be included in the morpheme sememe. These sets are the

---

cannot be done without knowledge of the two language systems (their units), the translation procedure is directly concerned with items:

    Source language   Target language
    total syntagm meaning → total syntagm meaning
    ↕   ↓
    syntagm   syntagm

[126] Compare the phones of the expression side which also exist in enormous numbers.

morpheme allosemes. The semes of *high*, considered as a morpheme could be grouped so as to fall under the allosemes (1) "having the dimension height", (2) "high on the pitch scale", (3) "intoxicated" (and certainly yet some others). (These three allosemes belong to a given morpheme sememe.)

Note that each allomorph within a given morpheme does not have a separate sememe, as allomorphs of a morpheme mean the same (at the α-level).

morpheme sememe = {morpheme alloseme$_1$, ..., morpheme alloseme$_n$}
morpheme alloseme = {morph seme$_1$, ..., morph seme$_n$}.

5. *Units: lexeme allosemes.* The semes of a lexeme often fall into sets, here called lexeme allosemes. (Allosemes of a given lexeme form a lexeme sememe.)

When a lexeme consists of one morpheme (allomorph) only, the morpheme sememe and the lexeme sememe, as well as the morpheme allosemes and the lexeme allosemes are in practice the same. The three (or more) lexeme allosemes of the lexeme *high* are the three or more variants just mentioned (as morpheme allosemes). They form the lexeme sememe "high".

What has just been said about *blackberries* considered as a varilex also holds for the lexeme *blackberries* (mutatis mutandis). When the lexeme has amalgamated segments at the content level, i.e. two or more amalgamated morpheme allosemes, these form just one lexeme sememe. *Blackberry*, with two segments at the morphemic level, has one lexeme sememe.

It should be noted that the amalgamated segments are morpheme allosemes rather than morpheme sememes. For instance, the first segment in *blackberry* is "of black colour" rather than "unfortunate" (as in *a black day*) or any other alloseme.

Although sememes and allosemes are, in various respects, treated independently of their expression units, they depend to a great extent on expression units when they are established. The three allosemes of *high* are grouped together as a morpheme sememe or a lexeme sememe because they are related to a given morpheme or a given lexeme. If one wanted to consider meaning without letting the expression side have any influence at all, one would not group together the three allosemes of *high* as one easily finds allosemes from other expression units which are closer to these than they are among themselves. For instance, an alloseme of *drugged* would be closer to the third alloseme of *high* than this alloseme is to the first alloseme ("having the dimension height"). On the other hand, in most cases allosemes of a given lexeme have some feature in common: the three allosemes just mentioned each involve some kind of height.

lexeme sememe = {lexeme alloseme$_1$, ..., lexeme alloseme$_n$}
lexeme alloseme = {lex seme$_1$, ..., lex seme$_n$}.

6. *Units: morpheme allosememes and lexeme allosememes.* Morpheme allosemes and lexeme allosemes can be grouped together in different ways so as to form different morpheme allosememes and lexeme allosememes respectively. These two kinds of allosememes are, in practice, the same as long as the lexemes have one morphemic segment only. (Any alloseme of *high* will be grouped with other relevant allosemes in a similar way whether it is considered as morpheme alloseme or lexeme alloseme.)

A (morpheme or lexeme) allosememe can be called "grammatical". The alloseme of *to* in *I want to do it* belongs clearly to this kind of set. Another allosememe includes all "general" (or "semantic") allosemes such as the ones of *high, go, red* etc. As some lexemes (morphemes) have grammatical as well as general allosemes (*a, the, by* etc.), different allosemes of the same lexeme may belong to different allosememes.

All "main" allosemes (as the alloseme "having the dimension of height" of *high*) could form one allosememe as opposed to more peripheral allosemes (as "intoxicated" of *high*). Among the peripheral ones a substantial set would be formed by the metaphorical ones (as "intoxicated" of *high*).

When allosemes can be somehow associated they form a *semantic field*, which is here considered as an allosememe. Such an allosememe is well-defined when it coincides with a subset which is part of the semantic system (see below, 96—104). One such allosememe would be the one defined by the component 'human': "man", "woman", "child", "girl" etc. Another allosememe would be defined by the component 'young': "child", "girl", "calf", "pup" etc. It is seen that these sets are overlapping: "child" and "girl" belong to both allosememes. It is possible for one set to be completely included in another. The 'human'-allosememe (as well as the 'animal'-allosememe, and others) is completely included in the 'animate'-allosememe.

A semantic field can, however, also be established in a very loose way. In this case there is no limit to the number of allosemes which can be associated: "cow" — "ruminate" — "eat" — "restaurant" — "house" ... As a matter of fact it is possible to consider "the whole lexicon" as associated[127].

It is often interesting to compare various semantic fields (kinship terms, "the names of the colours" etc.) in different languages.

A "set of synonyms" does not seem to be anything but a "semantic field". The field can be very narrow as in the case of the relevant allosemes of *liberty* and *freedom*[128]. It can also be very wide. For instance it has even been thought that *savoury, discriminate, exact, good, pleasing, fastidious* and *honourable* are "synonymous with *nice*"[129].

In practically every case, where two synonyms may have been thought of as being *completely* synonymous, a detailed linguistic analysis reveals differences between them[130].

Although it does not make a great deal of difference in English if morphemes or lexemes are considered when allosememes are established, two facts of some interest can be noted: (1) The set of all "grammatical" allosemes is larger if morphemes, rather than lexemes in their uninflected form are considered, as in this case "bound" morphemes such as substantive or verb endings will be included. (2) The set of "general" allosemes will be larger if all lexemes are considered rather than just all morphemes as many lexemes consist of two or more morphemes the meanings of which amalgamate to give a new meaning.

morpheme allosememe = {morpheme alloseme$_1$, ..., morpheme alloseme$_n$}
lexeme allosememe   = {lexeme alloseme$_1$, ..., lexeme alloseme$_n$}

---

[127] E. Coseriu (according to the stencilled lecture notes from 1965—1966) points out that "man bei entsprechender Ausweitung das ganze Lexikon als assoziiert auffassen kann" (p. 22).
[128] J. Lyons, *Introduction to theoretical linguistics*, Cambridge 1968, p. 449, provides this example. He does not, however, call a set of synonyms a semantic field.
[129] *Ibidem*, p. 446, where Lyons quotes *Roget's Thesaurus*.
[130] B. Brodda and H. Karlgren have searched for complete synonyms in various languages but only found one example, the Swedish pair *mer — mera* (p. 2 of *Synonymer och synonymers synonymer*, KVAL PM 335, Stockholm 1967). It is, however, doubtful if even this example is adequate.

7. Units: morpheme sememes and lexeme sememes. The allosemes of a morpheme and the allosemes of a lexeme form a morpheme sememe and a lexeme sememe respectively.

A dictionary provides allosemes of lexemes whether these are expressed in words from the same language (monolingual dictionary) or in words from another language (bilingual dictionary).

Although an inflected lexeme (such as a substantive in plural) can be thought of as having a lexeme sememe, this case is somewhat special. Thus it would be uneconomical to record it in a dictionary. The "added" grammatical morpheme is described in detail in morphemics, and in lexemics the "segmented" lexemes would not have to be accounted for in each particular case.

morpheme sememe = {morpheme alloseme$_1$, ..., morpheme alloseme$_n$}
lexeme sememe   = {lexeme alloseme$_1$, ..., lexeme alloseme$_n$}.

8. Units: syntagmeme sememes. A *syntagmeme sememe* is the sum of all the semes of all syntagms which belong to some particular syntagmeme (e.g. all the semes of some allosubject). This notion seems to be of little practical use.

syntagmeme sememe = {syntagm seme$_1$, ..., syntagm seme$_n$}.

9. Affiliation. Two or more syntagm semes, or varisyntagm sememes, are affiliated if they mean roughly the same. In this case they form an affiliation sememe or an affiliation semememe, respectively.

The boy hit the girl and *the girl was hit by the boy* have affiliated syntagm semes which belong to the same affiliation sememe. In this example the syntactic constructions are also affiliated (see above, p. 75–77). However, affiliation at the syntactic and at the semantic level do not presuppose one another. While *the boy lent the book to the girl* and *the girl borrowed the book from the boy* having affiliated semes would also show a certain syntactic affiliation, there would be little syntactic affiliation between *come!* and *I request you to come* although the two sentences have a high degree of semantic affiliation.

a-sememe   = {a-syntagm seme$_1$, ..., a-syntagm seme$_n$}
a-semememe = {a-varisyntagm sememe$_1$, ..., a-varisyntagm sememe$_n$}.

10. Interselection. It is often difficult to determine to what extent many problems about meaning and combinations of meanings belong to linguistics or not.

There seem, however, to be cases which should clearly not be dealt with in linguistics. Treating the unacceptability of *two and two equals five, the elephant in the Zoo weighs one gramme* or *the sky is always purple* involves problems of mathematics, biology and meteorology or is perhaps just a question of "common sense". No linguistic problem would be involved. (If the three periods just quoted had been thought of as linguistic problems, they would have been problems of purely semantic horizontal interselection as they do not offer any syntactic problem. In this respect none of them is irregular.) As a matter of fact, periods similar to the three just mentioned would not be of great interest to anybody except for an expert on literature if found in a poem or for a psychiatrist if coming from the mouth of a patient. However, in normal conversation utterances may also have content which does not correspond with "reality" (in irony, tales, jokes etc.).

In other instances, where syntax is again not involved in any significant way, there is, however, semantic horizontal interselection to be dealt with by linguists.

The adjective *blonde* has a component 'to be said about human hair', which accounts for the normal speaker's correct use: *blonde hair* but not *blonde car*. If, however, a child or a foreigner saw a table with the colour he had previously heard referred to as blonde (in the case of somebody's hair), he might say *the car is blonde*. If so, one would naturally think that his language was imperfect but not that there was anything wrong with his common sense or his knowledge of reality.

When there is interselection between syntax and semantics it seems clear that the problem is authentically linguistic. Although this principle may help us to see if a problem should be treated at all in linguistics, it is not always adequate as it may be difficult to determine how much should be included in syntax. It seems, however, to be a linguistic problem to determine that a subject has allofuncts and also which sets of lexes are in interselection with different allofuncts. In *the mother may admire the boy* the lex *mother* belongs to a set which has vertical interselection with subjects with the diallofunct experiencer of the allofunct agent. This diallofunct is required by the predicate verb *admire*. If instead, one tries out the period *sincerity may admire the boy*[131], *sincerity* is not a word in interselection with the diallofunct experiencer[132]. (Despite this one may be tempted to say that it just takes common sense to see that *sincerity* cannot admire anything.)

11. *Units: semi-sememes. Items: semi-semes.* The "unclear" meanings of some morphemes (allomorphs, morphs) (cf. *cranberry*, p. 45, and *hallon, lingon, why, when, where*, p. 49) may be called *semi-sememes* (*semi-semes*) as they have less than a full meaning (but are not quite devoid of meaning).

As it has been assumed above (p. 87) that all lexemes (lexes) have clear meanings (even if they consist of two morphemes (morphs) with unclear meanings), lexemes (lexes) cannot have semi-sememes (semi-semes).

However, a semi-lexeme (semi-lex) would have a semi-sememe (semi-seme) which, so to speak, stands between a morpheme sememe (morph seme) and a lexeme sememe (lex seme). *Vobiscum* (cf. p. 54), which has two semi-lexemes would accordingly have two semi-lexeme sememes, which would both be semi-sememes. *Vobiscum* as a whole would be considered as a semi-syntagmeme.

Examples of other semi-syntagmemes (semi-syntagms) would be *wild animal tamer* or *car salesman*. As a semi-syntagmeme (semi-syntagm) as a whole comes close to a lexeme, the main segments (*wild, animal, tamer; car, salesman*) are semi-lexemes (semi-lexes) with semi-sememes.

12. It seems uncertain if *quasi-sememe* (*quasi-seme*) would be a useful notion.

Although it was explained above (p. 49–50) that *stood*, *took* and *men* could be considered as each having two quasi-morphemes, this does not seem to imply that each has two quasi-sememes. For instance, *stood* seems to have two morpheme sememes as clearly as has *painted* or *paid*. However, one might say that *stood* (*took* and *men*), not having the more normal consecutive sememes (as *painted* or *paid*), have instead two *entangled* sememes (which is different from having two simultaneous sememes).

---

[131] Cf. N. Chomsky, *Aspects of the theory of syntax*, p. 75.
[132] It is thus thought that a subjecteme has different allofuncts, one of which is the agent. An agent, in its turn, has different diallofuncts, some of which could be: *actor* (as in *the mother spanked the child*), experiencer, (as in *the mother loved the child*), originator (as in *sincerity may frighten the boy*).

13. *Pseudo-sememe (pseudo-seme)* does not seem to be a useful notion.

14. *Meta-units* at the level of content are perhaps less useful notions than meta-units at the level of expression. In a talk on meanings (by linguists or laymen) the "quoted" meanings would be meta-semes. For instance, somebody may say that the meaning of *table* is concrete but the meaning of *admiration* is abstract. Such meta-semes could eventually form meta-sememes.

15. *Items : morph seme components and lex seme components*. The alloseme components and sememe components mentioned in the next paragraph have as elements seme components, or, in other words, are realized as seme components. The primary seme components, occurring in different combinations, build the semes in much the same way as phone components build phones. Secondary components are often added as parts of realizations of alloseme and sememe components.

Different kinds of secondary components can (as mentioned) be added to the primary ones. They belong to the α- as well as to the β-level but sometimes it may be difficult to tell which is the appropriate level. For instance, the secondary components 'slightly scientific' of "male" (see p. 101) or 'metaphorical' of "mouth (of river)" (see p. 102–103) seem to be α-components. The secondary components 'slang' and 'attractive' in "bird" (when *bird* is used with a meaning similar to that of *girl;* see p. 102) would perhaps rather be β-components.

It has been explained that semes vary according to the kind of emphas and express by which they are accompanied (p. 88). Context and reference are also of importance (p. 89). This implies that seme components also vary. Emphas and express may make one component vary more noticeably than another. For instance, in *she is a girl*, either the component 'young' or the component 'female' of "girl" can receive an emphas and some, perhaps strong, express. (It is easy to imagine situations where one or the other would be appropriate.)

16. *Units : morpheme alloseme components and lexeme alloseme components*. Components of morpheme allosemes and components of lexeme allosemes are similar. One difference is, however, that it generally seems difficult to attribute any component at all to morpheme allosemes the meaning of which is unclear. This is particularly so if the lexeme has two unclear morpheme sememes and no clear morpheme sememe as the Swedish examples *hallon* and *lingon* (quoted above, p. 49). (Lexemes always have clear meanings, cf. p. 87).

"Added" grammatical morphemes (such as plural endings) would possess their own components on which to build systems of grammatical morpheme allosemes.

The allosemes of "general" morphemes form another system based on their components. However, (at least in a language such as English) the system of "general" lexeme allosemes, being enormously wide and little studied, deserves particular interest (see below, p. 98–102).

It would be appropriate to give special importance to those components which seem to establish, in the first instance, those distinctions and similarities between lexeme (and morpheme) allosemes on which the semantic system (see below, p. 97–98) is based. These primary components, when considered as belonging to some particular alloseme, are direct or indirect (see below, p. 100).

Grammatical lexeme allosemes would have components and build sub-systems of their own.

When semi-lexemes have no clear meaning they have no components. The French word *fur* in *au fur et à mesure* (see p. 103) is an example of this case.

The n-components of morpheme and lexeme allosemes sum up all possible variations among the corresponding seme components. It may seem reasonable to let b-components include primary components and the "main" secondary ones, i.e. secondary components excluding those conditioned by different kinds of emphas or express, or by different reference or context.

To some extent the components of the same alloseme (or seme) influence each other[133]. The component 'male', when combined with 'older than young' in "man", implies stronger masculinity than 'male', when combined with 'young' in "boy". Similar modifications would be taken into account when n-components, but not when b-components, are studied.

17. *Units: allolex sememes and allolex sememe components.* In the infrequent cases when a lexeme has allolexes one must consider if each allolex should have a sememe which would be an alloseme of the sememe of the lexeme to which the allolex belongs. It seems that allolex sememes within some particular lexeme sememe have the same primary and the same "main" secondary components. They differ, however, as to other secondary components. For instance, the Swedish imperfect *betala* is, among other things, more colloquial than *betalade* (cf. p. 52).

Different allolex sememes within some particular lexeme sememe can thus be established within a lexeme n-sememe but not within a lexeme b-sememe.

18. *Units: varisyntagm sememe components.* Items *: syntagm seme components.* All components of the varilex sememe included in a varisyntagm may be considered as the components of the varisyntagm sememe. For any varisyntagm a sequence of varilex sememes and components thereof, can be provided.

All components of the lex semes included in a syntagm may be considered as the components of the syntagm seme. For any syntagm, a sequence of lex semes, and components thereof, can be provided.

When components are written out, they could conveniently be shown under the appropriate lexeme alloseme (lex seme) of the varisyntagm (syntagm). This would be parallel to the way phoneme components are sometimes written under a string of phonemes[134].

An n-varisyntagm and a b-varisyntagm would have somewhat different sememe components. The former would have n-components, so to speak, including every little detail. The latter would have b-components. This implies that a syntagm seme has components containing details to be included in n-varisyntagm components but not in b-varisyntagm components.

19. *Units: morpheme and lexeme sememe components.* One may sum up all components of all allosemes of a morpheme or a lexeme. One thus obtains morpheme and lexeme sememe components. These may differ widely among themselves as allosemes of the same morpheme or lexeme may differ very much.

---

[133] One can compare, with this kind of mutual influence between *simultaneous* components, the amalgamation between *consecutive* morpheme allosemes (morph semes) accounted for above, p. 52.
[134] Cf. Jakobson-Fant-Halle, *Preliminaries to Speech Analysis* (Cambridge, Mass., 1951), p. 44-45.

20. *Paradigmatics*. Using the loose definition of semantic field provided above (associable allosemes or sememes form a field) not only the examples given above (p. 91) but also (I) *semantic systems*, (II) *subdivisions*, (III) *groups* and (IV) *classes*, which will be defined below, are semantic fields[135]. These four notions can however receive comparatively rigorous definitions.

I. *Semantic systems*. Various authors have been interested in the problem of establishing what is here called the *semantic system* of a language, but E. Coseriu is the linguist who has made the most valuable suggestions. Although matters are much more complicated in semantics than in phonology, the basic principles for establishing phonological systems as explained by N. S. Trubetzkoy in *Grundzüge der Phonologie* appear to hold also in semantics.

Within the overall semantic system, a huge network of subsystems and subsystems of subsystems can be assumed to exist in all languages but in no language has it been studied in any detail. The overall system consists of (a) the system of morpheme allosemes, (b) the system of lexeme allosemes. (Also the system of varisyntagm sememes can be imagined.) These subsystems can be compared with the subsystems of vowels and consonants in phonology.

For the purpose of establishing the semantic system the allosemes mentioned would be considered as b-allosemes rather than as n-allosemes.

(a) In the system of morpheme allosemes, comparatively little would be described, at least in a language such as English. The allosemes of "bound morphemes", i.e. derivational and inflectional affixes, and also the allosemes of morphemes with "unclear meaning" would, however, have to be dealt with here. Each of these three categories would form a subsystem with some describable structure. While it seems possible to discover a clear structure in the two first mentioned systems, it does not seem possible to structure the set of "unclear meanings". How is "cran" (in *cranberry*) related to "logan" (in *loganberry*) or "ceive" (in *receive*) to "spond" (in *respond*)[136]?

It seems to be of little value to describe the system of the allosemes of the independent ("free") morphemes. Each of these "clear" meanings is also the alloseme of a lexeme (the alloseme "black" is hardly different whether it belongs to a morpheme or to a lexeme) and will be described as such although in a wider system, as languages usually have more lexemes and lexeme allosemes than morphemes and morpheme allosemes (as lexemes may consist of more than one morpheme). If a language had only lexemes consisting of one morpheme, one would rather speak of the system of lexeme allosemes than of the one of morpheme allosemes[137].

(b) The system of word meanings, or, here, the system of lexeme allosemes has been dealt with by various authors but we will basically follow Coseriu[138]. This linguist starts from the observation that, as in phonology, items with similar distribu-

---

[135] Most of the details given on fields in 1,1,6,6 are paradigmatic and could have been given here (in 1,1,6,20). On the other hand the "groups" and "classes" (to a higher degree than the "systems") are clearly sets and could have been dealt with above (in 1,1,6,6: "allosemes").
[136] Although more precise notations have been suggested above, we shall use, in a simplified way, double quotation marks for (semes,) allosemes (and sememes) and single quotation marks for components in the text below.
[137] If one thinks that generally morphemes are segments of lexemes and lexemes are segments of syntagmemes, then one would rather keep the lexemes and discard the morphemes (than the other way round) as the lexemes are needed for the description of the syntagmemes.
[138] The terminology as well as many details are, however, our own.

tion can be opposed, analyzed as to common and different components and given a place in a system on the basis of these components. In phonology, [b] and [t] in English can be opposed, as in *ball* and *tall*, but not [b] and [ɪ], as in *ball* and *bill*, as these two have different distribution within syllables. Consequently /b/ and /t/ are described in one subsystem, the one of the consonants, and /ɪ/ in another subsystem, the one of the vowels. This means that there will be different systems for adjective allosemes, substantive allosemes, adverb allosemes etc. If an adjective, substantive, adverb etc., in particular cases, functions as something else, it will have allosemes in more than one system. For instance, *then* will not only have allosemes in the system of adverb allosemes (cf. *then he came*) but also in the system of adjective allosemes (cf. *the then premier*).

Each of these systems can be described basically in the same way as phonological systems. The privative, gradual and equipollent oppositions explained by N. S. Trubetzkoy can be used also in semantics:

(a) The opposition can be *privative*, or perhaps better: *bipolar*. Coseriu points out[139] that in semantics one finds privative oppositions similar to those in phonology[140]. The difference in meaning is then established by the presence or absence of a distinctive feature, or in our terms, a semantic component. Latin "albus" as opposed to "candidus" is explained by 'not brilliant' and 'brilliant'.

Other examples would be "day" versus "night" and "man" versus "woman". The component, the presence of which is found in one of the members of the opposition, is "marked". A suitable notation would then be for the Latin example + 'brilliant' and for the two English examples + 'female' and + 'dark' respectively. As shown by Coseriu[141], neutralization can in many cases, not only in phonology but also in semantics, show which member of the opposition is marked and which is unmarked. (The marked component is the one which is not present in the neutralized form.)

One may wonder if it would not be preferable to think that the "unmarked" member also has a "positive" component. In this case, the term bipolar would be more suitable. Rather than 'not brilliant' versus 'brilliant', or — and + 'brilliant', 'dull' would stand versus 'brilliant' in the Latin example. In the English examples 'male' would stand against 'female' and 'light' against 'dark'[142]. I.e. two positive qualities would form a clear cut contradistinction. If so the plus versus-minus terminology should be avoided.

(b) Oppositions are *gradual* when different degrees of the same property establish the difference between the members of a series of oppositions[143]. Coseriu[144] provides the German example: "eisig" — "kalt" — "kühl" — "lau" — "warm" — "heiß".

(c) A number of oppositions are *equipollent* when each term is in the same way distinguished from all others so that no particular order between them can be established. This is the case of the "elementary" colours: "red", "yellow", "blue", etc.[145].

---

[139] Cf. the lecture notes, p. 57–58.
[140] Many languages have a /b/ and a /p/ distinguished by presence and absence of voice.
[141] Lecture notes, p. 24.
[142] English /b/ and /p/ would be distinguished by voiceless quality against voiced quality, both considered as something positive that can be heard in realizations of these two phonemes.
[143] English /ɪ/ (as in *bit*) and /e/ (as in *bet*) form a gradual opposition.
[144] Lecture notes, p. 57.
[145] Lecture notes, p. 57.

The colours may be ordered in physics (the colour spectrum) but this order is not inherent in any language, i.e. it is not part of the content side[146]. (The case of the colours is actually more complicated than we have just implied. An individual knowing the colour spectrum from physics (or just from contemplating a rainbow), or being conscious of how particular colours can be mixed with other colours so as to form shades between two colours which are then felt to be contiguous, or having a sense of "warm" and "cold" colours, or perhaps being aware of all these facts, may have a certain order in his colours. Similar arguments would hold for equipollent oppositions in general. It seems, however, that such "minor" details should be kept away from the "normal" description of a language, i.e. a "b-description", but could be included in an "n-description".)

It should be noted that the terms of an opposition must have, in addition to the distinguishing components, also one or more common components. (It may be left to the reader to establish exactly what the common components are in the examples just provided.)

As a matter of fact, in order to understand the structure of the semantic system one must elucidate also the common components, the basis for the comparisons. In phonology, Trubetzkoy explains in *Grundzüge der Phonologie* that an opposition is *bilateral* if the common component(s) can only be found in one single opposition and *multilateral* if the common component(s) can be found in more than one opposition. Every semantic subsystem goes as far as there are allosemes having the same common component(s). For instance, the equipollent oppositions between the names of the "elementary" colours are oppositions between terms which all have the component 'colour'. Assuming that "red" has only two shades, "crimson" and "scarlet", these two would form the only opposition which has as common component 'red'. This opposition would then be bilateral. All colour terms would form a subsystem. Within this subsystem "red" with "crimson" and "scarlet" would form a small subsystem.

It is of importance, also, to establish to what extent oppositions are *isolated* or *proportional* in phonology and in semantics[147]. If "crimson" and "scarlet" were the only shades of "red" and the kind of difference between them were not found in any other pair of colour shades, they would form an isolated opposition. The opposition between "man" and "woman" is proportional as the components distinguishing them are found also in "boy" and "girl" (and others).

It is obvious that only small parts of the semantic system of a language have ever been described. It also seems clear that empirically one has to start from the establishment of single direct oppositions and then build out the system step by step, as suggested by Coseriu[148].

Although it may be difficult to establish a clear boundary between words from technical terminology and words from everyday language, these two kinds of words

---

[146] /s/ and /k/ in English would be in equipollent opposition.
[147] In English /r/ — /l/ is bilateral (if these two are thought to be the only "liquids") but /p/ — /t/ is multilateral (because of /p/ — /k/ and /k/ — /t/).
In English /r/ — /l/ is isolated but /p/ — /b/ is proportional (because of /t/ — /d/ etc.). It is obvious that an opposition can be bilateral and isolated, bilateral and proportional, multilateral and isolated, and multilateral and proportional.
[148] "Les structures lexématiques", p. 9.

should not be treated together. The latter kind of word is the primary interest of a linguist. The former kind of word may, however, also be studied by a linguist although the problem of the meanings of these seen as a semantic problem is only marginally linguistic.

Before any further details on semantic systems are given it may be of advantage to consider some details from the English system of substantive allosemes as shown

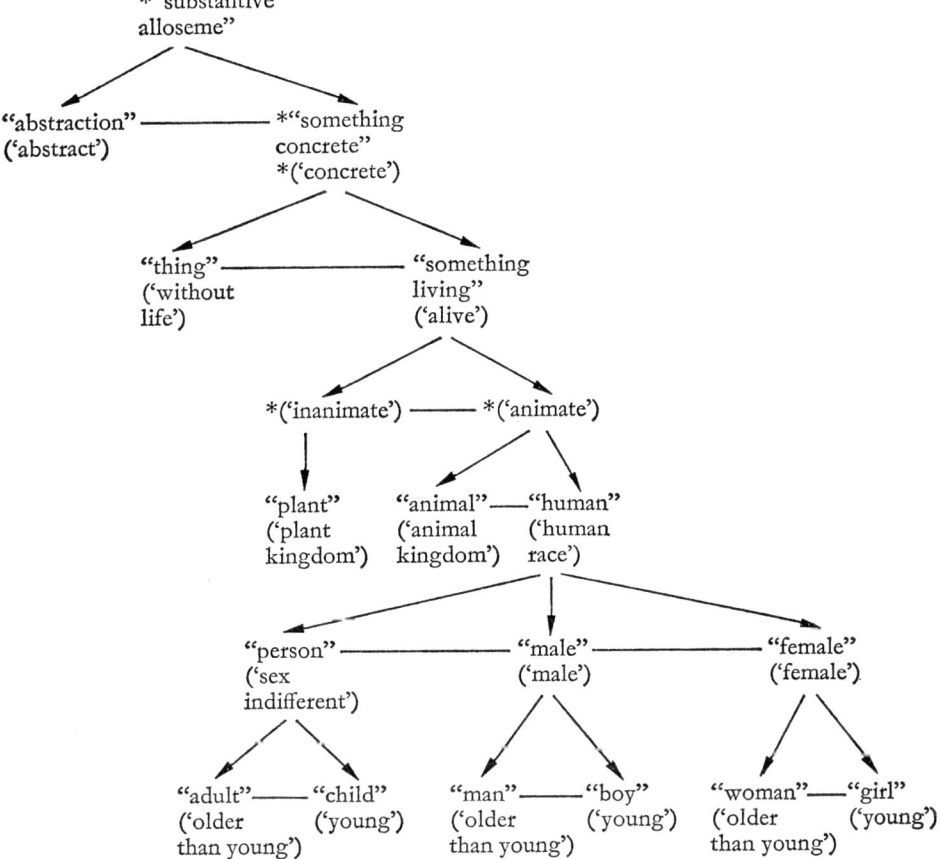

in the following graphic form where the components are shown in brackets after the allosemes. If the substantive the alloseme of which would have been capable of filling some place in the system does not exist, the component it would have had, or an expression explaining the missing alloseme, or both, appear in the graph. They are then provided with an asterisk.

The word having the highest alloseme in the hierarchy just diagrammed does not exist in common language. It does not exist either in the terminology used in this book but can be paraphrased as *substantive alloseme*. One step higher one would find *"alloseme", which does not exist either in common language. From *"alloseme" one can descend to *"adjective alloseme", *"verb alloseme" etc. which are at the same level as *"substantive alloseme". And from these one can obviously descend further.

99

The highest level having the alloseme of a common word is the one where *abstraction* is opposed to a meaning that can be expressed through a syntagm "something concrete", of which 'concrete' is the component opposed to 'abstract' in *abstraction*.

At each level the components distinguishing the allosemes at that level are shown in brackets. At each level the allosemes opposed obviously have also common components. These have, however, not been written out as they can be inferred from the general rule that a distinguishing component at one level is common component at the next lower level. Inversely, one can say that a common component at some particular level becomes distinguishing component at the next higher level. This means that not only the distinguishing components but also the allosemes become "more general" or "wider" the higher they occur in the hierarchy.

Each alloseme pointing by an arrow to one or more allosemes at a lower level dominates this or these allosemes. The alloseme here called *dominating* is called superordinate by Lyons[149]. *Dominated* allosemes are also called hyponyms.

Starting from a dominating alloseme and descending more than one level one comes to allosemes *indirectly* dominated by the first-mentioned alloseme.

The overall semantic system of a language is here called its semantic system. However, if nothing larger than a dominating alloseme with its dominated allosemes is under consideration, this can also be called a system. This kind of microsystem, seen as part of a larger system, is a *subsystem*.

There is (direct) opposition between all terms (directly) dominated by the same dominating alloseme. In the graph (p. 99) such terms are connected by horizontal lines. In the diagram there is clearly bipolar opposition between "adult" and "child" and there seem to be equipollent oppositions between "person", "male" and "female" (which is perhaps a somewhat unsatisfactory solution)[150].

As already stated, it is assumed that instead of a lexeme alloseme missing in the system the meaning of a longer expression (such as "something concrete" in opposition to "abstraction") can take its place in an opposition to one or more other terms at the same level.

Only terms at the same level, and similarly dominated, are in direct opposition, but a term at one level can be in indirect opposition to a term at another level. "Girl" is in direct opposition to "woman" but over "female", its dominating alloseme, it is also in indirect opposition to "male".

An alloseme has directly its "own" components but it also has as *indirect* components all components of dominating allosemes. For instance, "girl" has the direct components 'female' (common component) and 'young' (distinguishing component) and the indirect components 'human race', 'animate', 'alive', 'concrete'. Similarly a hierarchically higher alloseme has, in addition to its "own" direct components, indirectly the components of the dominated allosemes.

Sometimes one may doubt which should be the dominating and which the dominated term. In such cases one could give alternatives. For instance an alternative solution, to be considered as equivalent or perhaps rather as "secondary", of the lower part of the system just provided would be to let "adult" dominate "man"

---

[149] *Op. cit.*, p. 455.
[150] It is doubtful if these three terms should be at the same level. Another, perhaps better solution would be to let "person" dominate "adult" and "child" and *"human with definite sex" dominate "male" and "female".

and "woman", and "child" dominate "boy" and "girl" as it seems to be a possible alternative way of looking at human beings to think that basically they are *children* and *grown ups* and that these two categories can then be subdivided. In this case, however, "male" and "female" are difficult to accomodate in the system.

As in phonology one may be tempted to simplify one's task by using only the smallest possible number of components when building the system. This kind of "minimal" system may, however, be made more complete if other components are added. In the subsystem just discussed the most important components, which could be called primary components, are stated. It is, however, not shown that "adult" is somewhat less familiar than "child" or that "male" is also less familiar than "man" and, in addition, slightly scientific (see below, p. 102–103).

The same alloseme may be found in more than one subsystem. Quoting a French example provided by B. Pottier but giving it a somewhat different interpretation, Coseriu[151] notes that one "field" (= our (sub)system) "siège pour s'asseoir" contains "pouf", "chaise", "fauteuil" etc. Another field "meuble" contains "chaise", "fauteuil" etc. I.e. "pouf" is a seat but not a piece of furniture and "chaise", "fauteuil" etc. belong not only to the subsystem dominated by "meuble" (which in its turn would dominate "seat") but also to the subsystem dominated by "seat" (in a more general way, not dominated by "meuble"). As these allosemes would be opposed to other partly different allosemes according to the subsystem in which they were included, they may have to be characterized (partly) differently in terms of components in each subsystem.

In the graphs of semantic subsystems provided (p. 99 and below), oppositions are shown by lines connecting the two terms. "Additional" differences, such as the ones between "adult" and "child" and between "male" and "man" just mentioned, could be shown (in a more complete system) by some suitable additional convention.

It is also conceivable that allosemes of the same sememe would be connected, e.g. by dashed lines. Even the same component recurring in different allosemes could be signalled.

An example of rearranging allosemes in such a way that one obtains an alternative and particularly wide system would be to make *"sex indifferent being" (instead of "person") — "male" — "female" more general by not letting them be dominated by "human"). A very simplified subsystem[152] would then be:

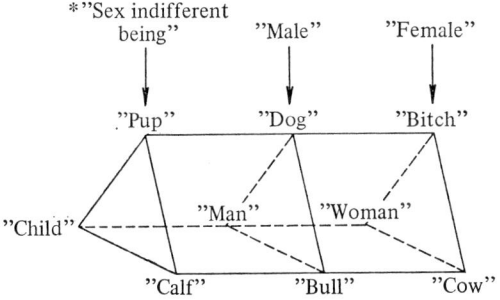

---
[151] Lecture notes, p. 63.
[152] Among other things, the distinction "child" — "adult", "pup" — "grown dog" (an alloseme other than the one accounted for on the graph!), "calf" — *"grown bull or cow", has been neglected.

101

It is obvious that if this system were built out it would yield some very long series of proportional oppositions. One such series would be "man" — "woman", "bull" — "cow", "dog" — "bitch", "rooster" — "hen" etc. All animals would, however, not be included as "he-wombat" versus "she-wombat", and similar expressions would rather be considered as gap-filling explanations than integral parts of the "semantic system".

Even without this kind of rearrangement the opposition "man" — "woman", dominated by "human", could be connected in some arbitrary way (for instance by the use of dotted lines) with "bull" — "cow", "dog" — "bitch" etc., dominated by "animal".

At various points in the system more than one subsystem would be dominated by the same term and each subsystem could be represented in some arbitrary direction in relation to the dominating term. "Human" would dominate not only the terms provided but also a large set of "occupations": "lecturer", "secretary", "minister" etc. (Some occupations would be dominated by "man" or "woman" only.)

Although (as just mentioned) it seems clear that terminologies used by experts should not be included in the "semantic system" of a language (see below, p. 104)[153], it seems difficult to know exactly what should be included in the semantic system. For instance an attempt to make a system of all possible professions would perhaps be outside linguistics. Anybody saying *at Australian universities, teaching fellow is higher than lecturer* would have got his facts wrong but he would not have made a language error and the relation between *lecturer* and *teaching fellow* would be of marginal interest in semantics.

It would seem that in the system, different professions could appear as an unordered list rather than being ordered in a subsystem.

As "compounds" (*doorknob, footstep*) and derived lexemes have lexeme allosemes in a way sufficiently similar to lexemes containing one morpheme only, this kind of alloseme should be included in the system.

Through their primary components, the allosemes of slang words are usually in one-to-one correspondence with allosemes of the normal words. "Bird" would have a place similar to "woman". There might, however, be some interest in establishing the semantic system of a slang code to see what parts of the basic semantic system it covers and what parts it does not cover. Also, the slang words have not only the component 'slang' but, in addition, in a particularly clear way components with β-function: appreciative, depreciative, scornful, funny etc. (When *bird* is said **for** *woman* or *girl*, the additional component is something like 'attractive'.)

Metaphoric words are somewhat special. If the metaphor is fixed, then through their primary components their allosemes just fit into the semantic system in the same way as any other alloseme. This would be the case of the allosemes of *mouth* (*of a river*) or *hand* (*of a clock*). It seems, however, appropriate to provide them with an extra

---

[153] With emphasis on properties of their expression side "special languages" could still be investigated by a linguist. Investigating every content detail of these "languages" he would have to transform himself into a specialist in the particular field in question and become a physicist, a biologist, a chess player etc. himself.
It must be admitted that frequently one runs into the difficulty of determining what is expert knowledge and what is common knowledge.

"metaphorical component", in the examples quoted: 'mouth like' and 'signalling as a hand'.

Occasional metaphors (like *the road was a ribbon of silver*, or *the big cigar* when speaking of a *zeppelin*) occur on the spur of the moment. They are very numerous and should not be catered for in the "semantic system". It is, however, still interesting to investigate the principles governing their use, which would be somewhat different in different idiolects, sociolects, dialects and glottolects.

There are fixed expressions or idioms which may be as long as periods, clauses or phrases. At the level of semantics these may be equated with lexemes. They are "ready made" and not constructed in the act of communication. They have allosemes which are part of the semantic system. Sometimes their meaning is more or less difficult to infer even if one has a normal knowledge of the words and the grammar of a language but does not know the particular expression in question[154]. This could be the case of *to break the ice* (= to put people at ease with each other). The same would apply to a period such as *barking dogs seldom bite* (= people making too many threats seldom carry them out).

Sometimes words are involved, which do not exist outside the idiom in question, as *fur* in the French *au fur et à mesure* (= *gradually*)[155].

If there is doubt about some cases being one lexeme with two widely differing allosemes or two homonymous lexemes, there is automatically doubt about in what capacity to introduce these two allosemes into the semantic system. Considering the way we have suggested of establishing the semantic system, this doubt is, however, of little practical consequence. The same two allosemes would be included whether they are related to one or two lexemes. On the basis of *John married Betty* and *the priest married John and Betty*, would one establish one or two verbs *marry*? (Probably one only!) Whatever solution, there would be (at least) two allosemes of *marry* to be included in the system.

To these basic considerations, several remarks can be made:

(1) Our "systems" and "subsystems" are called "fields" by Coseriu.

(2) As we have given to "semantic field" a wide and loose definition all our systems and subsystems are fields (cf. above, p. 96).

(3) Coseriu speaks of words and their meanings, of which a word can have more than one. This is one reason why a word can function in more than one field (= our subsystem)[156]. We have expressed the same thing in a somewhat more elaborate way: a lexeme often has more than one alloseme and each of these allosemes may belong to a different subsystem.

---

[154] Idioms are to be distinguished from often repeated "normal" syntagms of the kind which are probably stored as such in the brain (cf. above, p. 71). The meaning of these can be inferred by a speaker with sufficient knowledge of the separate words and the grammar of the language.

[155] Example provided by Coseriu, lecture notes, p. 31–32.

[156] In lecture notes, p. 60, Coseriu remarks that usually a phoneme functions in one system only. It is usually either a vowel or a consonant. (However, sometimes it is both.) He then continues: "Im Wortschatz dagegen kann eine Einheit ohne weiteres in zwei Wortfeldern funktionieren: "frais" gehört sowohl zum Wortfeld der Temperaturangaben als auch zum Feld des Alters im allgemeinen (neben "récent, neuf, nouveau" etc.)."

In a subsystem, an alloseme may dominate another alloseme of the same lexeme. In French the alloseme "human" of the lexeme *homme* dominates the alloseme "man" of *homme* (and, in addition the alloseme "woman" of *femme*).

Coseriu comments on this example (and similar ones): In French ((*femme*) *homme*) may be called an "inclusive opposition" but Latin having "einen neutralen Gesamtbegriff", *homo*, has the exclusive opposition *vir-femina*[157].

Or, it can also be said that the term of the opposition which can be used for the whole zone of meaning ("Bedeutungszone") is the extensive term, and a term used for only part of this "zone" is intensive. *Homo* (or *Mensch* in German) is extensive and *vir (Mann)* and *femina (Frau, Weib)* are intensive[158].

Note that in the example given Coseriu considers the whole lexeme sememe whereas on the preceding pages we have assumed that isolated allosemes are the basic units when semantic systems are established.

(4) Coseriu observes that a gap in the semantic system of a language can usually be filled by a paraphrase. It is not to be compared with a gap in the phonological system which cannot be filled as easily. If standard Italian has no /y/, this phoneme can not be supplemented[159]. Using a /y/ would serve no purpose in Italian.

If Swedish opposes *farfar* and *morfar* and English has only *grandfather*, whenever the need is felt, one can in English express the two meanings habitual in Swedish by using *paternal grandfather* and *maternal grandfather*.

This means that all languages can express approximately the same meanings but habitually they do not as their semantic systems are different.

(5) "Special languages" have already been mentioned. In this regard Coseriu speaks of "Wörter, die eine übersprachliche Gestaltung der Realität aufweisen, d. h., die Sprache wird zwar zur Gestaltung benutzt, doch geht die Gestaltung selbst über die Sprache hinaus. Es handelt sich hierbei um Terminologien und Nomenklaturen der Wissenschaften, also um Fachwörter, die sprachlich nicht abgrenzbar sind. Man muss sich hier auf die jeweiligen Wissenschaften beziehen. Dasselbe gilt auch für die populären Terminologien der Biologie oder Zoologie, etc. Eine sprachliche Gestaltung ist nur bei großen Klassen anzutreffen, die je nach Sprache verschieden sein können. So entspricht dem französischen "oiseau" im Spanischen "ave" und "pájaro" ('großer Vogel'/'kleiner Vogel' oder nicht definiert). [...] Auf Grund ihrer Unanalysierbarkeit in der Sprache bleiben diese populären Terminologien von der Struktur des Wortschatzes ausgeschlossen"[160].

Thus these "languages" are in one-to-one relation to what we believe are the "things". They are in principle universal and this is one of the reasons why they are of little interest in the description of a particular language.

(6) It is obvious that the semantic system of a language has not only, synchronically, an intrinsic interest but also an interest through its intimate relation to many linguistic problems. It also has, diatopically, a great importance in the theory of translation of written texts and in discussions of difficulties of individuals speaking a foreign language.

---

[157] Lecture notes, p. 24–25.
[158] Lecture notes, p. 54.
[159] "Les structures léxematiques", p. 10.
[160] Lecture notes, p. 14–15. See also p. 10.

II. *Semantic subdivisions.* We suggest the term subdivision for a systematic account of the allosemes of some particular lexeme sememe (or of some particular morpheme sememe). This is a problem that authors of dictionaries have had to tackle. Although an investigation into their strategies would probably show many inconsistencies, these authors often make the structure of their interpretation quite clear. One sees how the "main significations", perhaps shown as I, II, III, ..., may dominate other "significations" perhaps shown as 1, 2, 3, ..., and, if needed, also a, b, c, ..., can be used. For instance some particular "signification", i.e. alloseme, could be I, 2, b.

Opening my own school dictionary[161] at a random page, I find, *knight* explained as follows: I. 1. *riddare* i olika bet[162]. a) ..., b) ..., c) ..., d) ...[163], 2. *springare* (i schack)[164]. II. dubba till riddare[165].

Similar descriptions have recently been given by J. J. Katz and J. A. Fodor in the form of trees.

It is clear that the way dictionaries (be they mono- or bilingual) set out their subdivisions and a tree are equivalent. The first mentioned way is, however, more economical (paper saving) as it is more "compact"[166].

The tree for *knight* would be:

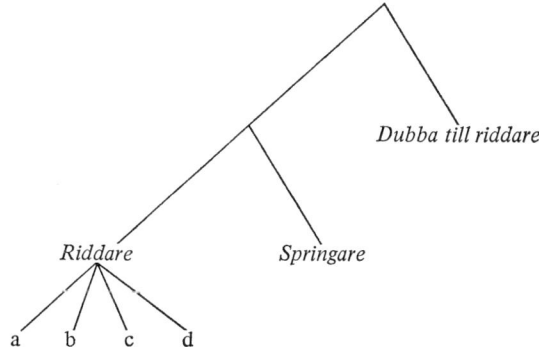

(We will not discuss the details as such of this tree).

III. *Semantic groups.* It is suggested that a number of allosemes having one, or more, components in common but not being a subsystem form a *semantic group*. For instance, "young", and "blonde" belong to different subsystems, the former being dominated by "age" and the latter by "colour". Within their subsystems they would both have the component 'referring to humans'. More exactly "young" has this component by

---

[161] *Engelsk-svensk ordbok* by Kärre-Lindkvist-Nöjd-Redin.
[162] *Knight* in different senses.
[163] We do not provide "the different senses".
[164] *Knight* (in chess).
[165] [*dub...a*] *knight*.
[166] Coseriu points out that far from being a "revolution" in structural semantics the suggestions by these authors are not even structural or functional (*lecture notes*, p. 37, 51–52 and "Les structures lexématiques", p. 4–6). In a somewhat more detailed way we would say that there is little new in the semantic trees but that they are, to some extent, structural although they do not describe the semantic structure (= our semantic system) of a language. Implicitly they presuppose knowledge of the semantic system. In this sense they are a secondary problem in semantics.

implication (which is a possibility we would like to accept) as in the subsystem the component would really be 'referring to living beings'. "Blonde" has directly the component 'referring to humans'. Thus "young" and "blonde" would belong to a given group (which would have further members than these two).

Coseriu mentions the group French "adlative" verbs (*acheter, reçevoir, prendre, saisir* etc.) and the group of "ablative" verbs (*vendre, donner, laisser, lâcher* etc.)[167].

A group may include allosemes of lexemes from different "word classes": allosemes of *beautiful, beauty, beautification* have all the component 'beautiful'.

IV. *Semantic classes*. It is suggested that a *semantic class* be defined as a number of allosemes which can occur in some particular place in some particular syntactic construction, i.e. a class is syntactically determined.

A class may or may not coincide with a subsystem or a group.

If one takes the syntactic notion of agent in a wide sense *man, dog, fire* and *machine* can function as agents: *this was done (made) by the man, dog, fire, machine*, i.e. these four belong to a particular class in English as they can all be agents but there is no subsystem and (probably) no group including just these. However, if agent is subdivided into "actor", "originator", "experiencer", "instrument" etc., then the class defined by "actor" seems to coincide with the subsystems where the terms are dominated directly or indirectly by 'animate' (cf. p. 99), or with the group defined by the component 'animate' (both including the same allosemes). There is certainly no subsystem dominated by something like "originator" and such that it would coincide with the class (*fire, storm, mistake* etc.). There would most certainly be a subsystem and a group including all allosemes referring to instruments. However, things other than instruments function as instruments so that the class determined by the syntactic notion "instrument" is very large and could include, it seems, almost any 'concrete' thing. If one throws a stone or a dog, one may say *the stick was broken by the stone* or *by the dog*[168].

When two (or more) allofuncts (diallofuncts etc.) from different functemes are similar, the classes established by these allofuncts seem to be the same. The class "girl", "man", "gift" etc. determined by the allofunct "target" as realized in *I appreciate the girl, man, gift* etc. is the same as the class "girl", "man", "gift" etc. as determined by the allofunct "target" as realized in *my appreciation of the girl, man, gift*.

It should be noted that we have concentrated on the heads of the constructions. In our discussion these have been in the focus of interest. However, taking semantic class in a wider sense, not only "man", "dog", "fire" etc. would be discussed but whole syntagm semes (varisyntagm sememes): "the man", "the little man" etc., would be taken into account.

---

[167] P. 11 of "Les structures lexématiques". Coseriu does not use the term "group" but the term "class", which, however, has a rather wide definition as it includes facts called by us "semantic classes" in addition to our groups.

[168] C. J. Fillmore discusses a similar problem and says (*The Grammar of hitting and breaking* in *Readings in English Transformational Grammar*, p. 132): "A sentence like *The dog broke the stick*, when it is used to refer to what happened to the stick when we threw the dog at it, must then be interpreted as containing in its deep structure the noun phrase *the dog's body*. The word *body*, then, being inanimate, is capable of fulfilling an instrumental function in the clause." This is a good example of the kind of nonsense conclusions that preconceived ideas and "deep structure" may lead to. Any sensible layman would have understood, quite correctly, that the unfortunate dog in question was as animate as any other dog.

21. *Syntagmatics*. It has already been explained how morpheme allosemes (morph semes) amalgamate to form lexeme allosemes (lex semes) (cf. p. 52). It has also been mentioned how components follow one another (p. 95). They would then, to some extent, modify each other.

Mention has also been made of semantic and semantic-syntactic interselection, which are syntagmatic facts as long as they are horizontal or diagonal (but not when they are vertical)[169].

In the description of various languages, as well as in the theory, combination (amalgamation) of morpheme allosemes has been pushed into the background in favour of the problem of combining morphemes into lexemes and sometimes the difference between the two problems does not seem to be clearly seen. It is, however, obvious that the difference between content and expression is always important. From the viewpoint of lexemes *yellowish* can be derived from *yellow* and *gardener* from *garden*. They are thus similar. Considering the level of content they are, however, not similar. In "yellowish", "yellow" is determined by "ish" but in "gardener", "er" is determined by "garden". (To "yellow" is added "ish" meaning something like "close to" or "indistinct". The meaning of "er" is "somebody carrying out some action" and "garden" says that this action is "connected with the garden"[170].)

22.1. *Units : glotto-, dia-, socio-, idiosememes of lexemes*. To simplify our task we will only consider lexeme sememes in their capacity as glotto-, dia-, socio- and idiounits (and leave out morpheme sememes, different kinds of components etc. in their capacity as similar units). As differences and similarities between diaunits, sociounits and idiounits are similar, we will only exemplify some differences and similarities between diaunits. The following relevant correspondences seem to be those which one would have to consider in the first instance:

Dialect A (Sociolect A) (Idiolect A)	Dialect B (Sociolect B) (Idiolect B)
1. lexeme$_a$ sememe$_a$	lexeme$_a$ sememe$_a$
2. lexeme$_a$ sememe$_a$	lexeme$_a$ sememe$_{partly\ a}$
3. lexeme$_a$ sememe$_a$	lexeme$_a$ sememe$_b$
4. lexeme$_a$ sememe$_a$	lexeme$_b$ sememe$_a$
5. lexeme$_a$ sememe$_a$	lexeme$_b$ sememe$_{partly\ a}$
6. lexeme sememe	∅

1. Two (or more) dialects (sociolects, idiolects) usually have many instances of corresponding lexemes which also have corresponding sememes. Many English dialects have the lexeme *table* with the sememe "table". This kind of correspondence is lexemic and sememic.

2. Two corresponding lexemes in two dialects may have only partly corresponding sememes. They have then at least one alloseme in common but the rest may be different. Both British and Australian English have the lexeme *bush* but in Australia,

---
[169] Further remarks can be found in Coseriu, "Les structures lexématiques", p. 15–16.
[170] Instead of taking similar problems any further we refer to Coseriu's important remarks in the lecture notes, p. 46–48, 76–92 and in "Les structures lexématiques", p. 13–15.

in addition to the allosemes it has in Britain, it has an alloseme referring to woods or forest. The correspondence is lexemic and partly sememic.

3. Two dialects may have corresponding lexemes with non-corresponding sememes. (In interdialectal communication this easily leads to misunderstandings, as sometimes do cases 2 and 5.) In French *déjeuner* usually refers to the second meal in the day (lunch) but in some dialects it is the first meal (breakfast). The correspondence is lexemic and non-sememic.

4. Two dialects have corresponding sememes but their lexemes are not corresponding. The Swedish sememe with which "bucket" would correspond in English would be expressed by *spann* in some Southern Swedish dialect and by *hink* in some Central Swedish dialect. The correspondence is non-lexemic and sememic.

5. Two dialects may have two different words with partly the same meaning. As, in Australia, *bush* has partly taken over the meaning of British *woods*, British *woods* and Australian *bush* have partly the same sememe. The correspondence is non-lexemic and partly sememic.

6. A word in one dialect may be non-existent in another dialect as its meaning does not need to be expressed at all or, perhaps, not often enough to warrant a lexeme. A *pavlova* is a well known cake in Australia but the word does not belong to British dialects. The correspondence is between a lexeme with its sememe and zero.

If we now want to establish glottosememes of various kinds, we will have to consider again the six kinds of correspondences just accounted for. First we may base our considerations on the content side:

1. If we believe that there are no other diasememes than those we have just assumed, "table" would be an English glottosememe such that one would either say that it has no diasememes, or (rather) that it has several diasememes but that they are the same. If we also believe that there is no variation between dialects at the level of expression, the glottosememe is *monolexemic*.

2. The British sememe "bush" and the Australian "bush" would possibly most conveniently have to form a glottosememe each, but under each, one would have to state that it has the other as a partly overlapping glottosememe. Each would presumably be monolexemic, but under each it would have to be stated that it is also *homolexemic* with the other, i.e. the other glottosememe is expressed in the same way.

3. There is a French glottosememe "breakfast" and a French glottosememe "lunch". As "breakfast" can be expressed by *déjeuner* or *petit déjeuner*, it is *polylexemic*. "Lunch", which can be expressed by *dîner* or *déjeuner*, is also *polylexemic*. "Breakfast" and "lunch" can also be said to be partly homolexemic.

4. In the Swedish example "bucket" is a glottosememe. As it can be expressed either by *spann* or *hink*, it is polylexemic (which should be stated). "Bucket" is homolexemic through *spann* (which expresses also glottosememes other than "bucket") but not through *hink*.

5. There is in English a glottosememe "bush" (or, perhaps, even two "bush" glottosememes, see above) and a glottosememe "woods". Each has the other as a partly overlapping glottosememe. Each glottosememe is monolexemic.

6. There would be a glottosememe "pavlova". It would have one diasememe "pavlova" and, in addition, it would have, in most dialects, zero-diasememes. The glottosememe is (presumably) monolexemic.

It is doubtful if this attempt at establishing glottosememes is the most interesting in a semantic study. The variants within each glottosememe consist of nothing more interesting than (a) diasememes which are the same (case 1, 3, 4), (b) a diasememe in one dialect to which there is nothing corresponding in other dialects (case 6), or (c) diasememes with partial correspondences in other dialects. It may, therefore, seem more interesting to do a different kind of analysis and to define the diasememes of some particular glottosememe as the sememes of all dialects belonging to some particular (glotto)lexeme. Using this definition, the examples just provided would be accounted for in the following way:

1. There would be a glottosememe *table*[171] with diasememes "table", which are not different from each other.

2. The glottosememe *bush* would have a British diasememe "bush" and an Australian diasememe "bush", which, having partly different allosemes, would be considerably different. Considered as parts of diasememes these allosememes would be diaallosemes. It could be explicitly stated which dialloseme of one diasememe corresponds with a dialloseme of the other diasememe (and which not).

3. The French glottosememe *déjeuner* would have diasememes as different as "breakfast" and "lunch". It should be stated that both diasememes correspond with diasememes within other glottosememes. ("Breakfast" is also found within the glottosememe *petit déjeuner* and "lunch" is also found within the glottosememe *dîner*.) These glottosememes could be called *partly homosememic*.

4. There would be the Swedish glottosememes *spann* and *hink* but they would have the "same" sememe. One would say that each has the other as a corresponding sememe. (When *spann* has meanings other than "bucket" it is a different homonymous word.)

5. In addition to the English glottosememe *bush* (cf. point 2) one would have the glottosememe *woods*. Diaallosemes of the former would correspond with diaallosemes of the latter.

6. The glottosememe *pavlova* would have the diasememe "pavlova" in Australia and zero-diasememes in many other dialects.

If we introduce some new abbreviations, add a detail concerning the expression side (ph-ph-units versus m-ph-units) and discard some details such as part correspondences, it seems that one can define the three most important kinds of semantic glotto-units in the following way:

22.2. *Definition*: All lexeme diasememes which are corresponding form a lexemic *se-glottosememe* regardless of possible relations between dialexemes. Such glottosememes may be monolexemic or polylexemic. The English glottosememe "bucket", which may be expressed by the dialexemes /bʌkɪt/ (bucket) or /peɪl/ (pail), is polylexemic.

The different dialexemes expressing an se-glottosememe form an se-glottolexeme (see above 1.1.5.11.3.), which poses a basically "onomasiological" problem: "which is the lexeme, or which are the lexemes, in different dialects, for some given meaning?".

22.3. *Definition*: All diasememes of corresponding ph-ph-lexemes form a *lexemic ph-ph-glottosememe*.

---

[171] As an abbreviation we write "glottosememe *table*" for "the glottosememe which includes all diasememes of the (glotto)lexeme *table*".

This kind of glottosememe concerns the problem "which are the meanings, in different dialects, of a lexeme defined as a string of phonemes which is the same in all dialects". This problem is "semasiological".

In many cases the corresponding dialexemes will have corresponding sememes. In two different English dialects /bi:/ (bee) may have the same meaning. There is, however, a possibility that a glottosememe includes non-corresponding diasemes. According to U. Weinreich[172] (p. 394) /futer/ has the meaning "father" in one variety of Yiddish and "fur" in another variety. This means that the glottosememe /futer/[173] has one diasememe "father" and another diasememe "fur". These diasememes belong to the same ph-ph-glottosememe, but are non-corresponding as to meaning[174]. As mentioned above the French word *déjeuner* also has different diasememes. It should, however, be noted that *déjeuner* is "the same word" in various dialects but that the two *futer* are "different words".

The problem would perhaps not be of primary interest to dialectologists, but it would be of definite importance in the study of interference phenomena between speakers of different dialects.

22.4. *Definition*: All diasememes of corresponding m-ph-lexemes form a *lexemic m-ph-glottosememe*.

As the notion of corresponding meaning was used in the definition of m-ph-lexemes, it is clear that by and large the diasememes of some m-ph-glottosememe will be corresponding. A Scottish *arm* with /r/ is m-ph- (but not ph-ph-)corresponding with *arm* from some dialect without /r/ (see above, 1.1.5.11.2.). The meanings or the diasememes of the two (which are probably corresponding) belong to the same glottosememe.

One can, however, imagine that the diasememes are different. Such an example would be similar to the two *futer* just mentioned but with the difference that one would have to imagine that one or more phonemes (variphones) were morphemically, without being phonemically, corresponding (e.g. *futer* versus **fuser*).

This kind of glottosememe concerns the problem "which are the meanings, in different dialects, of a lexeme, which may or may not take different phonemic shapes in different dialects". This again is a "semasiological" problem. It is of interest in dialectology as well as interference studies.

A (ph-ph-, or m-ph-)glottosememe may be called monosememic if the diasememes are corresponding and polysememic if they are non-corresponding.

A lexeme of one dialect does not normally have a one-to-many m-ph-correspondence with lexemes of another dialect (as a word of a particular dialect has usually not more than one phonemic form).

22.5. As mentioned there are part correspondences. Therefore, sememes may correspond one-to-many. In an imagined language the greeting could be *good day* in one dialect, and *good morning*, *good afternoon* and *good evening* in another. Mutatis mutandis

---

[172] "Is structural dialectology possible?" *Linguistics Today* (= Word 10:2/3, 1954, p. 388–400).
[173] "glottosememe /futer/" is used as an abbreviation for the glottosememe of the "ph-ph-glottolexeme /futer/".
[174] The case has some similarity with homonyms. However, the term homonym should be limited to the description of one single language system.

this problem would be treated exactly as the one of one-to-many corresponding m-diaphonemes (see above, 1.1.1.12.2.).

23. *Inventories of semantic units and items.* It is clear that inventories of any of the units or items mentioned above could be established.

The inventory of the morpheme allosemes of a language would be very large. An inventory of lexeme allosemes is in most languages still larger (as lexeme allosemes may consist of morpheme allosemes in different combinations).

Subinventories such as the one of "functional" or "grammatical" morpheme or lexeme allosemes may be quite limited and could therefore be provided in a complete form.

Dictionaries (unless they are just "orthographic") provide much information about allosemes and allosemes within sememes.

As morpheme and lexeme allosemes usually consist of components each of which usually recurs many times, the number of components is considerably smaller than the number of allosemes. It would be of considerable interest to possess an inventory of components.

24. *Discovery procedures.* As pointed out above (p. 51, 52), it is assumed that a linguist, knowing the language, can generally assign meanings to words and, in addition, establish components. The assistance of informants may, however, be of considerable importance.

1.2. β-Level

0. Up to this point our account has been rather detailed. The remarks provided below will, however, be limited to some hints about other parts of the description of languages.

1. As was noted above, the term β-level is here used for all language facts which signal "how something is said".

Said in a somewhat more explicit way, β-variants are different expressions for affiliated contents. (Affiliated contents may refer to exactly the same "thing", or have the same "referent".) For instance, *girl* and *bird* (both referring to a young woman) have affiliated meaning. The difference between them consists in their different β-value. The two words, or rather their contents, have the same "referent" (a young woman), the description of which is not within the domain of linguistics.

Both the expression side and the content side of the β-elements belong to the β-level.

It seems reasonable to subdivide the β-level into β_1, attitudes, and β_2, registers. β_1-facts would be conditioned by the sometimes swiftly changing "internal circumstances" of the speaker. β_2-facts would be conditioned by the somewhat more stable "external circumstances" (participants, place, topic etc.).

Contouremes (units) and contours (items) would be the most important β-facts in phonetics. The β-facts of syntax and semantics could be called stylistic.

Contours may have the "length" of a phone, a syllab, a morph (see above, p. 13, 33, 40, 48), a lex or a syntagm (see p. 88).

Contouremes may resemble prosodemes as to their sound properties but they are quite different in function. The discrete prosodemes have α-function ("constructive", "distinctive" or "emphatic" function) but the non discrete contouremes have different β-functions, or different expressemes: abrupt, affable, affected, affectionate, aggressive, etc.

While the whole meaning of a contoureme is called expresseme, there can be meaning variants between different contours of a contoureme. Something can be said in an abrupt way but according to the particular contour "abrupt" may be signalled in a strong or a weak way, i.e. with an express "strongly abrupt" or with an express "slightly abrupt". This means that several expresses form an expresseme.

(See above p. 2, 30, 33 and my paper "Towards more exhaustive descriptions of languages"[175].)

1.3. γ-Level

In this work the γ_1- ("idiolectal"), γ_2- ("sociolectal") and γ_3- ("dialectal") functions have been included in a framework for the description of synchronic language facts as they convey meanings from speaker to hearer in the act of communication.

In precise terms, idiolectal, sociolectal and dialectal would rather refer to idiolects, sociolects and dialects as wholes whereas γ_1, γ_2 and γ_3 would refer to the properties which characterize and distinguish these wholes.

Idiolects can usually be grouped into sociolects; which can be grouped into dialects; which can be grouped into a glottolect. (Glottolects can usually be grouped into "families" of glottolects.) This means that idiounits can be grouped into larger units. For instance, idiophonemes will belong to sociophonemes, which will belong to diaphonemes, which will belong to a glottophoneme (as has been shown above).

As a complete idiolect possesses not only γ_1- but also γ_2- and γ_3-properties, these three kinds of properties will be found in sociolects, dialects and glottolects. In some given study one may isolate γ_1-properties, whereby γ_2- and γ_3-properties will modify them, at least to some extent. If one isolates γ_2-properties there will be variants conditioned by γ_1- and γ_2-properties. And if one isolates γ_3-properties there will be variants according to γ_1- and γ_2-properties. This kind of variation would only be catered for in a narrow description (n-description).

Generally, linguistic descriptions are broad (b-descriptions). This means that in a less detailed way γ_1-properties (e.g. "voice qualities") are studied without regard to γ_2 and γ_3, γ_2-properties are studied without regard to γ_1 and γ_3, and γ_3-properties are studied without regard to γ_1 and γ_2. And a language as a whole, or some particular problem of a language, is described without regard to γ_1, γ_2 and γ_3. For instance, this is usually the case in school grammars of given languages or in a paper or book on a syntactic problem.

However, in an n-description there would be a network of influences between variants of the α-, β-, γ_1-, γ_2-, γ_3-levels. Often there would be *mutual conditioning of variants*. If, for instance, a language has a contoureme (β-level) signalling that some-

---

[175] Umeå University, Department of Phonetics, Publication 6.

thing is said in anger, this will modify the prosodeme (α-level) of *ímport* (as distinct from *impórt*) and the contoureme "anger" would have variants according to the prosodemes of the words with which it coincided. If a double-headed arrow is defined as showing variants which have MCV (mutual conditioning of variants) one would write in this case $\alpha \leftrightarrow \beta$.

(For further details see my paper "Towards more exhaustive descriptions of languages".)

1.4. Phonetics, Morphology, Semantics and Syntax

Phonetics includes phonemes, syllabemes and prosodemes.

Morphology includes morphemes and lexemes.

Semantics includes sememes.

Syntax includes syntagmemes.

As was mentioned above (p. 9) the author is of the opinion that in a description of α-facts it is not more appropriate to start from any one of these four main parts of linguistics rather than from any other.

If we assume (a) that the basic description should be "neutral" in relation to speaker and hearer (which, on the whole, grammars have usually been) and (b) that the framework will make provision for a high number of details (n-description), there will be conditioning of variants originating in each part of the description and affecting each other part. This could be shown as:

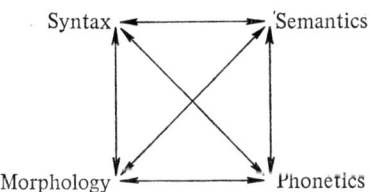

Consequently the description of each part presupposes the (n-)description of all other parts. (The description will have to have many cross-references, see above, p. 9.)

It is clear that for certain "high level" problems ("b-problems") one does not have to take facts from more than one or two levels into account. If one states that one language has 30 phonemes in contradistinction to some other language which has only 20 phonemes one abstracts away not only all relations to the three other main parts but also the parts of phonetics which deal with distribution and exact realizations of phonemes.

All arguments in favour of, or against, taking syntax, semantics or phonetics as the exclusive starting point in a description are considered by the present author to concern non-problems. (Morphology does not seem to have been involved in this discussion.)

Except, perhaps, for some special cases, all kinds of "processes", including "transformations", are considered as "empirically inadequate" (see my paper "Generative phonology: A critical appraisal", p. 157, 161–163)[176].

Processes which are inappropriate in the basic part of linguistic description, are, however, adequate in discovery procedures, speaker's grammar, hearer's grammar, comparing different languages, diachrony and machine translation (see my paper "The direct object nexeme in English")[177].

2. Written Language

Written language can, and should, be described as a system in its own right.

(a) In *typemics*, letters, typemes, have certain similarities with phonemes, although the "substance" is not sounds but lines. Both typemes and phonemes have distinctive components, both have positional variants etc. (see p. 333–338 of my paper "Type et typème, graphe et graphème"[178]).

(b) In *written morphology* morphemes, and words, will be accounted for in terms of typemes (and not phonemes).

(c) In *written syntax* the words constituting constructions will consist of written words. When spoken syntax has been studied in more detail, a comparison will probably show that written and spoken syntax are somewhat more different than one would imagine.

(d) At least if one limits oneself to considering the most basic facts about *the semantics of written morphemes, words and syntactic constructions*, these will be little different from the spoken counter-parts.

3. Written Language in Relation to Spoken Language

A written language can be described in terms of its relations to the spoken language.

The way many letters are related to phonemes can be described in terms of "graphemes". All letters writing a given phoneme form a grapheme. (For further details see my paper "Graphemes and nuncemes of English"[179].)

---

[176] Phonetica **27**: 3, 1973, p. 157–184.
[177] Forthcoming. Cp. above, p. VI.
[178] Studia neophilologica **36**: 2, 1964, p. 332–340. See also Hans Peter Althaus, *Graphetik*, p. 105–110 of *Lexikon der Germanistischen Linguistik*.
[179] Studia linguistica **26**: 1, 1972, p. 14–25. See also Hans Peter Althaus, *Graphemik*, p. 118–132 of *Lexikon der Germanistischen Linguistik*.

4. Spoken Language in Relation to Written Language

A spoken language can be described in terms of its relations to the written language. The written language is then "the point of departure" for one's considerations or, in other words, the units and items of the spoken language are "seen through" the units and items of the written language.

The way spoken phonemes are related to letters (typemes) could be described in terms of "nuncemes". All pronunciations of a letter (typeme), or of certain combinations of letters, form a nunceme. (For further details see my paper "Graphemes and nuncemes of English".)

We shall not attempt to take this kind of consideration into morphology, syntax and semantics. It is, however, clear that there are many facts to be accounted for. It has just been said that written and spoken syntax are rather different but that similarities could be greater in semantics. In morphology there would be many simple correspondences between written and spoken forms. Sometimes correspondences are more complicated. For instance, in written language there is a set of segments written *wh-* (*when, where, who* ...). In spoken language most of these are /w/ but *who* has the spoken corresponding form /h/.

5. The Tasks of Linguistics

The most basic task of linguistics is to describe idio-, socio-, dia- and glottosystems. These are the systems of communication which make it possible for human beings to carry out speech acts.

The descriptions of such systems will contain the *units* described above. These units are named by terms ending in *-eme* and *-ememe*, or beginning with *allo-, diallo-*, etc. or *vari-, divari-* etc.

Knowledge of the systems is based largely on investigation of speech acts whereas the *items* realized in the speech are of little interest for their own sake. When the linguist is a native speaker of the language under investigation, or if he knows this language well, he will consult his intuitive knowledge in very significant ways.

Linguists, and sometimes laymen, occupy themselves with languages in an "extra-communicative" way (see Ungeheuer, "Kommunikative und extrakommunikative Betrachtungsweisen in der Phonetik")[180].

This book has dealt with the "basic and neutral" part of the description of a language.

In addition there are other less known parts of the description of a language. These are "directional" (as "processes" will largely describe them): (1.a) "syntheti). grammar" and (1.b) "speaker's grammar", and (2.a) "analytic grammar" and (2.bc "hearer's grammar" (cf. above p. 114).

---

[180] P. 73–86 of *Proceedings of the Sixth international congress of phonetic sciences*. München-Prague-Philadelphia, 1970.

In *synthetic grammar* (1.a) it is explicitly shown how sentences are put together on the basis of the neutral description. Synthesis would start at the level of semantics and proceed through syntax and morphology to phonetics (or typetics if the message were written). Synthesis would be part of machine translation or used by somebody putting together a message in a foreign language using a grammar and a lexicon (although it is doubtful if he needs an explicit synthetic grammar as the basic neutral grammar seems to be sufficient). A "pure"[181] synthetic grammar would be written in the most purposeful way in relation to its aim but would not have to be exactly the same as a "speaker's grammar".

A *speaker's grammar* (1.b) is a kind of synthetic grammar but to be adequate it would ideally have to describe exactly what happens in the mind of a speaker when he produces ("encodes") utterances in his own language. It would also be of interest to know how a speaker produces utterances in a foreign language which he knows more or less well. Although there would be more than one direction to account for, there would, perhaps, be something like a "general direction": semantics — syntax — morphology — phonetics (typetics).

In *analytic grammar* (2.a) it is shown how sentences are analyzed as to their phonetic, morphological, syntactic and semantic properties. It could be used by somebody in search of a linguistic description of given sentences or as part of machine translation. Its aim would be purposefulness but not adequacy in relation to what is going on in a hearer taking part in language communication.

A *hearer's grammar* (2.b) is a kind of analytic grammar which would describe what happens in the mind of a speaker when he understands ("decodes") utterances in his own (or in a foreign) language. There would be a general direction: phonetics[182] — morphology — syntax — semantics. However, in a similar manner to what is true about the speaker's grammar, it is not likely that any of these parts is processed in the mind in isolation from the others. For instance, to interpret some sounds as a word one probably uses one's knowledge about how phonemes are habitually realized, what sequences of phonemes are possible, which morphemes and words exist and which not, what syntactic constructions are possible, what meaning sequences are possible and what content the interlocutor is likely to express.

A linguist intending to describe a spoken (eventually taped and notated) text, or a written text, will do it in terms of items (phones, syllabs ...). Each item is clearly and explicitly relatable to a unit of the basic description: a phone belongs to a phoneme, a syllab to a syllabeme etc. The order in which various kinds of items are described is of no great importance (cf. above p. 113) but one may as well use the widespread convention: phonetics — morphology — syntax — semantics.

One knows beforehand that every text will contain items which are relatable to all different kinds of units. At the α-level (if the text is spoken) it will be describable in terms of phones, syllabs, prosodes, morphs, lexes, syntagms and semes. In addition, $\beta_1, \beta_2, \gamma_1, \gamma_2, \gamma_3$ will have to be considered for every utterance if one aims at exhaustiveness.

---

[181] I.e. not explicitly relatable to the activity of a speaker speaking his own language.
[182] Sounds, not meanings, are sent through the air and strike the eardrum of the listeners.

Bibliography

Althaus, H. P.: *Graphetik.* Pp. 105—110 in *Lexikon der Germanistischen Linguistik*, Althaus, H. P., Henne, H., Wiegand, H. E. (eds). Tübingen 1973.
— *Graphemik.* Pp. 118—132 in *Lexikon der Germanistischen Linguistik*, Althaus, H. P., Henne, H., Wiegand, H. E. (eds). Tübingen 1973.
Bausch, K.-H.: *Soziolekte.* Pp. 254—262 in *Lexikon der Germanistischen Linguistik*, Althaus, H. P., Henne, H., Wiegand, H. E. (eds). Tübingen 1973.
Borgstrøm, C. H.: *Innføring i sprogvidenskap.* Oslo 1958.
Brodda, B., Karlgren, H.: *Synonymer och synonymers synonymer.* KVAL PM 335. Stockholm 1967.
Chomsky, N.: *Aspects of the theory of syntax.* Cambridge (Mass.) 1965.
— *Current issues in linguistic theory.* The Hague 1964. Also pp. 50—118 in *The structure of language. Readings in the philosophy of language*, Fodor, J. A., Katz, J. J. (eds). Englewood Cliffs (New Jersey) 1964.
— *Language and mind.* New York-Chicago-San Francisco-Atlanta 1972.
— Review of Skinner, B. F. *Verbal behavior.* Language **35:1**, 26—58 (1959). Also pp. 547 —578 in *The structure of language. Readings in the philosophy of language*, Fodor, J. A., Katz, J. J. (eds). Englewood Cliffs (New Jersey) 1964.
— *Topics in the theory of generative grammar.* The Hague 1966.
— *Syntactic structures.* The Hague 1957.
Chomsky, N., Halle, M.: *The sound pattern of English.* New York-Evanston-London 1968.
Collinder, B.: *Noam Chomsky und die generative Grammatik. Eine kritische Betrachtung.* Acta Societatis Linguisticae Upsaliensis, Nova series **2:1**. Uppsala 1970.
Cooper, W. S.: *Set theory and syntactic description.* The Hague 1964.
Coseriu, E.: *Lecture Notes*, abbreviation for *Probleme der romanischen Semantik. Vorlesung gehalten im WS 1965/66 an der Universität Tübingen.* Autorisierte Nachschrift besorgt von D. Kastovsky und W. Müller.
— Les structures lexématiques. Zeitschrift für französische Sprache und Literatur, Beiheft, Neue Folge. Heft 1, 3—16 (1968).
Elert, C.-C.: *Ljud och ord i svenskan.* Uppsala 1970.
Fillmore, C. J.: *The grammar of hitting and breaking.* Pp. 120—133 in *Readings in English transformational grammar*, Jacobs, R. A., Rosenbaum, P. S. (eds). Waltham-Toronto-London 1970.
Fischer-Jørgensen, E.: Remarques sur les principes de l'analyse phonémique. Travaux du Cercle linguistique de Copenhague V, 214—234 (1949).
Gleason, H. A.: *An introduction to descriptive linguistics.* New York, rev. ed., 1961.
Hall, R. A., Jr.: Some recent developments in American linguistics. Neuphilologische Mitteilungen **70**, 192—227 (1969).
— Underlying representation and observable fact in phonology. Journal of English Linguistics **7**, 21—42 (1973).
Hammarström, G.: Dialectal and sociolectal facts within the description of a language. Language Sciencies **34**, 13—18 (1975).
— Dialektologiska undersökningar. Nordisk tidsskrift for tale og stemme **24**, 27—51 (1964).
— *Étude de phonétique auditive sur les parlers de l'Algarve.* Uppsala 1953.
— Generative phonology. A critical appraisal. Phonetica **27**, 157—184 (1973).
— Graphemes and nuncemes of English. Studia linguistica **26:1**, 14—25 (1972).

Hammarström, G.: *Idiolekt.* Pp. 312—314 in *Lexikon der Germanistischen Linguistik*, Althaus, H. P., Henne, H., Wiegand, H. E. (eds). Tübingen 1973.
— Inquéritos linguísticos II. Revista de Portugal, Série A, Língua Portuguesa **26**, 9—32 (1961).
— L'historique et le programme d'activité de l'Institut de phonétique d'Upsal. Pp. 152—156 in *Communications et rapports du Premier Congrès International de Dialectologie générale*. Louvain 1965.
— *Linguistische Einheiten im Rahmen der modernen Sprachwissenschaft.* (Kommunikation und Kybernetik in Einzeldarstellungen **5**.) Berlin-Heidelberg-New York 1966. (Spanish translation: *Las unidades lingüísticas en el marco de la lingüística moderna*. Madrid 1974.)
— Monophthongemes and diphthongemes. Linguistics **87**, 50—53 (1972) = Talanya **1**.
— On linguistic terminology. Pp. 321—325 in *Actes du Xe Congrès International des Linguistes*. Bucharest 1969.
— On terminology in genetic, gennemic and energemic phonetics. Word **23:1-2-3**, 254—256 (1967).
— Prosodeme und Kontureme. Phonetica **10**, 194—202 (1963).
— Pseudo-units in phonetics. Pp. 411—413 in *Proceedings of the Sixth International Congress of Phonetic Sciences*, 1967. Prague 1970.
— Review of Hadding-Koch, K. *Acoustico-phonetic studies in the intonation of Southern Swedish*. Phonetica **7**, 245—251 (1961).
— Sur la durée des phonèmes en suédois. Revista do Laboratório de Fonética Experimental da Faculdade de Letras da Universidade de Coimbra **1**, 9—27 (1952).
— Sur l'inventaire des phonèmes français. Pp. 343—346 in *Omagiu lui Alexandru Rosetti*. Bucharest 1965.
— *The problem of nonsense linguistics*. Acta Societatis Linguisticae Upsaliensis, Nova series, **2:4**. Uppsala 1971.
— Towards more exhaustive descriptions of languages. Umeå University, Department of Phonetics, Publication 6, 1973, pp. 1—30.
— Type et typème, graphe et graphème. Studia neophilologica **36:2**, 332—340 (1964).
— Über Palatographie, anatomische Bedingungen der Lautunterschiede und schwedische Vokalphoneme. Zeitschrift für Phonetik **17:5**, 397—407 (1964).
— Zur soziolektalen und dialektalen Funktion der Sprache. Zeitschrift für Mundartforschung **34:3/4**, 205—216 (1967).
Hanson, G.: *Dimensions in speech sound perception*. Ericsson Technics No. 1. Stockholm 1967.
Harris, Z. S.: *Methods in structural linguistics*. Chicago 1951. (Later title: *Structural linguistics*, Chicago 1963.)
Hill, A. A.: Review of Quirk, R., Svartvik, J., *Investigating linguistic acceptability*. Language **45:3**, 622—624 (1969).
Hockett, C.: Problems of morphemic analysis. Language **23**, 321—343 (1947). Also pp. 229—242 in *Readings in linguistics I*, Joos, M. (ed.). Chicago and London 1957.
Itkonen, E.: Concerning the methodological status of linguistic descriptions. Pp. 31—41 in *Derivational Processes*. KVAL PM 729, Kiefer, F. (ed.). Stockholm 1972.
— *Linguistics and metascience*. Studia Philosophica Turkuensia Fasc. II. Kokemäki 1974.
Jakobson, R., Fant, G., Halle, M.: *Preliminaries to speech analysis*. Cambridge (Mass.) 1951.
Juilland, A. G., Lieb, H. H.: „*Klasse*" *und Klassifikation in der Sprachwissenschaft*. The Hague 1968.
Lindblom, B.: Spectrographic study of vowel reduction. The Journal of the Acoustical Society of America **35:11**, 1773—1781 (1963).
Lyons, J.: *Introduction to theoretical linguistics*. Cambridge 1968.
Martinet, A.: Un ou deux phonèmes? Acta linguistica **1**, 94—103 (1939). Also pp. 116—123 in *Readings in linguistics II*, Hamp, E. P., Householder, F. W., Austerlitz, R. (eds). Chicago 1966.
Paul, H.: *Prinzipien der Sprachgeschichte*. 5th ed. Halle 1920.
Pike, K. L.: *Language in relation to a unified theory of the structure of human behavior II*. Glendale (Calif.) 1955.
Pilch, H.: Modelle der englischen Wortbildung. Pp. 160—178 in *Festschrift H. Marchand*. The Hague 1967.

Author Index

Althaus, H. P. 114
Austerlitz, R. 21
Baudouin de Courtenay, J. V
Bausch, K.-H. 3
Beebe, R. VII
Bell, T. VII
Bloomfield, L. VI, 6
Borgstrøm, C. H. 57
Brodda, B. 91
Busby, P. VII
Chadwick, N. VII
Chomsky, N. VI, 64, 65, 72, 73, 76, 78, 88, 93
Clyne, M. VII
Collinder, B. VI, 71, 72
Cooper, W. S. 5
Coseriu, E. VI, 85, 91, 96—98, 101—107
Elert, C.-C. 20
Fant, G. 20, 21, 95
Fillmore, C. J. 106
Fischer-Jørgensen, E. 20, 77
Fodor, J. A. 78, 105
Gleason, H. A. 9, 57, 62, 64
Hall, R. A., Jr. VI
Halle, M. VI, 20, 21, 95
Hammarström, G. V, VI, 3, 4, 7—11, 15, 18, 19, 22—24, 28—32, 35, 36, 40, 42, 46, 52, 66, 71, 74, 76, 80, 81, 112—114
Hamp, E. 21
Hanson, G. 30
Harris, Z. S. 6, 11
Heike, G. VI
Hill, A. A. 85
Hjelmslev, L. V, 77
Hockett, C. 50

Householder, F. W. 21
Itkonen, E. 10, 11
Jacobs, R. A. 106
Jakobson, R. VI, 6, 20, 21, 95
Joos, M. 50
Juilland, A. G. 5
Karlgren, H. 91
Kärre, K. 105
Katz, J. J. 78, 105
Lieb, H.-H. 5
Lindblom, B. 81
Lindkvist, H. 105
Lyons, J. 91, 100
Martinet, A. VI, 21
Nöjd, R. 105
Paul, H. 70
Pike, K. 19
Pilch, H. 8, 30, 51
Platt, H. VII
Platt, J. VII
Pottier, B. 101
Quirk, R. 85
Redin, M. 105
Roget, P. M. 91
Rosenbaum, P. S. 106
Saussure, F. de V, VI, 2, 85
Shaw, E. VII
Sigurd, B. 29, 64
Skinner, B. F. 78
Svartvik, J. 85
Tillmann, H. G. VI
Trubetzkoy, N. S. V, VI, 6, 20, 96—98
Uldall, H. J. 77
Ungeheuer, G. VI, 30, 115
Weinreich, U. 110

Pilch, H.: Neue Wege der englischen Phonetik. Anglia **77**, 407—428 (1959).
Quirk, R., Svartvik, J.: *Investigating linguistic acceptability*. The Hague 1966.
Saussure, F. de: *Cours de linguistique générale*. Paris 1964 (1st ed. 1916).
Sigurd, B.: A note on the number of phonemes. Statistical Methods in Linguistics **2, 94**—99 (1963).
— Frågor och svar i lingvistiken. Pp. 83—98 in *Vetenskapliga perspektiv*. Stockholms universitet 1971.
Trubetzkoy, N. S.: *Grundzüge der Phonologie*. Göttingen 1958.
Ungeheuer, G.: Kommunikative und extrakommunikative Betrachtungsweisen in der Phonetik. Pp. 73—86 in *Proceedings of the Sixth International Congress of Phonetic Sciences*. München-Prague-Philadelphia 1970.
Weinreich, U.: Is a structural dialectology possible? Word **10:2-3**, 388—400 (1954).

Subject Index

abstract IV, 4, 113
accentuation 31, 36
acceptability 85
acoustic 7, 8, 11, 14, 16, 30, 31, 44
act 3
act of communication 19, 103, 112
active 74—77
actor 93, 106
added 65, 75, 87—89, 92, 94, 101
adjective 57, 58
adjectiveme 57
adverb 57, 58
adverbeme 57, 58
adverbial 58, 69, 73, 75
adverbialeme functeme 69, 73
affiliation 75—77, 92, 111
affix 96
affricate 16, 18, 21
affricateme 18
agent 65, 73, 75, 76, 78, 93, 106
agreement 61
allo- 4, 47
alloadjective 66, 77
alloadverb 58
allofunct 65, 66, 69, 72, 73, 83, 93, 106
allolex 35, 43, 52, 53, 89
— sememe 95
— — component 95
— varilex sememe 89
allometa-phone 19
allomorph 26, 34, 43, 46—53, 90
— boundary 43
— prosodeme 34
— — component 34, 35
allomorpheme 34, 47
— prosodeme 34, 35
— — component 35
allomorphememe 47, 48
allomorphically affiliated 15
allonex 74
alloperiod 36, 66, 69, 72, 73, 83, 84
allophone 13—16, 20, 21, 24, 25, 28, 30, 47
— component 20, 22
allophoneme 14

allopredicate 66
alloprosode 31, 34, 35, 37
allopseudo-phone 19
alloquasi-phone 18
alloseme 73, 85, 86, 90—92, 95—97, 99—109, 111
— component 85, 94, 111
allosememe 91
allosemi-phone 16
allosubject 36, 66, 68
allosubstantive 66
allosyllab 33, 41
— prosodeme 33
— — component 33
allosyllabeme 33
— prosodeme 33
— — component 34
allosyntagm 66, 68, 74, 75, 82
alloverb 77
amalgamation 52, 55, 87—91, 95, 107
ambiguous 37, 64, 72, 78, 79, 87
amorphous thought 88
anacoluthic 80
analytic grammar VI, 115, 116
appositive 58
arbitrary 1, 85
arrangement 69
articulator 16
articulatory 7, 8, 11, 14, 16, 30, 31, 44
ascending diagonal 79
attitude 2, 111
attribute 58
attributeme functeme 73
auditory 7, 8, 11, 16, 30, 36
automatic translation 85
autonomy 77
auxiliareme 57
auxiliary 57

basic VI, 31, 36, 50, 65, 66, 75, 102, 113, 115, 116
bilateral 98
binary feature 20, 21
biphonemic 21

121

bipolar   21, 97, 100
bound   48
boundary   51
— marker   31
bound morpheme   34, 96
box diagram   59, 67, 73
— structure   65
broad   4, 5, 32
— definition   36
b-syllabeme   41
b-unit   4, 14, 15, 19—22, 41, 46—48, 53, 54, 63, 66, 68—71, 80, 82, 95, 96, 98, 112, 113

cardinal   57
cardinaleme   57
centre   16
Chinese "tones"   35
class   96, 106
classification   V, 71
clause   58, 59, 69, 103
clauseme   69, 70, 74, 75
clear   19, 32, 44, 45, 49, 86, 87, 93, 96
clue   12
cluster   21
coarticulation   16
combinability   6
combination   77
common component   98, 100
— sense   93
communication   79
communicator   70, 79
commutation test   10, 29
comparative study   114
comparison   23
competence   VI
complement   58, 68, 74
complementarity   77
complementary distribution   14, 16, 48
completely synonymous   91
complex component   36
component   5, 6, 11, 19, 20, 29, 35, 91, 93—95, 97, 99, 101, 106, 107, 111
compound   102
compression substitution   68, 85
conditioning of variants   113
conjunction   57
conjunctioneme   57
consecutive   95
consonant   15, 16, 20, 22, 29, 39, 41, 47, 97
constituent analysis   87
— structure   65, 72
constructed period   71, 103
construction   106, 114
constructive   13, 32, 35, 37, 39, 43, 112
content   1—3, 10, 94, 107
— segment   52

content side   85
— unit   52
context   14, 47, 48, 51, 53, 63, 72, 73, 79, 81, 85, 94, 95
— of situation   85
continuous   17
contoid   17
contour   30, 33, 70, 73, 79, 111, 112
contoureme   30, 31, 33, 37, 79, 111, 112
conventional   1
coordination   74
corpus   10, 11, 79, 80
correct utterance   11
correspondence, see corresponding
corresponding   23—28, 39, 43, 44, 55, 82—84, 86, 88, 107—110, 115
course   8, 9, 31, 32
— of duration   9
— of length   9, 36
— of loudness   36
— of pitch   36
— of quality   36

decoder   77
decoding   7, 116
deep structure   VI, 64, 71, 75
definition   V, 10
degree   97
dependent morpheme 34
— morphememe   48
derived   50
— lexeme   102, 107
descending diagonal   78
description   9, 10, 11, 28, 40, 80, 111, 113
determiner   57
determinereme   57, 66
diaact   3
diaalloperiod   84
diaallophone   25, 28
diaalloseme   109
diaallosyllab   43
diachrony   VI, 11, 114
diafunct   83
diafuncteme   84
diagonal   64, 77, 78, 107
dia-idiophone   25
dialect   3, 22—28, 38, 39, 43, 44, 55, 56, 79, 82—86, 103, 107—110, 112
— A   27
— of place A   23
dialectologist   23, 110
dialectology   110
dialexeme   56, 109, 110
diallo-   4, 47
diallofunct   93
dialloperiod   36, 69, 71
diallophone   14

dialloprosode 33
diallosubject 36
diallosyllab 41
diallosyntagm 66, 74, 75
diaperiodeme 82
diaphone 13, 25
diaphoneme 22, 24—28, 112
diaprosode 38
— component 38
diaprosodeme 38, 39
— component 38
— functeme 39
diaseme 110
diasememe 56, 108—110
diasubjecteme 82
diasyllab 40, 43
— prosode 38
diasyllabeme 43, 44
— prosodeme 38
diasyllabememe 43
diasyntagm 82
diasyntagmeme 82, 83
diasystem 3, 115
diatext 3
diatopy 11, 104
diaunit 4
diavarisyllab 44
dictionary 56, 92, 105, 111
diphthong 16—18, 21
diphthongeme 16, 17
direct 66, 94
— object 58, 75
— opposition 100
— segment 59, 61, 66, 69
directly available period 70, 71
— dominated 100
disambiguate 37, 79
discontinuous syntagm 60
discovery procedure 9—11, 29, 39, 44, 51, 56, 84, 111, 114
discrete 30, 37, 112
distinctive 13, 32, 35, 37, 40, 46, 112
— component 114
— feature 7, 20, 22, 24
— function 39
distinguishing component 98, 100
distribution 6, 13, 14, 21, 22, 24, 46—48, 53, 57, 58, 63, 66, 67, 81, 82, 96
distributional 68
divari- 4, 47
divided 64
dividing substitution 30, 67, 68, 85
division 69
d-lexeme 57, 61
d-lexememe 53, 54, 66, 68, 69
dominate 104, 105
dominated 100—102, 106

dominating 100, 102
double arrow 50
duration 8, 9

economy VI, 64, 70, 101, 105
-eme 4
-ememe 4
emphas 37, 86, 88, 89, 94, 95
emphaseme 37
emphasis 18, 62, 63, 73, 88, 112
emphatic prosode 63, 88
— prosodeme 37
empirical 10, 11
— adequacy 10, 114
encoder 77
encoding 116
energemic 7, 8, 11, 12
entangled sememe 93
equipollent 97, 98, 100
equivalent 23
evaluation 23
exclusive opposition 104
exhaustiveness 116
expansion 59, 72
— substitution 67, 85
experiencer 93, 106
express 63, 86, 88, 89, 94, 95, 112
expresseme 10, 112
expression 2, 3, 10, 39, 45, 66, 85, 86, 94, 107
— segment 52
— side 1, 85, 89, 90, 102
— unit 77, 90
extensional 5
extensive 104
external circumstances 111
extracommunicative 115

facultative 20, 35, 41, 52
— variation 13, 32, 33, 35, 40, 46
falling diphthong 17
feature V, 30
f-glottofuncteme 83, 84
f-glottoprosodeme 39
f-glottosyntagmeme 83
field 96, 101
finite 71
— verb 58
fixed expression 103
— metaphor 102
force of articulation 8
form V
formant frequency 16
free 48
— morpheme 34, 96
— variation 13, 20, 32, 33, 35, 40, 41, 46, 70
frequency 62
— of the fundamental 8

frequency of the vocal cords 8
full form 71
funct 63, 65—68, 75, 78, 88
functeme 10, 39, 65, 66, 72, 82—84, 106
function 1, 3, 11, 12, 38, 39, 47—49, 56, 63, 65, 67, 68, 75, 78, 80, 83, 84, 87, 112
— word 61, 74
functional 12, 77, 89, 105, 111
— phonetics 12

gap 104
general V
— allosememe 91
— lexeme alloseme 94
— morpheme 94
generative V, VI
generativist 40
genetic 7, 8, 11, 12
gennemic 7, 8, 11, 12
glossary 56
glottoact 3
glottoallofunct 83
glottoallophone 25, 29
glottoallosyllab 43
glottodialloperiod 82
glotto-dia-socio-idiophone 25
glottofunct 83
glottofuncteme 83, 84
glotto-idiophone 25
glottolect 3, 5, 23, 26, 82, 83, 103, 112
glottolexeme 109
glottoperiodeme 82
glottophoneme 22, 24—26, 28, 29, 112
glottopredicateme 82
glottoprosode 38
glottoprosodeme 38, 39
glotto-sememe 108—110
glottosubjecteme 82
glottosyllab 43
glottosyllabeme 43
glottosyllabememe 43
glottosyntagm 82
glottosyntagmeme 82, 83
glottosystem 3, 115
glottotext 3
glottounit 4, 24, 109
government 61
gradual 97
grammar 46, 103, 113
grammatical alloseme 111
— allosememe 91
— function 44, 46, 49, 51, 86, 87
— lex seme 87
— lexeme alloseme 94
— morph 87, 88
— morpheme 49, 94
— varimorph 89

grapheme 114
group 96

habit 1
habitual 1
head 58, 67, 68, 74, 106
hearer VI, 7, 9, 12, 19, 51, 70, 112, 113, 116
hearer's grammar VI, 114—116
hearing act 3
— test 8
height 31
heterofunctemic 83
heterosyntagmemic 84
hierarchy 100
— of allosemes 99, 100
high level pattern 70
homofunctemic 83
homolexemic 108
homonym 110
homonymous 37, 64, 103
homosememic 109
homosyntagmemic 84
horizontal 5, 77, 78, 107
— interselection 64, 92
hyponym 100
hypotactical 74

identical 23
identification 12, 32
identity substitution 68, 85
idioact 3
idioallophone 25, 29
idioallosyllab 43
idiofunct 83
idiolect 3, 23, 35, 79, 82, 83, 85, 86, 103, 107, 112
idiolex prosode 38
idiolexeme prosodeme 38
idiom 103
idiomorph prosode 38
idiomorpheme prosodeme 38
idiophone 13, 25, 29
idiophoneme 22, 25, 28, 112
idioprosode 38
idioprosodeme 38
idiosyllab 40, 43
— prosode 38
— — component 38
idiosyllabeme 43
— prosodeme 38
— — component 38
idiosyllabememe 43
idiosyntagm 82
— prosode 38
idiosyntagmeme 82
— prosodeme 38
idiosystem 3, 115

idiotext 3
idiounit 4, 112
ill-formed 80
immediate constituent 59
includer 58
inclusive opposition 104
incoherent 80
incorrect utterance 11
indefinite article 86
— pronomineme 57
— pronoun 57
independent 48
— morpheme 34, 96
index 73
indirect 66, 94
— component 100
— object 58
— opposition 100
— segment 59
indirectly dominated alloseme 100
individual 3, 13, 25, 28, 40, 71, 79, 80, 83, 98, 104
— seme 89
infinite 71, 84
infix 47, 48
inflected lexeme 92
informant 30, 44, 51, 56, 80, 85, 111
instrument 8, 14, 106
intensional 5
intensity 8, 9
intensive 104
interdialectal communication 108
interference 100
interlocutor 116
internal circumstances 111
International Phonetic Association 21
interpretation 62, 72, 79, 116
interrogative pronomineme 57
— pronoun 57
interrogator 57
interrogatoreme 57
interrupted 80
interselection 73, 77—79, 85, 87, 88, 92, 93, 107
intonation 30, 31, 36
— pattern 30
introspection 10, 11, 44
intuition 10, 60, 64, 115
invariant 4, 15, 41
inventory 29, 39, 51, 56, 84, 111
isogloss 22
isolated 98
— word 81
item V, 1—7, 10, 16, 19, 25, 29, 32, 40—42, 44, 45, 49, 52, 55, 56, 63, 70, 77—79, 81—83, 86, 89, 93, 94—96, 111, 115, 116

juxtaposition 74

labelled arrow 76
— and directed arrow 50
— brackets 61, 62, 68
— double arrow 50
language 1—3, 5, 8—10, 23, 24, 64, 70, 82, 85, 104, 112
— communication 116
— error 102
— variety 79
layman 10, 12, 24, 81, 85, 94, 106, 115
learning 70
length 8, 9, 31, 32, 36
letter 114, 115
level 60, 99, 100
lex 12, 15, 18, 19, 33, 35, 43, 47, 49, 52—59, 61—63, 67, 69, 70, 80, 86—88, 93
lex-building function 40
lex component 35
— period 81
— prosode 12, 31, 35, 55
— — component 35, 36
— segment 52
— seme 52, 63, 64, 86—89, 93, 95, 107
— — component 94
lexeme 10, 15, 18, 19, 22, 35, 41—43, 45, 48, 49—56, 58, 63, 68, 88—93, 96, 102—104, 107—110, 113
— alloseme 89—92, 94—96, 100, 102, 107, 111
— — component 94
— — system 96
— allosememe 90, 91
— component 35
— diasememe 107
— glottosememe 107
— idiosememe 107
— prosodeme 30, 35, 36, 55
— — component 35, 36
— sememe 90, 92, 93, 95, 104, 105, 107
— — component 95
— sociosememe 107
lexememe 35, 53, 57, 61, 66
— prosodeme 36
— — component 36
lexemic 108
— ph-ph-glottosememe 109
— se-glottosememe 109
lexicon 56
linear 2
linguist 6, 7, 10, 16, 18, 19, 23, 25, 44, 45, 51, 56, 64, 67, 79—81, 84, 92, 94, 98, 99, 102, 115, 116
linguistic 1, 92, 93
— description 85, 112, 114, 116

linguistics   V, VI, 1—3, 7, 10, 21, 82, 92, 102, 111, 113, 115
listener   14, 16, 17, 32, 85
— test   16
loudness   8, 9, 31, 36

machine translation   VI, 114, 116
main alloseme   91
— component   95
— signification   105
margin   16
marked   97
matrix   21
MCV   113
m-diaphoneme   26—28, 111
m-diasyllabeme   44
meaning   1—3, 12, 13, 37, 44—46, 49, 51, 56, 64, 79, 85—94, 97, 99, 103, 104, 108—112, 116
means of communication   11
mediate constituent   59
medium   8
mentalistic   68
meta-lex   55
meta-lexeme   55
meta-morph   50, 86
meta-morpheme   50
meta-phone   19, 29, 45
meta-phoneme   19, 29, 30
metaphor   102
metaphorical alloseme   91
— component   103
meta-seme   94
meta-sememe   94
meta-syllab   33, 42
— prosode   33
meta-syllabeme   42
meta-syntagm   81
meta-syntagmeme   81, 82
meta-unit   94
meta-varisyntagm   81
m-glottophoneme   26, 27
m-glottosyllabeme   43
minimal pair   10, 29, 39
— system   101
minus   97
mistake   23
misunderstanding   108
monofunctemic   84
monolexemic   108, 109
monophonemic   21
monophthong   16—18
monophthongeme   16, 17
monosememic   110
monosyntagmemic   84
morph   13, 19, 43—49, 51, 52, 54, 57, 61, 86, 88

morph boundary   43
— contour   46, 111
— prosode   31, 34
— — component   34
— seme   44—46, 52, 86—89, 93, 107
— — component   94
morpheme   19, 26, 34, 43, 44, 48—54, 56, 57, 90, 91, 93, 96, 97, 113, 114
— alloseme   89—92, 94—96, 107, 111
— — component   94
— — seme   90
— — system   96
— allosememe   91
— prosodeme   30, 34, 35
— — component   34, 35
— seme   90
— sememe   44, 89, 90, 92—94, 105
— — component   95
morphememe   34, 47, 48
— prosodeme   34, 35
— — component   35
morphemically conditioned   48
— corresponding   26
morphology   9, 30, 51, 53, 87, 113, 116
morphophonemics   50
motivated   1
moving boundary   43
m-ph-dialexeme   56
m-ph-glottolexeme   55
m-ph-glottosememe   110
m-ph-lexeme   110
m-sociophoneme   26, 28
m-sociosyllabeme   44
multidimensional   20, 21
multilateral   98
multiple interselection   78
mutual conditioning of variants   112
m-variphone   28

narrow   4, 5, 32, 36
natural   10
— sciences   11
neogrammarian   23
neutral description   V, VI, 77, 113, 115, 116
neutralization   97
nexsyntagm   74
nexsyntagmememe   74
node   60
nomenclature   104
non discrete   30, 37, 112
notation   80, 87, 89
noun phrase   70
numbered brackets   76
nuncemes   114, 115
n-unit   4, 14, 15, 19—21, 41, 46—48, 52—54, 63, 66, 68, 69, 71, 80, 82, 95, 96, 98, 112, 113

object   58
observation   10
observer   11
occasional metaphor   103
one-to-many correspondence   26, 27
one-to-one correspondence   26
onomasiological   109
opposition   10, 39, 97, 98, 100—102, 104
order   69
ordinal   57
ordinaleme   57
originator   93, 106
over all pattern   71
overlapping   14
overt   78

paradigm   87
paradigmatics   V, 5, 6, 10, 16, 20, 42, 50, 53, 55, 82, 96
paraphrase   72, 104
paratactical syntagm   74
— syntagmememe   74
parole   3
part diaphoneme   26
participant   111
partly corresponding   26, 107
passive   74—77
pattern   31, 36, 40, 62, 70, 71, 76
pause   31, 36
pentalloperiod   69
period   12, 36, 58, 59, 63, 67—72, 76, 79, 81, 86, 103
— seme   88
periodeme   36, 68, 69, 71, 73
periodememe   68
peripheral alloseme   91
personal pronoun   57
— pronomineme   57
ph-diallophone   26
ph-diaphoneme   24, 26, 27
ph-diasyllabeme   43
ph-diavariphone   26
ph-glottophoneme   24, 26
ph-glottosyllabeme   43
phonation   7
phone   12, 13, 15, 16, 21, 22, 24—26, 28, 29, 40, 44, 45, 47, 51, 52, 89, 110
— component   19, 22, 29, 30, 94
— contour   13, 111
— dial   28
— idiol   28
— sociol   28
phoneme   10—12, 14—21, 24—30, 32, 39, 44—46, 51—53, 55, 103, 110, 113—115
— component   19—22, 29, 30
— dialeme   28
— idioleme   28

phoneme representative   25
— socioleme   28
phonememe   20, 22, 29, 47
— component   20
phonemic   12
phonemically conditioned   48
— corresponding   24, 26, 43
phonemics   12
phonetics   9, 12, 30, 51, 113, 116
phonic   12, 14, 53
— notation   57, 62
phonics   47
phonic similarity   14, 16, 19, 47
phonological opposition   29
— system   6, 20, 24, 30, 96, 103
phonology   12, 13, 32, 46, 70, 96, 98
ph-ph-dialexeme   55
ph-ph-glottolexeme   55, 110
ph-ph-lexeme   109
phrase   58, 103
phraseme   70
ph-sociophoneme   24
ph-sociosyllabeme   43
pitch   8, 31, 32, 36
— contour   30
pitchmeter   9
place   106, 111
p-lexememe   54
plus   97
polyfunctemic   84
polylexemic   108, 109
polysememic   110
polysyntagmemic   84
position   13, 14, 20, 26, 35, 36, 40, 41, 43, 47, 58, 63, 70
positional variant   114
— variation   13, 40
positive quality   97
possessive pronomineme   57
— pronoun   57
Prague School system   20
pr-diaprosodeme   39
predicate   58, 74
prefix   47, 48
prephonological system   20
preposition   57
prepositioneme   57
pr-glottoprosodeme   39
primary component   94, 95, 101, 102
— seme component   94
privative   97
process   50, 114, 115
production   71, 116
prominence   31
pronunciation   64, 79, 81
property   7
proportional   98

127

proportional opposition 102
prosode 12, 31, 42, 56, 64, 70, 85
— component 32, 36
— contour 111
prosodeme 12, 30—39, 42, 44, 45, 64, 79, 85, 112, 113
— component 31, 32
— pattern 31
prosodemic f-glottofuncteme 39
— pr-glottofuncteme 39
prosodemics 12
prosodic 51
pseudo-component 22
pseudo-item 50
pseudo-lex 55
pseudo-lexeme 55
pseudo-period 81
pseudo-phone 18, 19, 29, 45, 52
pseudo-phoneme 19, 29, 30
pseudo-prosode 81
pseudo-seme 94
pseudo-sememe 94
pseudo-syllab 42, 52
pseudo-syllabeme 42
pseudo-syllab prosode 33
pseudo-syntagm 80, 81
pseudo-syntagmeme 80—82
pseudo-unit 18, 50
pseudo-varisyntagm 81
psychological subject 88

quality 8, 9, 31, 32, 36
quasi-allomorph 49
quasi-lex 54
quasi-lexeme 54
quasi-morph 49
quasi-morpheme 49, 93
quasi-phone 18, 29, 45, 52
quasi-phoneme 16, 18, 21, 29, 30, 46
quasi-seme 93
quasi-sememe 93
quasi-syntagm 79, 80
quasi-syntagmeme 79
quasi-syllab 42, 52
quasi-syllabeme 42

random variation 13
reading 3
real speech 30
reality 93
realization V, 4, 16—18, 22, 25, 31—33, 35—38, 40, 42, 47, 63, 86, 94
recorded language 2
rection 61
recurring 70
reference 86, 89, 94, 95
referent 85, 86, 89, 111

regional 35
register 111
related 50
relation V, 7, 8
relative pronomineme 57
— pronoun 57
relevant feature 24
repeated segment 69
rewrite rule 60
rhythm 31
rising diphthong 17

same 23
scalar relationship 21
school grammar 112
secondary component 94, 95
— function 15, 62
— seme component 94
se-dialexeme 56
se-glottolexeme 56, 109
se-glottosememe 109
segment 2, 5, 6, 9, 11—13, 16—19, 25, 31, 40, 42, 44—49, 51—53, 56—59, 62, 63, 66—71, 75, 76, 81, 82, 89, 90, 96
segmentable 2
segmental phoneme 12
segmentation 6, 16
segmented 16
selection 77, 88
semantic 78, 79, 88, 92, 109
— allosememe 91
— class 106
— component 78, 97, 101
— feature 54
— field 91, 96, 103
— group 105
— interselection 107
— items 111
— subdivision 105
— subsystem 98, 101
— system 91, 94, 96, 98, 99, 100, 102—105
— tree 105
— unit 77, 111
semantics 9, 77, 78, 85, 92, 93, 96—98, 102, 103, 111, 113, 116
semasiological 110
seme 46, 51, 61, 63, 64, 73, 78, 85, 86, 88—90, 92, 94, 95
— component 85, 95
sememe 10, 26, 46, 48, 51, 52, 55, 73, 85, 89, 90, 93, 96, 101, 107—110, 113
— component 85, 94—96
semememe 92
sememic 108
semi-lex 54, 93
semi-lexeme 54, 93, 95
— sememe 93

128

semi-morph 49
semi-morpheme 49
semi-phone 16, 21, 29, 52
semi-phoneme 15, 16, 29, 30, 46
semi-seme 93
semi-sememe 93
semi-syllab 52
semi-syllabeme 42
semi-syntagm 79, 80, 93
semi-syntagmeme 79, 93
sentence 12, 33, 36, 58, 80, 116
set 4—6, 13—15, 19, 20, 24—26, 31, 33, 35, 36, 38, 41, 47, 52, 53, 57—59, 63, 68—71, 74, 75, 82, 90, 91, 96
— theory 4, 5, 73
signification 105
silent language 2
similarity 23
— substitution 68, 85
simple interselection 78
simplicity 40
simultaneous 46, 86, 87, 93, 95
situation of communication 79, 81
slang 102
s-lexememe 54
socioact 3
socioallophone 25, 29
socioallosyllab 43
sociofunct 83
socio-idiophone 25
sociolect 3, 22—28, 35, 38, 39, 43, 56, 79, 82, 83, 85, 86, 103, 107, 112
sociophone 13, 25
sociophoneme 22—25, 26, 28, 112
socioprosode 38
— component 38
socioprosodeme 38, 39
— component 38
sociosyllab 40, 43
— prosode 38
sociosyllabeme 43
— prosodeme 38
sociosyllabememe 43
sociosyntagm 82
sociosyntagmeme 82
sociosystem 3, 115
sociotext 3
sociounit 4
solidarity 77
sonagram 30
sound 7, 20, 24, 116
— property 8, 20
— substance 11
— symbolic function 15
source language 89
speaker VI, 3, 7, 9, 13, 22—24, 27—29, 38, 70, 71, 78, 79, 81, 88, 89, 110, 112, 113, 116

speaker-hearer 8
speaker's grammar VI, 114—116
special language 102, 104
specification 77
spectrum 8, 9
speech 19, 70
— act 3, 9, 11, 115
— community 23
spelling pronunciation 19
spoken 1—3, 7, 11, 12, 18, 49, 51, 80, 84, 114—116
standard language 27
statistical 54, 57
stem 48
stimulus 8, 30
stress 31, 41
structural 105
structuralist 9, 40
structure 5, 6, 36, 47, 49, 62, 67, 96, 98
style 2, 111
subdivision 60, 67—69, 96
subfunction 65
subinventory 29, 111
subject 36, 58, 74, 75
— allofunct 93
— complement 58
subjecteme 36, 65, 68, 93
— allofunct 65
— functeme 65
subjective 28
— judgement 14
subpattern 70, 71
subset 4, 5, 14, 36, 47, 54, 58, 66—68, 70, 72, 74, 75, 89, 91
substance V, 114
substantive 57, 58, 81
— allophrase 77
— alloseme 99
— — system 99
— phrase 70, 86
— phraseme 70
substantiveme 57, 66
substantivized 72
substitution 10, 60, 67
— test 67
subsystem 96, 97, 100—106
sub-unit 5
suffix 47, 48
superordinate 100
suprasegmental 8, 30
— phoneme 12
Swedish "accents" 35, 39
— supradentals 18
sy-diasyntagmeme 83
sy-glottosyntagmeme 83
syllab 12, 13, 19, 32, 33, 36, 40—45, 52
— boundary 43, 44

129

syllab component 32, 35
— contour 40, 111
— inventory 44
— prosode 12, 31—34, 40—42
— — component 32—34
syllabeme 10, 16, 19, 22, 32, 33, 39, 40—44, 46, 53, 113
— boundary 43
— component 32, 35
— inventory 44
— prosodeme 30, 32—34, 42
— — component 32—34
syllabememe 33, 41, 42, 44, 47
— prosodeme 33, 34, 42
— — component 34
syllable 12, 22, 31, 32, 39, 42
— boundary 40
— division 17
symbol 7
synchrony 11
synonym 48, 91
syntactic 78, 79, 84, 88, 92, 112
— analysis 80
— construction 31, 51, 53, 54, 57, 66, 71, 84, 92
— fact 85
— functeme 66
— function 67, 68, 83, 85, 86
— functional unit 77
— pattern 70, 71
— prosode 36, 37, 62
— prosodeme 36, 37
— relationship 61, 71
— structure 62, 67, 68
— system 70
syntagm 12, 33, 36, 56—82, 86, 88, 95
— boundary 61
— funct 63—65, 79, 82, 86
— function 56, 61
— prosode 12, 31, 36, 37, 57, 81
— — component 36, 37
— seme 63, 65, 86—88, 92, 95, 106
— — component 95
— structure 82
syntagmatic structure 40, 66, 82
syntagmatics V, 5, 6, 17, 18, 21, 22, 35, 43, 51, 55, 82, 107
syntagmeme 10, 36, 38, 54, 56, 63—77, 79, 82—84, 86, 96, 113
— allofunct 65
— functeme 65, 82, 84
— function 56
— prosodeme 30, 36—38, 81
— — component 36, 37
— sememe 92
syntagmememe 74, 75, 77, 82
— prosodeme 38

syntagmemic diafuncteme 83, 84
— f-glottofuncteme 84
— glottofuncteme 83
— idiofuncteme 83
— sociofuncteme 83
— sy-glottofuncteme 84
syntagmic structure 66
syntax 9, 30, 36, 57, 71, 77, 78, 83, 92, 93, 106, 111, 113, 116
synthetic grammar VI, 115, 116
— speech 30
system V, 3, 4, 16, 23, 24, 96, 97, 99, 101, 103, 115
— of communication 1, 115
— of signs 3
— of vowels 21

table 21
— of vowels and consonants 20
tagmemicist 60
tape recording 80, 84
target 65, 73, 75, 106
— language 89
technical terminology 98
tempo 31
term 8
terminology 102, 104
test 9, 10, 44, 67, 86
— sentence 81
tetrallo- 4
tetralloperiod 36, 69, 71
tetraphthong 17, 18
tetraphthongeme 18
text 3, 86, 116
thing 62, 85, 104, 111
thinking 2
T. M. 86
topic 111
total meaning 63—65, 76, 89
— syntagm 86
— — meaning 63, 86
transformation 50, 75, 114
transformational V, VI
translation 88, 104
translator 85
tree 60, 61, 105
— structure 65
triallo- 4, 47
trialloperiod 36, 69, 71
triallophone 14
triallosyntagm 66
triphthong 17, 18
triphthongeme 16—18
trivari- 4, 47
"two-dialect" phoneme 27
"two-sociolect" phoneme 27
type 4

typeme 114, 115
typemics 114
typetics 116

ultimate 71
— constituents 57
unacceptability 92
unamalgamated 54
unamalgamated seme 52
unclear 12, 19
— meaning 44, 45, 49, 86, 87, 93—96
— segment 45, 52
underlying abstraction VI, 50, 76
understood 71
unit V, 1, 2, 4—6, 9, 10, 13—16, 19, 23, 25, 29, 30, 32, 33, 38, 40, 42, 44, 48—50, 52, 53, 63—66, 74, 77—79, 81—83, 85, 89, 90, 92—95, 104, 107, 111, 115, 116
universal V, VI, 14, 64, 85, 104
unmarked 97
utterance 1

vague boundary 49
vari- 4, 47
variant 4, 13, 15, 26, 35, 40, 41, 47, 70
variation 35, 40, 70
variclause 75
varilex 35, 53, 63, 90
— prosodeme 35, 36
— — component 36
— sememe 89, 95
— — component 95
varilexeme 35, 53
— prosodeme 35, 36
— — component 36
varimorph 26, 47, 89
— prosodeme 34
— — component 34, 35
— sememe 89
varimorpheme 47
— prosodeme 34
variperiod 68, 69
— sememe 89
variphone 15, 21, 25, 26, 28, 32, 46, 53, 55
varisyllab 40, 41, 44, 46, 53
— prosodeme 33, 34
— — component 34
varisyntagm 37, 63, 65—68, 70, 71, 74—77, 86, 95
— component 95
— functeme 63—65
— prosodeme 37, 38, 63

varisyntagm prosodeme component 37, 38
— seme component 95
— sememe 63, 64, 89, 92, 95, 106
varisyntagmeme prosodeme 37, 38
— — component 38
verb 57
verbeme 57
vertical 5, 77, 78, 107
— interselection 64
vocabulary 56
vocal tract 8
voice quality 112
vowel 15, 17, 20, 22, 29, 39, 41, 47, 97

well-formed 80
word 15, 18, 22, 25, 31, 35, 42, 49, 51, 52, 54, 56, 67, 85, 92, 98, 102, 103, 108, 111, 114, 116
— class 53, 54, 57, 61, 62, 66
— meaning 96
— order 61
— prosodeme 39
— seme 65
— sememe 65
writer 3
written 1—3, 7, 49, 51, 80, 114, 115

zero 20, 22, 25, 32, 42, 50, 65, 82, 83, 108
$\emptyset$-diaphoneme 27
zero-diasememe 108, 109
$\emptyset$-variant 43
zone of meaning 104

α-function 2, 3, 11—13, 18, 19, 28, 30, 32, 85, 94, 112, 113, 116
α-level, see α-function
α-unit, see α-function

β-function 2, 3, 12, 13, 18, 19, 30, 32, 35, 40, 48, 62, 64, 70, 80, 81, 85, 94, 102, 111, 112
β-level, see β-function
β-unit, see β-function
β_1-function 111, 116
β_2-function 48, 111, 116

γ-function 3, 12, 13, 21, 28, 35, 40, 48, 70, 85, 112
γ-level, see γ-function
γ-variation, see γ-function
γ_1-function 32, 40, 112, 116
γ_2-function 32, 40, 112, 116
γ_3-function 32, 40, 48, 112, 116

Communication and Cybernetics

Editors: K. S. Fu, W. D. Keidel, H. Wolter

Vol. 1 W. Meyer-Eppler
Grundlagen und Anwendungen der Informationstheorie
2. Auflage, neu bearbeitet und erweitert von G. Heike und K. Löhn

Vol. 2 B. Malmberg
Structural Linguistics and Human Communication
An Introduction into the Mechanism of Language and the Methodology of Linguistics
2nd revised edition

Vol. 3 J. L. Flanagan
Speech Analysis / Synthesis and Perception
2nd edition

Vol. 4 G. Herdan
The Advanced Theory of Language as Choice and Chance

Vol. 5 G. Hammarström
Linguistische Einheiten im Rahmen der modernen Sprachwissenschaft

Vol. 6 J. Peters
Einführung in die allgemeine Informationstheorie

Vol. 7 K. Weltner
The Measurement of Verbal Information in Psychology and Education
Translated from the German by B. M. Crook

Vol. 8 *Facts and Models in Hearing*
Proceedings of the Symposium on Psychophysical Models and Physiological Facts in Hearing, held at Tutzing, Oberbayern, Federal Republic of Germany, April 22–26, 1974
Edited by E. Zwicker, E. Terhardt

Some Related Titles

Communication and Cybernetics
Editors: K. S. Fu, W. D. Keidel, H. Wolter

Vol. 10 *Pattern Recognition*
Edited by K. S. Fu
With contributions by numerous experts
Contents: Topics in Statistical Pattern Recognition. – Clustering Analysis. – Syntactic (Linguistic) Pattern Recognition. – Picture Recognition. – Speech Recognition and Understanding.

Vol. 11 *Structure and Process in Speech Perception*
Proceedings of the Symposium on Dynamic Aspects of Speech Perception, held at I.P.O., Eindhoven, Netherlands, August 4 — 6, 1975
Edited by A. Cohen and S. G. Nooteboom
Contents: Theoretical Issues in Speech Perception Research. – Prosody in Speech Perception. – Some Storage Properties of Speech Perception. – Short-Term Context Effects, Dichotic Listening, Speech Perception in the Very Young. – General Discussion and Tentative Conclusions.

Vol. 12 J. D. Markel, A. H. Gray
Linear Prediction of Speech
In preparation

Topics in Applied Physics
Founded by H. K. V. Lotsch

Vol. 6 *Picture Processing and Digital Filtering*
Edited by T. S. Huang
With contributions by numerous experts
Contents: Two-Dimensional Transforms. – Two-Dimensional Nonrecursive Filters. – Two-Dimensional Recursive Filtering. – Image Enhancement and Restoration. – Noise Considerations in Digital Image Processing Hardware.

Vol. 11 *Digital Picture Analysis*
Edited by A. Rosenfeld
In preparation

Springer-Verlag Berlin Heidelberg New York